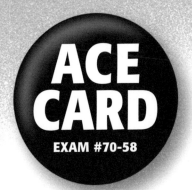

ACE CARD
EXAM #70-58

M...
N...
Essentials
Ace It!

CW00972542

STANDARDS

▶ Know the layers of the OSI Model:

- **Physical layer** – Handles bit conversion for data transmission across the physical media.
- **Data Link layer** – Consists of the following two sublayers: Media Access Control, which is responsible for error-free network transmissions, and Logical Link Control, which controls data-link communications.
- **Network layer** – Responsible for routing data across an internetwork.
- **Transport layer** – Manages reliable data transmissions across the network.
- **Session layer** – Handles connections between devices.
- **Presentation layer** – Negotiates and establishes the format in which data is exchanged.
- **Application layer** – Acts as the interface between the user's application and the network.

▶ Know the 802 standards:

- **802.1** – Spanning tree algorithm
- **802.2** – LLC portion of the Data Link layer
- **802.3** – Ethernet
- **802.4** – Token Bus
- **802.5** – Token Ring
- **802.6** – Distributed Queue Dual Bus
- **802.7** – Broadband technology
- **802.8** – Fiber-optic technology
- **802.9** – Integrated data and voice
- **802.10** – Network security
- **802.11** – Wireless networks
- **802.12** – 100VG-AnyLAN

IMPLEMENTATION

▶ Choose an administrative plan to meet specific needs, including performance management, account management, and security.

▶ Choose a disaster recovery plan for various situations. Disaster recovery plans can include the following backup types:
  - Full
  - Incremental
  - Differential

▶ Given the manufacturer's documentation for the network adapter, install, configure, and resolve hardware conflicts for multiple network adapters in a Token Ring and Ethernet network.

▶ Implement a NetBIOS naming scheme for all computers on a given network.

▶ Select the appropriate hardware and software tools to use to monitor trends in the network. Some common tools to use are:
  - Digital volt meters
  - Time-domain reflectometers
  - Advanced cable testers
  - Oscilloscopes
  - Network monitors
  - Protocol analyzers

TROUBLESHOOTING

▶ Identify common errors associated with components required for communications, such as network adapters with incorrect IRQs.

▶ Diagnose and resolve common connectivity problems with cards, cables, and related hardware.

▶ Resolve broadcast storms.

▶ Identify and resolve network performance problems.

▶ RAID levels:
- **RAID 0** – Disk striping without parity
- **RAID 1** – Disk mirroring and duplexing
- **RAID 5** – Disk striping with parity

TERMINOLOGY

▶ NDIS and ODI allow binding of multiple adapters and protocols.

▶ Understand the protocols used on networks:
- **TCP/IP** – Internet
- **IPX/SPX** – Novell NetWare
- **AppleTalk** – Macintosh Networks
- **DLC** – Commonly used for network printers
- **NFS** – File sharing over TCP/IP
- **SMB** – Microsoft Networks

▶ Understand which layers of the OSI model network devices function at:
- **Physical layer** – TDRs, oscilloscopes, repeaters, hubs
- **Data Link layer** – advanced cable testers, NICs, bridges
- **Network layer** – advanced cable testers, routers
- **Transport layer** – advanced cable testers, gateways
- **Session layer** – gateways
- **Presentation layer** – gateways
- **Application layer** – gateways

▶ Understand how IRQs, DMAs, and I/O addresses are used.

▶ Know the various connectors, such as BNC and T-connectors.

▶ Understand the differences between server-based networks and peer-to-peer networks.

▶ Understand the network topologies such as mesh, ring, bus, and star.

▶ Know the advantages and disadvantages of FAT and NTFS.

▶ Compare a file-and-print server with an application server.

▶ Know that user-level security is based on user accounts, whereas share-level security uses a password to determine the type of access granted to a resource.

▶ Understand that connectionless communications are quicker with less overhead than connection-oriented protocols. However, connection-oriented protocols can be more reliable.

▶ Distinguish whether SLIP or PPP is used as the communications protocol for various situations.

PLANNING connectivity devices to use in a given situation:

- **Repeaters** – Extend segment range
- **Bridges** – Filter network traffic
- **Routers** – Make intelligent data forwarding decisions
- **Brouters** – Bridging routers
- **Gateways** – Protocol or system conversions

▶ Choose the appropriate media type when given various requirements.
Media choices are:
- Coaxial cable
- Twisted-pair cable
- Fiber-optic cable
- Satellite
- Wireless

Requirements are:
- Speed
- Distance limitations
- Number of nodes

▶ List the characteristics, requirements, and appropriate situations for WAN connection services. WAN services include:
- X.25
- ISDN
- Frame relay
- ATM

MCSE
Networking
Essentials
Ace It!

MCSE
Networking
Essentials
Ace It!

Jason Nash

IDG Books Worldwide, Inc.
An International Data Group Company
Foster City, CA • Chicago, IL • Indianapolis, IN • New York, NY

MCSE Networking Essentials Ace It!

Published by
IDG Books Worldwide, Inc.
An International Data Group Company
919 E. Hillsdale Blvd., Suite 400
Foster City, CA 94404
www.idgbooks.com (IDG Books Worldwide Web site)

Library of Congress Catalog Card Number: 98-73336

ISBN: 0-7645-3257-X

Printed in the United States of America

10 9 8 7 6 5 4 3 2 1

1P/RW/QZ/ZY/FC

Distributed in the United States by IDG Books Worldwide, Inc.

Distributed by Macmillan Canada for Canada; by Transworld Publishers Limited in the United Kingdom; by IDG Norge Books for Norway; by IDG Sweden Books for Sweden; by Woodslane Pty. Ltd. for Australia; by Woodslane (NZ) Ltd. for New Zealand; by Addison Wesley Longman Singapore Pte Ltd. for Singapore, Malaysia, Thailand, Indonesia, and Korea; by Norma Comunicaciones S.A. for Colombia; by Intersoft for South Africa; by International Thomson Publishing for Germany, Austria, and Switzerland; by Toppan Company Ltd. for Japan; by Distribuidora Cuspide for Argentina; by Livraria Cultura for Brazil; by Ediciencia S.A. for Ecuador; by Ediciones ZETA S.C.R. Ltda. for Peru; by WS Computer Publishing Corporation, Inc., for the Philippines; by Unalis Corporation for Taiwan; by Contemporanea de Ediciones for Venezuela; by Computer Book & Magazine Store for Puerto Rico; by Express Computer Distributors for the Caribbean and West Indies. Authorized Sales Agent: Anthony Rudkin Associates for the Middle East and North Africa.

For general information on IDG Books Worldwide's books in the U.S., please call our Consumer Customer Service department at 800-762-2974. For reseller information, including discounts and premium sales, please call our Reseller Customer Service department at 800-434-3422.

For information on where to purchase IDG Books Worldwide's books outside the U.S., please contact our International Sales department at 650-655-3172 or fax 650-655-3297.

For information on foreign language translations, please contact our Foreign & Subsidiary Rights department at 650-655-3021 or fax 650-655-3281.

For sales inquiries and special prices for bulk quantities, please contact our Sales department at 650-655-3200 or write to the address above.

For information on using IDG Books Worldwide's books in the classroom or for ordering examination copies, please contact our Educational Sales department at 800-434-2086 or fax 317-596-5499.

For press review copies, author interviews, or other publicity information, please contact our Public Relations department at 650-655-3000 or fax 650-655-3299.

For authorization to photocopy items for corporate, personal, or educational use, please contact Copyright Clearance Center, 222 Rosewood Drive, Danvers, MA 01923, or fax 978-750-4470.

is a trademark under exclusive license
to IDG Books Worldwide, Inc.,
from International Data Group, Inc.

ABOUT IDG BOOKS WORLDWIDE

Welcome to the world of IDG Books Worldwide.

IDG Books Worldwide, Inc., is a subsidiary of International Data Group, the world's largest publisher of computer-related information and the leading global provider of information services on information technology. IDG was founded more than 25 years ago and now employs more than 8,500 people worldwide. IDG publishes more than 275 computer publications in over 75 countries (see listing below). More than 90 million people read one or more IDG publications each month.

Launched in 1990, IDG Books Worldwide is today the #1 publisher of best-selling computer books in the United States. We are proud to have received eight awards from the Computer Press Association in recognition of editorial excellence and three from *Computer Currents'* First Annual Readers' Choice Awards. Our best-selling *...For Dummies®* series has more than 50 million copies in print with translations in 38 languages. IDG Books Worldwide, through a joint venture with IDG's Hi-Tech Beijing, became the first U.S. publisher to publish a computer book in the People's Republic of China. In record time, IDG Books Worldwide has become the first choice for millions of readers around the world who want to learn how to better manage their businesses.

Our mission is simple: Every one of our books is designed to bring extra value and skill-building instructions to the reader. Our books are written by experts who understand and care about our readers. The knowledge base of our editorial staff comes from years of experience in publishing, education, and journalism — experience we use to produce books for the '90s. In short, we care about books, so we attract the best people. We devote special attention to details such as audience, interior design, use of icons, and illustrations. And because we use an efficient process of authoring, editing, and desktop publishing our books electronically, we can spend more time ensuring superior content and spend less time on the technicalities of making books.

You can count on our commitment to deliver high-quality books at competitive prices on topics you want to read about. At IDG Books Worldwide, we continue in the IDG tradition of delivering quality for more than 25 years. You'll find no better book on a subject than one from IDG Books Worldwide.

John Kilcullen
CEO
IDG Books Worldwide, Inc.

Steven Berkowitz
President and Publisher
IDG Books Worldwide, Inc.

Eighth Annual Computer Press Awards ≥1992

Ninth Annual Computer Press Awards ≥1993

Tenth Annual Computer Press Awards ≥1994

Eleventh Annual Computer Press Awards ≥1995

IDG Books Worldwide, Inc., is a subsidiary of International Data Group, the world's largest publisher of computer-related information and the leading global provider of information services on information technology. International Data Group publishes over 275 computer publications in over 75 countries. More than 90 million people read one or more International Data Group publications each month. International Data Group's publications include: **ARGENTINA:** Buyer's Guide, Computerworld Argentina, PC World Argentina; **AUSTRALIA:** Australian Macworld, Australian PC World, Australian Reseller News, Computerworld, IT Casebook, Network World, Publish, Webmaster; **AUSTRIA:** Computerwelt Österreich, Networks Austria, PC Tip Austria; **BANGLADESH:** PC World Bangladesh; **BELARUS:** PC World Belarus; **BELGIUM:** Data News; **BRAZIL:** Annuário de Informática, Computerworld, Connections, Macworld, PC Player, PC World, Publish, Reseller News, Supergamepower; **BULGARIA:** Computerworld Bulgaria, Network World Bulgaria, PC & MacWorld Bulgaria; **CANADA:** CIO Canada, Client/Server World, ComputerWorld Canada, InfoWorld Canada, NetworkWorld Canada, WebWorld; **CHILE:** Computerworld Chile, PC World Chile; **COLOMBIA:** Computerworld Colombia, PC World Colombia; **COSTA RICA:** PC World Centro America; **THE CZECH AND SLOVAK REPUBLICS:** Computerworld Czechoslovakia, Macworld Czech Republic, PC World Czechoslovakia; **DENMARK:** Communications World Danmark, Computerworld Danmark, Macworld Danmark, PC World Danmark, Techworld Denmark; **DOMINICAN REPUBLIC:** PC World Republica Dominicana; **ECUADOR:** PC World Ecuador; **EGYPT:** Computerworld Middle East, PC World Middle East; **EL SALVADOR:** PC World Centro America; **FINLAND:** MikroPC, Tietoverkko, Tietoviikko; **FRANCE:** Distributique, Hebdo, Info PC, Le Monde Informatique, Macworld, Reseaux & Telecoms, WebMaster France; **GERMANY:** Computer Partner, Computerwoche, Computerwoche Extra, Computerwoche FOCUS, Global Online, Macwelt, PC Welt; **GREECE:** Amiga Computing, GamePro Greece, Multimedia World; **GUATEMALA:** PC World Centro America; **HONDURAS:** PC World Centro America; **HONG KONG:** Computerworld Hong Kong, PC World Hong Kong, Publish in Asia; **HUNGARY:** ABCD CD-ROM, Computerworld Szamitastechnika, Internetto online Magazine, PC World Hungary, PC-X Magazin Hungary; **ICELAND:** Tolvuheimur PC World Island; **INDIA:** Information Communications World, Information Systems Computerworld, PC World India, Publish in Asia; **INDONESIA:** InfoKomputer PC World, Komputek Computerworld, Publish in Asia; **IRELAND:** ComputerScope, PC Live!; **ISRAEL:** Macworld Israel, People & Computers/Computerworld; **ITALY:** Computerworld Italia, Macworld Italia, Networking Italia, PC World Italia; **JAPAN:** DTP World, Macworld Japan, Nikkei Personal Computing, OS/2 World Japan, SunWorld Japan, Windows NT World, Windows World Japan; **KENYA:** PC World East African; **KOREA:** Hi-Tech Information, Macworld Korea, PC World Korea; **MACEDONIA:** PC World Macedonia; **MALAYSIA:** Computerworld Malaysia, PC World Malaysia, Publish in Asia; **MALTA:** PC World Malta; **MEXICO:** Computerworld Mexico, PC World Mexico; **MYANMAR:** PC World Myanmar; **NETHERLANDS:** Computer! Totaal, LAN Internetworking Magazine, LAN World Buyers Guide, Macworld Netherlands, Net, WebWereld; **NEW ZEALAND:** Absolute Beginners Guide and Plain & Simple Series, Computer Buyer, Computer Industry Directory, Computerworld New Zealand, MTB, Network World, PC World New Zealand; **NICARAGUA:** PC World Centro America; **NORWAY:** Computerworld Norge, CW Rapport, Datamagasinet, Financial Rapport, Kursguide Norge, Macworld Norge, Multimediaworld Norge, PC World Ekspress Norge, PC World Nettverk, PC World Norge, PC World ProduktGuide Norge; **PAKISTAN:** Computerworld Pakistan; **PANAMA:** PC World Panama; **PEOPLE'S REPUBLIC OF CHINA:** China Computer Users, China Computerworld, China InfoWorld, China Telecom World Weekly, Computer & Communication, Electronic Design China, Electronics Today, Electronics Weekly, Game Software, PC World China, Popular Computer Week, Software Weekly, Software World, Telecom World; **PERU:** Computerworld Peru, PC World Profesional Peru, PC World SoHo Peru; **PHILIPPINES:** Click!, Computerworld Philippines, PC World Philippines, Publish in Asia; **POLAND:** Computerworld Poland, Computerworld Special Report Poland, Cyber, Macworld Poland, Networld Poland, PC World Komputer; **PORTUGAL:** Cerebro/PC World, Computerworld/Correio Informático, Dealer World Portugal, Mac*In/PC*In Portugal, Multimedia World; **PUERTO RICO:** PC World Puerto Rico; **ROMANIA:** Computerworld Romania, PC World Romania, Telecom Romania; **RUSSIA:** Computerworld Russia, Mir PK, Publish, Seti; **SINGAPORE:** Computerworld Singapore, PC World Singapore, Publish in Asia; **SLOVENIA:** Monitor; **SOUTH AFRICA:** Computing SA, Network World SA, Software World SA; **SPAIN:** Communicaciones World España, Computerworld España, Dealer World España, Macworld España, PC World España; **SRI LANKA:** Infolink PC World; **SWEDEN:** CAP&Design, Computer Sweden, Corporate Computing Sweden, Internetworld Sweden, it.branschen, Macworld Sweden, MaxiData Sweden, MikroDatorn, Nätverk & Kommunikation, PC World Sweden, PCaktiv, Windows World Sweden; **SWITZERLAND:** Computerworld Schweiz, Macworld Schweiz, PCtip; **TAIWAN:** Computerworld Taiwan, Macworld Taiwan, NEW ViSiON/Publish, PC World Taiwan, Windows World Taiwan; **THAILAND:** Publish in Asia, Thai Computerworld; **TURKEY:** Computerworld Turkiye, Macworld Turkiye, Network World Turkiye, PC World Turkiye; **UKRAINE:** Computerworld Kiev, Multimedia World Ukraine, PC World Ukraine; **UNITED KINGDOM:** Acorn User UK, Amiga Action UK, Amiga Computing UK, Apple Talk UK, Computing, Macworld, Parents and Computers UK, PC Advisor, PC Home, PSX Pro, The WEB; **UNITED STATES:** Cable in the Classroom, CIO Magazine, Computerworld, DOS World, Federal Computer Week, GamePro Magazine, InfoWorld, I-Way, Macworld, Network World, PC Games, PC World, Publish, Video Event, THE WEB Magazine, and WebMaster; online webzines: JavaWorld, NetscapeWorld, and SunWorld Online; **URUGUAY:** InfoWorld Uruguay; **VENEZUELA:** Computerworld Venezuela, PC World Venezuela; and **VIETNAM:** PC World Vietnam.   5/7/98

Welcome to *Ace It!*

Looking to get certified? The *Ace It!* series is what you're looking for! The *Ace It!* series has been designed to meet your need for a quick, easy-to-use study tool that helps you save time, prioritize your study, and cram for the exam. *Ace It!* books serve as a supplement to other certification resources, such as our award-winning *Study Guide* and *MCSE . . . For Dummies* series. With these two series and *Ace It!*, IDG Books offers a full suite of study tools to meet your certification needs, from complete tutorial and reference materials to quick exam prep tools.

Ace It's exam-expert authors give you the ace in the hole: our unique insider's perspective on the exam itself — how it works, what topics are really important, and *how you really need to think* to ace the exam. Our features train your brain to understand not only the essential topics covered in the exam, but how to decipher the exam itself. By demystifying the exam, we give you that extra confidence to know that you're really prepared!

Ace It! books help you study with a wealth of truly valuable features in each chapter:

- **Official Word** lists the official certification exam objectives covered in the chapter.

- **Inside Scoop** immediately follows the Official Word and gives you the author's insight and expertise about the exam content covered in the chapter.

- **Are You Prepared?** is a chapter pretest that lets you check your knowledge beforehand: if you score well on the pretest, you may not need to review the chapter! This helps you focus your study. The questions are immediately followed by answers with cross-references to the information in the chapter, helping you further target your review.

- **Have You Mastered?** is a chapter post-test that includes five to ten multiple-choice questions with answers, analysis, and cross-references to the chapter discussion. The questions help you check your progress and pinpoint what you've learned and what you still need to study.

- **Practice Your Skills** consists of three to five exercises related to specific exam objectives. They provide an opportunity to relate exam concepts to real-world situations by presenting a hypothetical problem or guiding you through a task at the computer. These exercises enable you to take what you've learned for the exam and put it to work.

Within each chapter, icons call your attention to the following features:

Test Tips give hints and strategies for passing the exam to help strengthen your test-taking skills.

Test Traps warn you of pitfalls and loopholes you're likely to see in actual exam questions.

Pop Quizzes offer instant testing of hot exam topics.

Know This provides a quick summary of essential elements of topics you *will* see on the exam.

In the front and back of the book, you'll find even more features to give you that extra confidence and prepare you to get certified:

- **Ace Card:** Tear out this quick-review card for a distilled breakdown of essential exam-related terms and concepts to take with you and review before the exam.

- **Insider's Guide:** This helpful certification profile describes the certification process in general, and discusses the specific exam this book covers. It explains the exam development process, provides tips for preparing for and taking the exams, describes the testing process (how to register for an exam, what to expect at the testing center, how to obtain and evaluate test scores, and how to retake the exam if necessary), and tells you where to go for more information about the certification you're after.

- **Practice Exam:** A full-length multiple choice practice exam. Questions and answer selections mimic the certification exam in style, number of questions, and content to give you the closest experience to the real thing.

- **Exam Key** and **Exam Analysis:** These features tell you not only what the right answers are on the Practice Exam, but why they're right, and where to look in the book for the material you need to review.

- **Exam Revealed:** Here's your ace in the hole — the real deal on how the exam works. Our exam-expert authors deconstruct the questions on the Practice Exam, examining their structure, style, and wording to reveal subtleties, loopholes, and pitfalls that can entrap or mislead you when you take the real test. For each question, the author highlights part of the question or answer choices and then, in a sentence or two, identifies the possible problem and explains how to avoid it.

- **Glossary:** Not familiar with a word or concept? Just look it up! The Glossary covers all the essential terminology you need to know.

With this wealth of features and the exclusive insider's perspective provided by our authors, you can be sure that *Ace It!* completes your set of certification study tools. No matter what you've got, you still need an *Ace It!*

Credits

Acquisitions Editor
Tracy Thomsic

Development Editor
Jennifer Rowe

Copy Editors
Larisa North
Nicole Fountain

Project Coordinator
Susan Parini

Cover Coordinator
Cyndra Robbins

Book Designer
Dan Ziegler

Graphics & Production Specialists
Vincent F. Burns
Laura Carpenter
Stephanie Hollier
Linda Marousek
Hector Mendoza

Quality Control Specialists
Mick Arellano
Mark Schumann

Proofreader
Sharon Duffy

Indexer
C² Editorial Services

About the Author

Jason Nash currently lives in Raleigh, North Carolina with his wife and coauthor Angie. He works for Wang Global (www.wang.com). His certifications include MCSE, MCT, Novell CNE, and the Network Professional Association's CNP. Outside of writing and work, he and Angie enjoy playing paintball on the weekends and going to the beach. He welcomes comments from readers; his e-mail address is jnash@intrex.net, and his home page is at www.intrex.net/nash.

To Peggy Franks, thank you for everything.

Insider's Guide to MCP Certification

The Microsoft Certified Professional Exams are *not* easy, and require a great deal of preparation. The exam questions measure real-world skills. Your ability to answer these questions correctly will be greatly enhanced by as much hands-on experience with the product as you can get.

About the Exams

An important aspect of passing the MCP Certification Exams is understanding the big picture. This includes understanding how the exams are developed and scored.

Every job function requires different levels of cognitive skills, from memorization of facts and definitions to the comprehensive ability to analyze scenarios, design solutions, and evaluate options. To make the exams relevant in the real world, Microsoft Certified Professional exams test the specific cognitive skills needed for the job functions being tested. These exams go beyond testing rote knowledge — you need to *apply* your knowledge, analyze technical solutions, solve problems, and make decisions — just like you would on the job.

Exam Items and Scoring

Microsoft certification exams consist of three types of items: multiple-choice, multiple-rating, and enhanced. The way you indicate your answer and the number of points you receive differ depending on the type of item.

Multiple-choice item

A traditional multiple-choice item presents a problem and asks you to select either the best answer (single response) or the best set of answers (multiple response) to the given item from a list of possible answers.

For a multiple-choice item, your response is scored as either correct or incorrect. A correct answer receives a score of 1 point and an incorrect answer receives a score of 0 points.

In the case of a multiple-choice, multiple-response item (for which the correct response consists of more than one answer), the item is scored as being correct only if all the correct answers are selected. No partial credit is given for a response that does not include all the correct answers for the item.

For consistency purposes, the question in a multiple-choice, multiple-response item is always presented in singular form, regardless of how many answers are correct. Always follow the instructions displayed at the bottom of the window.

Multiple-rating item

A multiple-rating item presents a task similar to those presented in multiple-choice items. In a multiple-choice item, you are asked to select the best answer or answers from a selection of several potential answers. In contrast, a multiple-rating item presents a task, along with a proposed solution. Each time the task is presented, a different solution is proposed. In each multiple-rating item, you are asked to choose the answer that best describes the results produced by one proposed solution.

Enhanced item

An enhanced item is similar to a multiple-choice item because it asks you to select your response from a number of possible responses. However, unlike the traditional multiple-choice item that presents you with a list of possible answers from which to choose, an enhanced item may ask you to indicate your answer in one of three ways:

- Type the correct response, such as a command name.
- Review an exhibit (such as a screen shot, a network configuration drawing, or a code sample), and then use the mouse to select the area of the exhibit that represents the correct response.

- Review an exhibit, and then select the correct response from the list of possible responses.

As with a multiple-choice item, your response to an enhanced item is scored as either correct or incorrect. A correct answer receives full credit of 1 point, and an incorrect answer receives a score of 0 points.

Preparing for a Microsoft Certified Professional Exam

The best way to prepare for an exam is to study, learn, and master the job function on which you'll be tested. For any certification exam, you should follow these important preparation steps:

1. Identify the objectives on which you'll be tested.
2. Assess your current mastery of those objectives.
3. Practice tasks and study the areas you haven't mastered.

This section describes tools and techniques that may be helpful as you perform these steps to prepare for the exam.

Exam Preparation Guides

For each certification exam, an Exam Preparation Guide provides important, specific information about what you'll be tested on and how best to prepare. These guides are essential tools for preparing to take certification exams. You'll find the following types of valuable information in the exam preparation guides:

- **Tasks you should master:** Outlines the overall job function tasks you should master
- **Exam objectives:** Lists the specific skills and abilities on which you should expect to be measured
- **Product resources:** Tells you the products and technologies with which you should be experienced

- **Suggested reading:** Points you to specific reference materials and other publications that discuss one or more of the exam objectives
- **Suggested curriculum:** Provides a specific list of instructor-led and self-paced courses relating to the job function tasks and topics in the exam

You'll also find pointers to additional information that may help you prepare for the exams, such as *Microsoft TechNet, Microsoft Developer Network* (MSDN), online forums, and other sources.

By paying attention to the verbs used in the "Exam Objectives" section of the Exam Preparation Guide, you can get an idea of the level at which you'll be tested on that objective.

To view the most recent version of the exam preparation guides, which include the exam's objectives, check out Microsoft's Training and Certification Web site at `www.microsoft.com/train_cert/`.

Assessment Exams

When preparing for the exams, take lots of assessment exams. Assessment exams are self-paced exams that you take at your own computer. When you complete an assessment exam, you receive instant score feedback so you can determine areas in which additional study may be helpful before you take the certification exam. Although your score on an assessment exam doesn't necessarily indicate what your score will be on the certification exam, assessment exams give you the opportunity to answer items that are similar to those on the certification exams. The assessment exams also use the same computer-based testing tool as the certification exams, so you don't have to learn the tool on exam day.

An assessment exam exists for almost every certification exam.

Taking a Microsoft Certified Professional Exam

This section contains information about registering for and taking an MCP exam, including what to expect when you arrive at the Sylvan Prometric testing center to take the exam.

How to Register for an Exam

Candidates may take exams at any of more than 700 Sylvan Prometric testing centers around the world. For the location of a Sylvan Prometric testing center near you, call (800) 755-EXAM (755-3926). Outside the United States and Canada, contact your local Sylvan Prometric Registration Center.

To register for an MCP exam:

1. Determine which exam you want to take and note the exam number.

2. Register with the Sylvan Prometric Registration Center nearest to you. A part of the registration process is advance payment for the exam.

3. After you receive the registration and payment confirmation letter from Sylvan Prometric, call a Sylvan Prometric testing center to schedule your exam.

When you schedule the exam, you'll be provided instructions regarding the appointment, cancellation procedures, and ID requirements, as well as information about the testing center location.

Exams must be taken within one year of payment. You can schedule exams up to six weeks in advance, or as late as one working day prior to the date of the exam. You can cancel or reschedule your exam if you contact Sylvan Prometric at least two working days prior to the exam.

Although subject to space availability, same-day registration is available in some locations. Where same-day registration is available, you must register a minimum of two hours before test time.

What to Expect at the Testing Center

As you prepare for your certification exam, it may be helpful to know what to expect when you arrive at the testing center on the day of your exam. The following information gives you a preview of the general procedure you'll go through at the testing center:

- You will be asked to sign the log book upon arrival and departure.

- You will be required to show two forms of identification, including one photo ID (such as a driver's license or company security ID), before you may take the exam.

- The test administrator will give you a Testing Center Regulations form that explains the rules you will be expected to comply with during the test. You will be asked to sign the form, indicating that you understand the regulations and will comply.

- The test administrator will show you to your test computer and will handle any preparations necessary to start the testing tool and display the exam on the computer.

- You will be provided a set amount of scratch paper for use during the exam. All scratch paper will be collected from you at the end of the exam.

- The exams are all closed-book. You may not use a laptop computer or have any notes or printed material with you during the exam session.

- Some exams may include additional materials, or exhibits. If any exhibits are required for your exam, the test administrator will provide you with them before you begin the exam and collect them from you at the end of the exam.

- Before you begin the exam, the test administrator will tell you what to do when you complete the exam. If the test administrator doesn't explain this to you, or if you are unclear about what you should do, ask the administrator before beginning the exam.

- The number of items on each exam varies, as does the amount of time allotted for each exam. Generally, certification exams consist of about 50 to 100 items and have durations of 60 to 90 minutes. You can verify the number of items and time allotted for your exam when you register.

Because you'll be given a specific amount of time to complete the exam once you begin, if you have any questions or concerns, don't hesitate to ask the test administrator before the exam begins.

As an exam candidate, you are entitled to the best support and environment possible for your exam. In particular, you are entitled to following:

- A quiet, uncluttered test environment
- Scratch paper
- The tutorial for using the online testing tool, and time to take the tutorial
- A knowledgeable and professional test administrator
- The opportunity to submit comments about the testing center and staff or the test itself

The Certification Development Team will investigate any problems or issues you raise and make every effort to resolve them quickly.

Your Exam Results

Once you have completed an exam, you will be given immediate, online notification of your pass or fail status. You will also receive a printed Examination Score Report indicating your pass or fail status and your exam results by section. (The test administrator will give you the printed score report.) Test scores are automatically forwarded to Microsoft within five working days after you take the test. You do not need to send your score to Microsoft.

If you pass the exam, you will receive confirmation from Microsoft, typically within two to four weeks.

If You Don't Receive a Passing Score

If you do not pass a certification exam, you may call Sylvan Prometric to schedule a time to retake the exam. Before retaking the exam, you should review the appropriate Exam Preparation Guide and focus additional study on the topic areas where your exam results could be improved. Please note that you must pay again for each exam retake.

One way to determine areas where additional study may be helpful is to carefully review your individual section scores. Generally, the section titles in your score report correlate to specific groups of exam objectives listed in the Exam Preparation Guide.

Here are some specific ways you can prepare to retake an exam:

- Go over the section-by-section scores on your exam results, noting objective areas where your score could be improved.
- Review the Exam Preparation Guide for the exam, with a special focus on the tasks and objective areas that correspond to the exam sections where your score could be improved.
- Increase your real-world, hands-on experience and practice performing the listed job tasks with the relevant products and technologies.
- Consider taking or retaking one or more of the suggested courses listed in the Exam Preparation Guide.
- Review the suggested readings listed in the Exam Preparation Guide.
- After you review the materials, retake the corresponding Assessment Exam.

For More Information

To find out more about Microsoft Education and Certification materials and programs, to register with Sylvan Prometric, or to get other useful information, check the following resources. Outside the United States or Canada, contact your local Microsoft office or Sylvan Prometric testing center.

- **Microsoft Certified Professional Program:**
  (800) 636-7544. Call for information about the Microsoft
  Certified Professional program and exams, and to order
  the *Microsoft Certified Professional Program Exam Study
  Guide* or the Microsoft Train_Cert Offline CD-ROM.

- **Sylvan Prometric Testing Centers: (800) 755-EXAM.**
  Call to register to take a Microsoft Certified Professional
  exam at any of more than 700 Sylvan Prometric testing
  centers around the world, or to order the *Microsoft
  Certified Professional Program Exam Study Guide.*

- **Microsoft Sales Fax Service: (800) 727-3351.** Call for
  Microsoft Certified Professional Exam Preparation
  Guides, Microsoft Official Curriculum course
  descriptions and schedules, or the *Microsoft Certified
  Professional Program Exam Study Guide.*

- **Education Program and Course Information:**
  (800) SOLPROV. Call for information about Microsoft
  Official Curriculum courses, Microsoft education products,
  and the Microsoft Solution Provider Authorized Technical
  Education Center (ATEC) program, where you can attend
  a Microsoft Official Curriculum course, or to order the
  Microsoft Certified Professional Program Exam Study Guide.

- **Microsoft Certification Development Team: Fax #:**
  (425) 936-1311. Use this fax number to volunteer for
  participation in one or more exam development phases
  or to report a problem with an exam. Address written
  correspondence to: Certification Development Team,
  Microsoft Education and Certification, One Microsoft
  Way, Redmond, WA 98052.

- **Microsoft TechNet Technical Information Network:**
  (800) 344-2121. Call for support professionals and system
  administrators. Outside the United States and Canada,
  call your local Microsoft subsidiary for information.

- **Microsoft Developer Network (MSDN): (800) 759-5474.**
  MSDN is the official source for software development kits, device driver kits, operating systems, and information about developing applications for Microsoft Windows and Windows NT.

- **Online Services: (800) 936-3500.** Call for information about Microsoft Connection on CompuServe, Microsoft Knowledge Base, Microsoft Software Library, Microsoft Download Service, and Internet.

This section contains excerpts from the Microsoft Certified Professional Exam Study Guide (Microsoft Corporation, 1998), reprinted with permission.

Preface

Welcome to *MCSE Networking Essentials Ace It!* This book is intended to help you hone your existing knowledge and gain a greater understanding of Networking Essentials so you have the ability to pass Microsoft Certified Professional Exam No. 70-58: Networking Essentials.

Consider this book your strategy guide as you prepare for the exam. It supplements any other materials you already have and helps you decide how to make best use of your study time leading up to the exam. Throughout this book I assume you are familiar with Networking Essentials concepts, or that you have other study materials to help you understand these concepts. With that in mind, I cover Networking Essentials to the depth of the exam objectives, but not beyond that point.

How to Use This Book

The chapters of this book are designed to be studied sequentially. In other words, it would be best if you complete Chapter 1 before you proceed to Chapter 2. A few chapters could probably stand alone, but all in all, I recommend a sequential approach.

For best results (and we both know that the only acceptable result is a passing score on the Networking Essentials exam), I recommend the following plan of attack as you use this book. First, take the Are You Prepared? self-test at the beginning of the chapter to see if you've already mastered the topic. Next, if your self-test score tells you that you need more study, read the chapter and the Test Tips and Test Traps highlights, paying particular attention to the Inside Scoop section for pointers on what topics to concentrate on. Then use the Have You Mastered? and Practice Your Skills sections to see if you really have the key concepts under your belt. If you don't, go back and reread the section(s) you're not clear on. If your self-test score indicates you are prepared on this topic, you may want to move on to the next chapter.

After you've completed your study of the chapters, reviewed the Have You Mastered? questions, and done the Practice Your Skills exercises, take the Practice Exam included in the back of the book. The Practice Exam will help you assess how much you've learned from your study and will familiarize you with the types of questions you'll face when you take the real exam. Once you identify a weak area, you can use the cross-references to the corresponding chapters (including the Have You Mastered? questions) to improve your knowledge and skills in that area.

Before you take the Networking Essentials exam, tear out the *Ace Card* and use its quick run-down of essential concepts to refresh your memory and focus your review just before the test.

Prerequisites

This book is an exam preparation guide, but it does not start at ground zero. I do assume you have the following knowledge and skills at the outset:

1. Basic terminology and basic skills to use a Microsoft Windows product. (This could be Windows 95, Windows for Workgroups, or a Windows NT product.)
2. Basic mouse skills: being able to left-click, right-click, use the pointer, and so on.

If you meet these prerequisites, you're ready to begin this book.

If you don't have the basic Windows experience or mouse skills, I recommend you either take a one-day Windows application course or work through a self-study book to acquire these skills *before* you begin this book.

What You Learn

MCSE Networking Essentials Ace It! gives you the quickest review of all the essential topics on Exam 70-58. Here's a rundown of what you learn:

- **Basics of Networking**
- **OSI Model**
- **Network Media**

- **Network Designs**
- **Network Protocols**
- **Connecting Networks**
- **Administration**
- **Troubleshooting**
- **Adding Services to Your Network**

Let's Get Started!

That concludes the owner's manual on how to operate this book. It's time to get started, and get you on your way to passing the Networking Essentials exam. Now, let's get certified!

Acknowledgments

First, I would like to thank the people at IDG Books Worldwide. They are all great people and have been nothing but helpful. I also thank them for giving me the wonderful opportunity to write for them. A special thanks goes to Tracy Thomsic and Jennifer Rowe on this one.

The most important person to thank is my wife. She is the most important thing to me, and as I said in my last book, everything I do, I do for her. She helped me greatly in writing this book and is a wonderful coauthor.

Next is my family. Without the help and support of my mother and stepfather, Peggy and Timmy Franks, and my grandmother Marie Ward, there is no way I would be where I am today. I would also like to thank my sister, Jeanie, my father, Bill Nash, and my grandparents, Homer and Frances Nash.

Finally, all the other people on my list to thank. The people at work: John, Blain, Dave, Chuck, Joe, Mike, Missy, Kris, Tim, and Drew. A few non-work related friends: Todd Shanaberger, Jacob Hall, Robert Mowlds, Derek Stutsman, Paul Ward, Johannes and Joakim Erdfelt, Yossarian Hulmberg, Andy Scherrer, and Scott Bessler.

Contents
at a Glance

Contents

Basics of Networking

WELCOME TO THE FIRST CHAPTER in your study of the Networking Essentials exam. This chapter reviews the basics of networking to help you get up to speed quickly. The chapter starts off with a quick overview of the definition of networking. Next, components of a network are discussed, followed by the different network models and types. After that, we cover the different services networks offer to their users. We wrap up the chapter with a discussion on LANs, MANs, and WANs. Good luck on your quest!

Exam Material in This Chapter

Based on Microsoft Objectives

- Compare a file-and-print server with an application server
- Define common networking terms for LANs and WANs
- Compare a client/server network with a peer-to-peer network

Based on Author Experience

- Components of a network
- Centralized computing
- Distributed computing
- Collaborative computing
- Peer-to-peer networks
- Server-based networks
- File services
- Print services
- Message services
- Directory services
- Application services
- Database services
- Local area networks
- Metropolitan area networks
- Wide area networks

Are You Prepared?

These questions will help you determine whether you're prepared for the material covered in this chapter or whether you need more review.

1. Which network component makes requests for network services?

- ☐ A. Server
- ☐ B. Client
- ☐ C. Resource
- ☐ D. Media

2. Which type of network has one or more large computers servicing requests from clients?

- ☐ A. Peer-to-peer
- ☐ B. Server-based
- ☐ C. Local area network
- ☐ D. Contention-based

3. Which network service would you use when you save a word processing file to a disk on the network server?

- ☐ A. File services
- ☐ B. Print services
- ☐ C. Storage services
- ☐ D. Disk services

4. Which type of network would fit in one office building?

- ☐ A. Local area network
- ☐ B. Wide area network
- ☐ C. Office area network
- ☐ D. File-based network

5. Which network model has one large computer do all of the processing?

- ☐ A. Collaborative
- ☐ B. Centralized
- ☐ C. Server-based
- ☐ D. Peer-to-peer

Answers:

1. *B.* Clients make requests to the server for resources. See section titled "Network Components."

2. *B.* Server-based networks have a large computer handling requests from client computers. See section titled "Different Network Types."

3. *A.* File services handle all requests for disk access to the file server. Print services only handle requests for printing. There is no such thing as a storage service. See section titled "Network Services."

4. *A.* LANs are small networks usually contained to one physical building. WANs can cover large areas covering many countries. Office area networks do not exist. See section titled "Differences Between LANs, MANs, and WANs."

5. *B.* Centralized networks use one mail computer, usually a mainframe, that does all processing for clients. The clients only display information. See section titled "Networking Models."

Networking Basics

No matter what the size or type of network, some things never change. Network components are similar wherever you go. Before we review the types of networks and their services, you need to be familiar with the different parts of a network. The following list explains some of these parts:

- **Server:** Powerful computer that provides services to the other computers on the network.
- **Client:** Computer that uses the services that a server provides. The client is usually less powerful than the server.
- **Peer:** A computer that acts as both a client and a server.
- **Media:** Physical connection between the devices on a network.
- **Resources:** Anything available to a client on a network is considered a resource. Printers, data, fax devices, and other networked devices and information are resources.
- **User:** Any person who uses a client to access resources on the network.
- **Protocol:** Protocols are written rules that are used for communications. They are the languages computers use to talk to each other over a network.

These components can be set up so the network operates in different ways, depending on what you need to provide for your users and how they access it. A few different networking models define the various setups for sharing and accessing data on a network.

Networking Models

Network models describe how information is processed by the computers on the network. Data can be processed by clients, by a central server, or by everyone. The best server model for your needs is generally determined by the applications you need to run.

There are three basic network models:

- Centralized
- Distributed
- Collaborative

Centralized Computing

Centralized networks are used today for a variety of reasons. This type of computing keeps all the data in one location and does the processing there, ensuring that everyone is working with the same information. It is also easy to back up data because it is all stored on the server; the servers are the only systems that need to be backed up. This also means that the servers are the only systems that need to be secured, because the terminals have no data. And because everything is done on the server, terminals do not require a floppy drive, so the chances of the network being infected with a virus are low. This type of network also costs less overall; although the servers need to be powerful systems with a lot of storage space, the terminals are inexpensive because they require no real processing or storage capability of their own.

A centralized network has disadvantages, as well. Because the computing is done on the server, this type of network can be somewhat slow. Additionally, if the users have a variety of needs, meeting these needs in a centralized computing network could be difficult because each user's applications and resources would have to be set up separately, and it would no longer be efficient to have them operate from the same centralized server. Also, connectivity can become a large problem on centralized networks because all users must connect to one central site. Due to these limitations, most networks today are based on either the distributed or collaborative network computing model.

Centralized Computing Characteristics

Advantages of centralized computing:

- Ease of backup
- Security
- Low cost

Disadvantages of centralized computing:

- Slow network access
- Fewer options

Distributed Computing

Unlike centralized computing, where all the work is done on the server, in a distributed network the data storage and processing are done on the local workstation. This allows for faster access to data. Because each computer can store and process data, the servers do not need to be as powerful and expensive. This type of network accommodates users with a variety of needs, and enables them to share data, resources, and services. The computers used in distributed computing are capable of working as stand-alone systems, but are networked together for increased functionality.

This type of system has many benefits, but it also has some drawbacks. A distributed network is more susceptible to viruses because any user could introduce an infected file and spread a virus throughout the network. Also, developing an effective backup plan is more difficult if users begin to store data on their individual systems instead of keeping all the data on a central system. This can also cause users to work with different versions of the same file.

Distributed computing is the preferred choice as many companies move from mainframes to intelligent desktops.

Distributed Computing Characteristics

Advantages of distributed computing:

- Quick access
- Allows for a variety of uses

Disadvantages of distributed computing:

- Susceptible to viruses
- Difficult to back up
- File synchronization

Collaborative Computing

Collaborative computing enables computers to share processing power across a network. Applications can be written to use the processing on other computers to complete jobs more quickly. This type of network can be faster because users are not limited to the processing power of one system to complete tasks. Aside from the capability to process tasks on multiple systems, this type of network is similar to distributed computing in its capability to share resources and data.

This likeness introduces many of the same advantages as distributed computing networks — for example, a variety of users can be accommodated on a collaborative network. This type of network also has many of the same drawbacks as distributed networks. First, viruses can be spread quickly throughout the network. Also, because data can be stored throughout the network, backing up all important data can be difficult. File synchronization is also an issue when several copies of a file are stored throughout the network.

Collaborative Computing Characteristics

Advantages of collaborative computing:

- Extremely fast
- Allows for a variety of uses

Disadvantages of collaborative computing:

- Susceptible to viruses
- Difficult to back up
- File synchronization

Different Network Types

A computer network can consist of two different types: server-based and peer-to-peer. A server-based network is the type that typically comes to mind when one mentions networks. These networks consist of clients that make requests to a server. In peer-to-peer networks, each machine can act as both a client and a server, both requesting and providing resources.

When answering questions on the exam concerning the type of network to use, always look at the projected growth! Too often, when people take the exam, they look at the initial size of the network. That is really not important. What is important is the final projected size.

Peer-to-Peer Networking

The simplest form of networking is *peer-to-peer*. In a peer-to-peer network, each workstation acts as a client and a server. There is no central repository for information and no central server to maintain. Data and resources are distributed throughout the network, and each user is responsible for sharing data and resources connected to his or her system.

A number of operating systems support peer-to-peer networking. Some operating systems have this capability built in, while others can have the capability added. The following Microsoft operating systems have peer-to-peer networking built in:

- Windows 95
- Windows for Workgroups
- Windows NT Workstation

For most operating systems without this capability, such as Windows 3.*x* and MS-DOS, you can add software such as NetWare Lite or LANtastic.

 TEST TRAP Watch for the type of operating system used in a question on the exam. Even though Windows NT Server can actually be used in a peer-to-peer environment, on the exam it should be considered a server-based operating system.

Although peer-to-peer networks may not always be the best choice, they do have their place and advantages. The peer-to-peer network model works well for small office networks. Once your network has reached about ten clients, it can become too difficult to maintain. Because the peer-to-peer model does not need a powerful dedicated server, it is usually the cheapest type of network to install. All you need to connect several individual systems are network adapters, cable or other transmission media, and the operating system.

The general rule is to stop using peer-to-peer networking once your total number of clients reaches about ten. With more than ten users, it becomes likely you'll find different revisions of documents on different client computers. Also, it becomes difficult to set up that many users because you have to connect to one client for your printer, another client for documents, and so on. If the network had a central server, you would only need to get information from one source.

Training is also difficult when you have a large number of clients, because your users need to be trained to share resources, and each user is responsible for acting as administrator of his or her system. Security is another issue because users need to know how to secure their own resources. Because there is no central administration, it is the users' responsibility to ensure that only authorized users can access their data. Most peer-to-peer security consists of a single password for each resource; this is known as *share-level security*. Share-level security requires that a user know the password for a resource before it can be accessed.

KNOW THIS — When to Use Peer-to-Peer

On the Networking Essentials exam, you will see questions concerning when to use peer-to-peer networking. The two keys to answering those questions usually have to do with the current or projected network size, and with security.

If the question states that there are fewer than ten computers on the network, then peer-to-peer would be a good choice. Be sure to keep in mind the projected growth, if that information is given to you. Additionally, if a network in an exam question needs share-level security, then peer-to-peer should be used.

Peer-to-Peer Network Characteristics

Advantages of peer-to-peer networks:

- Inexpensive
- Ease of setup
- Ease of maintenance

Disadvantages of peer-to-peer networks:

- No central administration
- Data is spread across the network
- Difficulty locating resources
- Weak security
- Dependent on user training

Server-based Networks

When a network comes to mind, most people think of the server-based network. In a server-based network, you have one computer, usually larger than the clients, that is dedicated to handing out files and/or information to clients. The server controls the data, as well as printers and other resources the clients need to access. The server is not only a faster computer with a better processor, but it also requires much more storage space to contain all the data that needs to be shared to the clients. Having these tasks handled by the server enables the clients to be less powerful, because they only request resources.

Because the server is dedicated to handing out files and/or information, it cannot be used as a workstation. Its purpose is strictly to provide services to other computers, not to request services. Servers are optimized at being able to hand out information as fast as possible.

Some servers, called Application Servers, are used specifically for one application. This is usually an e-mail server, or sometimes a server used for a gateway.

POP QUIZ — True or False?

1. The network component that carries the signals between devices is called media.

2. The TCP/IP protocol suite was created by Microsoft.

3. Routers are an inexpensive and easy way to extend network distance.

Answers: *1. True   2. False   3. False*

KNOW THIS — When to Use Server-based

The exam questions on server-based networks go along with those regarding peer-to-peer networks. Usually, they appear as either/or types of questions. The keys to knowing whether the answer relates to server-based networking are the opposite of the keys for peer-to-peer networking: if the network requires user-level security, or has more than ten clients, it should be a server-based network.

Another clue might be whether the proposed network has a central server. Remember that server-based networks must have a large central server with a server operating system of Windows NT or Novell's NetWare. If every computer on the network only has Windows 95, the only option is peer-to-peer.

If your network has more than ten to fifteen clients, you should consider a server-based network.

Security is also much easier to manage in a server-based network. Because you only need to create and maintain accounts on the server instead of on every workstation, you can assign rights to resources easily. Access to resources can be granted to user accounts. Specific users can be granted access to resources using their account on the server. This type of security is known as *user-level security*. Because the server on the network acts as the central repository for almost all your information, you only need to perform backups to the server. You can also replicate this information easily to other servers on your network, in case one server should go down. Using replication tools on the server is an effective way to synchronize files. These tools copy the most current version of a file to other servers, so those users are working from the same version of the file rather than many different versions.

This type of network can also be cost efficient. With the server storing almost all of the information on your network, you do not need large hard drives on the client computers. You also do not need extra RAM and processing power on your clients to provide server functions. This can help offset the price of the server, because each client computer can be a less powerful, less expensive system.

Server-based Network Characteristics

Advantages of server-based networks:

- Centralized security
- Dedicated servers
- Easy accessibility
- Ease of backup
- File synchronization

Disadvantages of server-based networks:

- Require an administrator
- Expensive server

Network Services

What good would a network be if it did not provide services to the user? Networks are meant to make us more productive by providing services to make us more efficient. Some common services are:

- **File services** — The primary reason for networking computers is for the file services a network can provide. File services include transfer, storage and migration, update synchronization, and archiving.

- **Print services** — Network print services enable companies to buy small numbers of printers and share them among all their users. Features of print services are queue-based printing and fax services. Queue-based printing enables a client's application to spool the print job off to a network server, so the application thinks the job has printed and enables the user to continue working. Print queues can be given different priorities.

- **Message services** — Message services allow for e-mails with attachment files. Attachments can now include video, sound, documents, and almost any other type of data. Groupware applications that use e-mail as their connection backbone are also becoming popular. This enables users to share calendars and scheduling information as well.

- **Directory services** — Directory services enable you to maintain information about all of the *objects* in your network. An object is anything about which you can store information, such as users, printers, servers, and so on. Before directory services were popular, you had to keep separate configuration information about users on each file server. With directory services, you only create one user account object for that user. Each server sees that object, and you can then assign resource rights to that user account. The network operating systems that support directory services have predefined methods to share and update this information.

POP QUIZ **True or False?**

1. All devices on a network with a star topology connect to a bridge.
2. Protocol Analyzers enable you to see what is happening between devices on a network.
3. Star networks have no single point of failure.

Answers: *1. False   2. True   3. False*

Differences Between LANs, MANs, and WANs

Networks are constantly being connected to each other to form larger *internets* (not to be confused with the popular Internet). An internet is a large network made up of connected smaller networks.

The sizes of networks are generally categorized into three different groups:

- **Local area network (LAN)** — This is the smallest network size; it is normally contained in a building or small group of buildings. Because LANs are contained to small areas, high-speed cable can be used. Also, since the media that is installed is usually high-quality, few or no errors are generated on the network. Prices of LAN equipment are fairly reasonable. Network cards for individual computers can be found for as little as $30 each.

- **Metropolitan area network (MAN)** — A group of LANs located in a geographical city. For example, if a college had campuses spread over the majority of a city, and networks existed on each campus, the networks could be connected to create a MAN. MANs are slower than LANs, but they usually generate few errors on the network. Because special equipment is needed to connect the different LANs together, MANs have a high price.

- **Wide area network (WAN)** — This is the largest network size. WANs can interconnect any number of LANs and WANs. They can connect networks across cities, states, countries, or even across the world. The term *Enterprise WAN* refers to a network that connects all the LANs and WANs within an entire organization. WANs normally use connections that travel all over the country or world. For this reason, they are usually slower than MANs and LANs, and more prone to errors. They also require a lot of specialized equipment, so their price is high.

KNOW THIS — LAN, MAN, and WAN Characteristics

LAN characteristics:

- Small areas, usually in one office or building
- High speed
- Equipment is the cheapest of the three

MAN characteristics:

- Larger area than a LAN; usually a large campus or organization spread over a city-sized area
- Lower speed than a LAN, but faster than a WAN
- Equipment has a high price
- Moderate error rates

Continued

WAN characteristics:

- WANs can connect networks worldwide
- Usually much slower than LAN speed
- Highest possible error rate of all three types
- Expensive equipment

Have You Mastered?

Now it's time to review the concepts in this chapter and apply your knowledge. These questions will test your mastery of networking basics.

1. Which of the following must you consider when planning a network?

- ☐ A. Security
- ☐ B. Number of users
- ☐ C. Growth capacity
- ☐ D. All of the above

D. All of these characteristics must be considered when planning a network. Security is important because it will impact how resources are stored and shared. The number of users on a network will help to decide the type of network and media needed. The final growth capacity needs to be considered, so the type of network that's built will grow and not need to be redone at a later time. This information is covered throughout this chapter.

2. Which network component represents the written rules for communication that all devices must understand in order to communicate?

- ☐ A. Protocol
- ☐ B. Media
- ☐ C. Specification

A. Protocols define how network devices communicate. All devices that want to communicate must support and understand the same protocol(s). Protocols use the media to get to other devices. Many protocols are written out in a specification that other manufacturers can follow. For more information, see the "Network Basics" section of this chapter.

3. Which networking model would be appropriate for a large project that required an extreme amount of processing power?

☐ A. Centralized
☐ B. Collaborative
☐ C. Distributed

B. With collaborative computing, you could get many computers to work on a single problem. This would greatly reduce the overall time needed to complete the task. Centralized and distributed computing would not provide enough power to solve the problem. For more information, see the "Networking Models" section of this chapter.

4. What is one disadvantage of server-based networking?

☐ A. Cost
☐ B. Administration overhead
☐ C. Growth potential

A. Server-based networks are more expensive than peer-to-peer networks, due to the cost of the extra large computer for the server, as well as the software the server uses. Many operating systems that come on computers today have peer-to-peer networking built in at no additional charge. Administration overhead is greater in a peer-to-peer network, and the growth potential is not as high. For more information, see the "Different Network Types" section of this chapter.

5. Which network service helps administrators with their job?

- ☐ A. Print services
- ☐ B. File services
- ☐ C. Directory services
- ☐ D. Message services

C. Directory services help administrators do their job by logically mapping out networks and creating objects for each device, user, printer, and so on. This enables administrators to make and track changes from one location. Print, File, and Message services all handle their respective services, but do not help administrators with their job. For more information, see the "Networking Services" section of this chapter.

6. What type of network would a company have if it had offices in Dallas, Charlotte, and New York?

- ☐ A. LAN
- ☐ B. MAN
- ☐ C. WAN

C. Because the company has several sites spread over a very large geographical area, it would require a WAN. LANs are contained in one building, and MANs cover an area the size of a city. Only a WAN would cover an area between three cities across the United States. For more information, see the "Differences Between LANs, MANs, and WANs" section of this chapter.

Practice Your Skills

This exercise will help you apply the material in this chapter through critical thinking.

A changing network

EXERCISE For the past few months, you've been in charge of a small but expanding network. You currently have ten users in an office of a law firm, and they all currently use Windows 95 on their desktop. They are taking advantage of Windows 95's built-in peer-to-peer networking capabilities. You will soon hire another 10 to 20 people who will become network users. Knowing this information, what changes might you make to the network? What components might you need to add?

ANALYSIS Because of the eventual size of the network, it would be in your best interest to switch from the current peer-to-peer network scheme and move to a server-based network. This would require adding a dedicated server, such as Windows NT Server, and sharing all resources from there. This would help with administration and security overhead.

The OSI
Model

Now it's time to review the more boring parts of the Networking Essentials Exam! We start out with a general review of protocols and protocol stacks, then we move over to OSI Model where we quickly cover the different layers and their functions. After that we wrap up this chapter with the different 802 standards. While the Official Word doesn't say much about this chapter, you will see this information on the exam.

Exam Material in this Chapter

Based on Microsoft Objectives

- Compare the implications of using connection-oriented communications with connectionless communications

Based on Author Experience

- Protocol stacks
- Connection-oriented protocols
- Connectionless protocols
- OSI model
- Physical layer
- Data Link layer
- Network layer
- Transport layer
- Session layer
- Presentation layer
- Application layer
- 802 standards

Are You Prepared?

These questions help you determine whether you're prepared for questions on the OSI model or if you need more review.

1. Which type of protocol is the most reliable?

☐ A. Connectionless
☐ B. Connection-oriented
☐ C. Streaming
☐ D. Datagram

2. The Data Link Layer is divided in to which two sublayers?

☐ A. Routing
☐ B. MAC
☐ C. LLC
☐ D. DLC

3. Which layer is responsible for routing?

☐ A. Data
☐ B. Presentation
☐ C. Network
☐ D. Communication

4. **Which form of communication only permits unidirectional conversation?**

   ☐ A. Simplex
   ☐ B. Connectionless
   ☐ C. Half-duplex
   ☐ D. Full-duplex

5. **Which 802 standard defines the 100Mbit standard by Hewlett-Packard?**

   ☐ A. 802.3
   ☐ B. 802.5
   ☐ C. 802.12
   ☐ D. 802.7

Answers:

1. *B.*   *See the section titled "Data Link Layer."*

2. *B&C.* *More information on this can be found in the section titled "Data Link Layer."*

3. *C.*   *More information on this can be found in the section titled "Network Layer."*

4. *A.*   *See the section titled "Session Layer."*

5. *C.*   *More information on this can be found in the section titled "IEEE 802 Standards."*

What Is a Protocol?

Before we can review the OSI Model we need to be sure you understand protocols and their function. In order for computers to communicate, a uniform language must be defined among them. This language is a *protocol*. A protocol defines almost every aspect of the language that computers use to communicate. Some common protocols discussed later are IPX, TCP/IP, and NetBEUI. Protocols can either be mandated by one company or organization or created, used, and maintained by the entire networking industry. A *de jure* standard, Latin for "according to law," indicates a protocol designed by one company or organization. Typically, this organization maintains control of the protocol and is responsible for any additions or changes. A *de facto* standard, Latin for "existing in fact," indicates a protocol controlled by the entire industry, and is thus also known as an "industry standard." Anyone can use a de facto standard free of charge but changes to these standards are sometimes hard to make, as you must convince the rest of the industry that the changes are needed.

When a company does not publish specifications for a protocol, it's considered a closed standard. If the specifications are published, it's an open standard. De jure standards can be either open or closed standards. Most de jure standards are now open and, by definition, all de facto standards are open. TCP/IP and IPX are both open protocols. DECnet and IBM's SNA were once closed protocols but are now open.

Each layer of the model has different protocols that define how information travels. The layered functionality of the different protocols in the OSI model is called a *protocol stack.*

When data is sent from a source device down the OSI model, each layer attaches its own header to that information. The process starts when the user's application sends data to the Application Layer. The Application Layer adds its information to the data and passes it down to the next layer. When the Presentation Layer receives the information, it does not distinguish the original data from the Application Layer's header. Everything that it receives is considered just data. The Presentation Layer then adds its own header to that "data" and forwards it to the Session Layer. This process continues all the way down the OSI model until it gets to the Physical Layer, where it is converted to 1's and 0's.

After the data is sent across the media to the destination device (in the form of frames), this process works in reverse. At each layer, the appropriate header is stripped and the data is passed up to the next layer. Each layer only removes its corresponding header.

The OSI Model

The OSI model depicts the stream of information down the seven layers of the model on the source device, across intermediate devices, and up through the seven layers on the destination device. These devices can be any type of network equipment. Networked computers, printers, and faxes, as well as internetworking devices (such as routers and switches), are all examples of these devices. The model is a theoretical object, most often followed loosely and not to the letter, that breaks down the functions of a network into seven layers. Most protocol standards can be placed into one of the seven layers. If you know the layer, or layers, that a protocol fits into in the model, you have some idea of its purpose and function. The layers are shown from bottom to top in Figure 2-1.

Figure 2-1 *OSI model*

For the exam, you need to know the layers of the OSI model. Here are a couple of ways to easily remember them:

All **P**eople **S**eem **T**o **N**eed **D**ata **P**rocessing

Please **D**o **N**ot **T**hrow **S**ausage **P**izza **A**way

The second line is preferable, as it follows the correct order of the layers.

As data moves through the various layers of the OSI model, it is referred to by different names. Table 2-1 shows what data is called at each OSI layer.

TABLE 2-1 Data Names at Different OSI Model Layers

OSI Layer	Data Name
Application	Messages
Presentation	Packets
Session	Packets
Transport	Datagrams and segments
Network	Datagrams
Data Link	Frames
Physical	Bits

Sometimes the term *packet* is used as a generic term in the test to describe data at any layer.

True Or False?

1. UDP is a connection-oriented protocol.

2. NLSP is a data transmission protocol.

3. FDDI uses fiber optic cable to reach great distances.

Answers: *1. False   2. False   3. True*

Physical Layer

The first layer of the OSI model is the *Physical Layer*. The function of this layer is the transmission of bits over the network media. It provides a physical connection for the transmission of data among the network devices. The Physical Layer is responsible for ensuring that data is read the same way on the destination device as it was sent from the source device.

The Physical Layer specifies the mechanical, electrical, and functional means to establish and maintain physical connections. For example, the Physical Layer specifications on a network include the amount of voltage on a cable, how a signal changed to signify a 1 or 0 being sent, and in what order a signal was sent.

Physical Layer Characteristics

For the exam, you should know what each layer of the OSI model handles. The Physical Layer:

- Is responsible for transmission of bits.
- Specifies requirements for how transmission occurs.
- Ensures compatible data transmission with other devices.

Data Link Layer

The second layer of the OSI model is the *Data Link Layer*. The main purpose of this layer is to provide a reliable method of transmitting data across the physical media. This layer breaks the input data into frames, transmits the frames sequentially, and processes the acknowledged frames sent back by the receiver. It adds a header and trailer to the frames it creates. These enable the destination device to see when a frame begins or ends on the physical media.

Data Link Layer Characteristics

For the exam, you should know the characteristics of the Data Link Layer:

- Packages data into frames.
- Transmits data sequentially.
- Processes acknowledged frames sent from the receiver.

The Data Link Layer is divided into two sublayers, the Logical Link Control (LLC) sublayer and the Media Access Control (MAC) sublayer.

The Logical Link Control sublayer of the Data Link Layer establishes and maintains data link connections between network devices. It is responsible for any flow control and error correction found in this layer.

The following is a list of connection services that the LLC sublayer supplies:

- **Unacknowledged connectionless service** — The fastest means to transfer data at the LLC layer. It is also the most unreliable, but it is commonly used because the upper layer protocols handle their own error checking.

- **Connection-oriented service** — The opposite of unacknowledged connectionless service is *connection-oriented service*, which uses a sliding-window flow control and acknowledgments for error checking.

I'll reiterate this, as it is an Official Word topic. Connectionless protocols do not guarantee that your data will get delivered. If a device is down and the data does not get sent, the application using the protocol will not know unless other checking has been built into the program.

The Media Access Control sublayer of the Data Link Layer is responsible for physical addressing and access to the network media. Only one device at a time may transmit on any type of media. If multiple devices attempt to transmit, they will scramble each other's signal. The two network types for controlling access to media are

- Contention-based
- Deterministic

Remember that Ethernet uses CSMA/CD and Token Ring uses token passing, a deterministic method. These are the two you will see most often on the exam.

In a *contention-based* network, any device can transmit whenever it needs to. An advantage to this system is that it provides equal access to the network media, but at the expense of possible collisions. Collisions occur when two devices try to transmit at the same time and disrupt each other's signaling.

On modern contention-based networks, devices listen for other signals on the media before transmitting. Collisions are not totally eliminated, but they are kept down to manageable levels. This is known as *Carrier Sense Multiple Access*, or CSMA.

The two types of CSMA are CSMA/CD and CSMA/CA (Carrier Sense Multiple Access/Collision Detection/Avoidance). CSMA/CD basically listens to the network media for other devices. If the media seems clear it sends the queued data it has. Once the data has been sent, the device listens to the media to see if there was a collision. If a collision did occur, each of the colliding devices back off for a random amount of time and try again. Ethernet uses CSMA/CD. CSMA/CA networks use a different method to avoid collisions. Before a device can transmit on the network it must send out a Request to Send message. If the network is clear, the network server replies with a Clear to Send message. The device then sends its data along with a signal at the end to signify that it is finished. CSMA/CA is most often used by Apple's LocalTalk network.

KNOW THIS **Contention-based Systems Characteristics**

Advantages of contention-based systems:

- Low overhead
- High speed on networks with less than 40 percent utilization

Disadvantages of contention-based networks:

- Degradation of performance due to collisions under moderate-to-high network loads
- Inability to assign priorities to special devices
- Channel access not always predictable

Unlike a contention-based network, where devices are free to transmit whenever they want to, a *deterministic* network has a system that determines transmitting order. The only deterministic system you may see on the exam is token passing. In a token-passing system, a small data frame is passed from device to device across the network in a predetermined order. The device that has control of the token frame has the capability to transmit data across the network. Even on large networks where contention would start to break down due to increased levels of collisions, token passing maintains an orderly network.

Deterministic Systems Characteristics

Advantages of token passing:

- Special devices can have higher priorities than normal devices.
- Token passing is much more efficient under high network loads than are contention-based networks.
- Network access is predictable due to the predetermined transmitting order.

Disadvantages of token passing:

- It's slower than contention-based systems on networks with low utilization.
- Network devices and interface cards are more expensive due to their increased intelligence.

Network Layer

The third layer of the OSI model is the *Network Layer*. This layer is responsible for routing information from one network device to another. The Network Layer decides what path data will take if the destination device is located on another network. Data passes through the network by devices called *intermediate devices*. The source and destination devices are *end systems*. The Network Layer uses network addresses to decide where to forward the information. These addresses are dependent on the protocol stack being used.

Network Layer Characteristics

Be sure to know the responsibilities of the Network Layer for the exam:

- Routes information from sender to receiver
- Converts data into packets
- Uses connectionless transmissions

Routing

The Network Layer is responsible for routing packets across a network. For packets to be correctly routed a table must be set up to show the shortest routes between two networks. These tables can either be dynamic or static.

Static routing tables are set up manually by administrators. Dynamic routing protocols use one of two methods to define the shortest route. Network administrators are not required to enter any information with the following two dynamic routing methods (all configuration settings can be detected by the network routers):

- **Distance vector** — This is the simplest method to use, as it calculates the shortest number of hops between two points. Distance vector can take a considerable amount of time to configure and change on a large network.

- **Link state** — Link state routing protocols are newer and more complex than is distance vector. Link state takes into account more than just hop count — it usually considers link speed, latency, and congestion.

Addressing

Because the Network Layer is concerned with getting data from one computer to another (even if they are on different networks), it uses network addresses. A device on a network has not only a device address, but also a network address that tells other computers where to locate that device. By using this address, the sending device can tell whether the destination device is on the same network segment (local) or on another network segment (remote). The fact that a device is local or remote may dictate certain sending parameters, such as protocols and timeout values.

Transport Layer

The *Transport Layer* is the fourth layer of the OSI model. It provides a transport service between the Session Layer and the Network Layer. This service takes information from the Session Layer and splits it up if necessary. It then passes this information to the Network Layer and checks to make sure the information arrived at the destination device successfully.

The Transport Layer is a true source-to-destination layer. This means that a program on the source device carries on a dialogue with another program on the destination device by using message headers and control messages. These message headers and control messages are used for error detection, sequencing, and flow control.

Unlike the Network Layer, the connections at the Transport Layer are considered connection oriented. Data passed through this layer will be acknowledged by the destination device. If an acknowledgment is not received in a specified time-out period, the data is re-sent.

KNOW THIS Transport Layer Characteristics

You should know the responsibilities of the Transport Layer for the exam:

- Breaks up and restores data
- Provides end-to-end reliability
- Uses connection-oriented transmission of data

Session Layer

The fifth layer of the OSI model is the *Session Layer*. This layer lets users establish a connection — called a *session* — between devices. Once the connection has been established, the Session Layer can manage the dialogue.

Sessions can be set up so that they are

- **Half-duplex** — A two-way alternate method of communication (one way at a time). This is like talking on a CB radio; while one device talks, the other must listen.

- **Simplex** — Simple, one-way communication. No two-way communications are permitted. Some examples include a speaker, television, or radio.

- **Full-duplex** — Provides a full, two-way, simultaneous connection. Either device can transmit and receive at will. A modern telephone uses full-duplex communications.

To establish a session, the user must provide the remote address to which they want to connect. These addresses are not like MAC or network addresses; they are intended for users and are easier to remember. Examples are DNS names (`www.microsoft.com`) or computer names (SERVER41).

 Session Layer Characteristics

For the exam, you should also know the characteristics of the Session Layer:

- Enables users to establish connections between devices
- Manages dialogue
- Uses remote address to establish connections

Presentation Layer

The sixth layer of the OSI model, the *Presentation Layer*, negotiates and establishes the format in which data is exchanged. This layer is responsible for any character set or numeric translations needed between devices. It is also responsible for data compression to reduce the amount of data transmitted, as well as encryption.

KNOW THIS **Presentation Layer Characteristics**

For the exam, you should know the responsibilities of the Presentation Layer:

- Establishes format for data exchange
- Handles character set and numeric translations
- Performs data compression

Application Layer

The top layer of the OSI model is the *Application Layer*. This layer is the interface between the user's application and the network. It enables the application (that the user sees) to transfer files, send e-mail, and do anything else it needs to on the network. This should not be confused with the actual application that the user is running.

KNOW THIS **Application Layer Characteristics**

An exam question might concern characteristics of the Application Layer, so be sure to review them:

- Serves as the interface between user applications and the network
- Permits user applications to interact with the network

Example of a Connection

Now that we've reviewed the seven layers of the OSI model, let's go through a sample connection between two devices to review the flow of information through the OSI model. Let us assume that a user is running some sort of chat application on her computer that enables her to connect to another person's computer and talk to that person over a network.

The user types the message "Good morning" into the chat application. The Application Layer passes the data from the user's application to the Presentation Layer. At the Presentation Layer the data is translated and encrypted. The data is then passed to the Session Layer, where the dialogue is set for full-duplex communication. The Transport Layer packages the data as segments. The recipient's name is resolved to the corresponding IP address. Checksums are added for error checking.

Next, the Network Layer packages the data as datagrams. After examining the IP address, the destination device is discovered to be on a remote network. The IP address for the intermediate device is then added as the next destination. Data is sent to the Data Link Layer, where it is packaged as frames. The physical address of the device is resolved. This is the address belonging to the intermediate device, which will forward the data on to its destination. The access type for the network is determined to be Ethernet.

The data is then passed on to the Physical Layer, where it is packaged as bits and sent from the network adapter across the transmission media. The intermediate device reads the bits off the network media at the Physical Layer. The Data Link Layer packages the data as frames. The physical address of the destination device is resolved to its IP address. The Network Layer packages the data as datagrams. After examining the IP address of the destination device, the location of this device on the network is determined. The data is passed back to the Data Link Layer, where it is again packaged as frames. The IP address is resolved to the MAC address. The access type for the network is determined to be Ethernet.

The data is then sent to the Physical Layer, packaged as bits, and sent across the network media. The destination device reads the bits off the network media at the Physical Layer. The Data Link Layer packages the data as frames. The physical address of the destination device is resolved into its IP address. The Network Layer packages the data as datagrams. It is determined that the device has reached its final destination, where it is reordered into the proper sequence.

It is then passed on to the Transport Layer. Data is compiled into segments and error checking is performed. Checksums are compared to determine that the data is error free. The Session Layer acknowledges that the data has been received. At the Presentation Layer the data is translated and unencrypted. The Application Layer then passes the data from the Presentation Layer on to the user's chat application. The message "Good morning" then appears on the recipient user's screen.

Now that you understand the flow of information through the OSI model, let's discuss the IEEE 802 standards.

POP QUIZ **True or False?**

1. Routers use MAC addresses to decide whether to pass data or not.
2. Coaxial cable uses light to transmit data.
3. IRQ 10 is free on most computers.

Answers: *1. False   2. False   3. True*

The IEEE 802 Standards

Unlike the theoretical OSI model, the 802 standards are documented, real-world standards that define different technologies, such as Ethernet. The Institute of Electrical and Electronic Engineers (IEEE) started a project, called Project 802, to create device standards for different LAN needs. The 12 different 802 standards are as follows:

- 802.1   The standard that created what is now known as the spanning tree algorithm. The spanning tree algorithm is used by transparent bridges (you learn about these bridges in Chapter 6). They use this algorithm to detect other bridges on the network, remove loops, and to detect when another bridge fails.

- 802.2   The Data Link Layer of the OSI model is made up of two parts: the LLC layer and the MAC layer. 802.2 defines the standards for the LLC layer of the Data Link Layer.

- 802.3   CSMA/CD (for example, Ethernet) is defined by the 802.3 standard.

- 802.4   Token-passing bus network systems are defined in 802.4. Almost all modern token-passing networks are rings, not bus types. This standard never really took off, and you will rarely see it used.

- 802.5   This standard is based on IBM's Token Ring network standard. This standard uses a logical ring topology running at 4Mbits or 16Mbits.

- 802.6   This defines standards for MANs (metropolitan area networks). The main purpose of this standard is to define Distributed Queue Dual Bus (DQDB, a network with two physical channels).

- 802.7   This standard simply defines Broadband Technology Advisory Group.

- 802.8   This standard is the Fiber Optic Technical Advisory.

- 802.9   This standard is the Integrated Data and Voice Networks.

- 802.10   Network security issues are defined in 802.10.

- 802.11   As users start to roam more, the idea of wireless networks unfolds. The 802.11 standard committee is currently working on the problems associated with this type of network.

- 802.12   Hewlett-Packard has developed its own 100Mbit standard for the next generation of networks. This new network type is called 100VG-AnyLAN. 802.12 defines the standards for this new technology.

Have You Mastered?

Now it's time to review the concepts in this chapter and apply your knowledge. These questions test your mastery of the OSI model.

1. Which 802 standard covers Token Ring?

☐ A. 802.6
☐ B. 802.5
☐ C. 802.11
☐ D. 802.4

B. The 802.5 spec defined the IBM Token Ring standard. 802.6, 802.11, and 802.4 covered MANs, wireless networks, and Token Passing respectively. See the IEEE 802 Standards section for more information.

2. Which OSI layer handles the media access method used by networking devices?

☐ A. Network
☐ B. Physical
☐ C. Data Link
☐ D. Signaling

C. The MAC sublayer of the Data Link Layer handles media access. The Network Layer handles routing information across the network. The Physical Layer handles the actual transmission of data over the physical cable. See the Data Link Layer section for more information.

3. Which layer provides the interface between the network and the user's applications?

☐ A. Session
☐ B. Application
☐ C. Transport
☐ D. Connection

B. The Application Layer handles the interface between the end user's application, such as an e-mail application, and the networking services. See the Application Layer section for more information.

4. Which routing method is the simplest?

☐ A. Link State
☐ B. Conditional
☐ C. Distance Vector
☐ D. Hop Count

C. Distance Vector uses the number of hops to the destination, and then chooses the best route. It does not consider link speed or other information. See the Network Layer section for more information.

5. Which type of media access works best under high load?

☐ A. CSMA/CD
☐ B. CSMA/CA
☐ C. Token Passing
☐ D. Queuing

C. While the token passing method is not the fastest under light load, it is the fastest under heavy load. With token passing, each device is guaranteed a chance to send its data. See the Data Link Layer section for more information.

6. The 802.3 standard deals with which subject?

    ☐ A. Token Ring
    ☐ B. Fiber Optic
    ☐ C. Network Security
    ☐ D. Ethernet

D. 802.3 covers the Ethernet standard. Token Ring is covered by 802.5. Fiber Optic is handled by 802.8, and Network Security is specified in 802.10. See the IEEE 802 Standards section for more information.

7. Which layer provides end-to-end reliability for data transfer?

    ☐ A. Session
    ☐ B. Communication
    ☐ C. Transfer
    ☐ D. Transport

D. The Transport Layer handles the error-checking and connection information between devices when reliability is needed. See the Transport Layer section for more information.

25

Practice Your Skills

These exercises will help you apply the material in this chapter with some critical thinking.

1. Communicating through the OSI model

EXERCISE Using what you know about the way layers communicate in the OSI model, draw a sample dialogue session between two devices. Be sure to note that all communication between layers is handled on a peer basis. For example, the Transport Layer on one device can only talk to the Transport Layer on another device. Also remember that each layer adds and removes its own header information.

ANALYSIS Your diagram should show that each layer adds its own header to the data. All of the header information from previous layers is considered data because the lower layer does not understand the information it contains. This is why the communication between layers across devices happens at the peer level. The Transport layer on one device cannot understand the header information from the session layer of another device.

2. Data reliability

EXERCISE You are designing a network application that will be used to process orders for a mail order company. Reliability is a key feature that is required by the company. Would you choose a protocol that uses connectionless or connection-oriented communications? What would be the drawback of using that method?

ANALYSIS Because reliability is a very important feature, you should use a connection-oriented protocol. This ensures that the order information is sent across the network successfully. The only drawback to using this method is performance because connectionless protocols are faster with less overhead.

Network
Media

C
HAPTER 3 STARTS REVIEWING THE REAL MEAT of the
Networking Essentials Exam. This chapter covers all the
information you need to know about network adapters
and how they are configured. Next is a quick section on
the many different types of buses you'll find in computers, and how they stack up. The review then moves to
the world of network media, where we cover both bound and unbound
media. Finally, this review addresses data transmission considerations.

Exam Material in This Chapter

Based on Microsoft Objectives

- Describe the characteristics and purpose of the media used in IEEE 802.3 and IEEE 802.5 standards
- Select the appropriate media for various situations
- Twisted-pair cable
- Coaxial cable
- Fiber-optic cable
- Wireless media
- Cover cost, distance limitations, and number of nodes
- Given the manufacturer's documentation for the network adapter, install, configure, and resolve hardware conflicts for multiple network adapters in a token-ring or Ethernet network
- Explain the purpose of NDIS and Novell ODI network standards

Based on Author Experience

- Network adapters
- IRQs
- I/O addresses
- DMA channels
- Shared memory addresses
- Jumpers
- Dip switches
- Software configuration
- NDIS drivers
- ODI drivers
- ISA bus
- MCA bus

- EISA bus
- VESA bus
- PCI bus
- PCMCIA cards
- Network adapter ports
- Bounded media
- Unbounded media
- Data transmission

Are You Prepared?

These questions will help you determine whether you're prepared for the exam questions on network media or whether you need more review.

1. Which bus was designed for the original IBM PC computer?

- ☐ A. PCI
- ☐ B. EISA
- ☐ C. MCA
- ☐ D. ISA

2. Which type of network connector is very similar to a telephone connector?

- ☐ A. UTP
- ☐ B. STP
- ☐ C. Coaxial
- ☐ D. Serial

3. Which IRQ is normally available in a computer?

- ☐ A. 0
- ☐ B. 13
- ☐ C. 8
- ☐ D. 11

4. Which type of driver was created by Novell?

☐ A. ODI
☐ B. NDIS
☐ C. Packet driver
☐ D. VLM

Answers:

1. *D.* *The original IBM computer used the 8-bit ISA bus. See section titled "Bus Architecture."*

2. *A.* *UTP is very similar to telephone cable. See section titled "Twisted-Pair Cabling."*

3. *D.* *IRQ 11 is free on most computers whereas the others are taken. See section titled "IRQ."*

4. *A.* *Novell created the ODI specification for drivers. See section titled "Interfacing the Adapter."*

Understanding Network Adapters

The *network adapters,* commonly known as *NICs (Network Interface Cards)* or simply network cards, are responsible for moving data from the computer to the transmission media. The network adapter transforms data into signals that are carried across the transmission media to its destination. Once the signals reach the destination device, the NICs translate the signals back into information that the computer can process. Exactly how the adapter functions can vary according to the type of adapter being used.

The circuitry on the card that does the conversion of the signal from computer data to the media is known as a *transceiver.* Ethernet can run over a few different cable types, but the main circuitry on all the Ethernet cards should be the same; only the transceiver should be different. Most Ethernet cards have built-in transceivers. Figure 3-1 shows the transceiver on a network adapter.

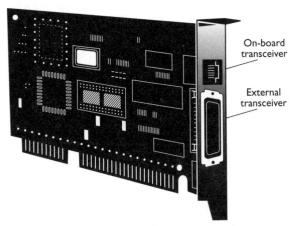

On-board transceiver

External transceiver

Figure 3-1 *Network card showing transceivers*

If you plug the cable directly into the card, you can be pretty sure the transceiver is built in, or *on-board* as it's called. Some Ethernet cards have what is known as an *AUI port,* which enables you to use an external transceiver. With an external transceiver, you could use your network card to run over fiber-optic, although there's no fiber-optic connector on the card.

Installing and Configuring Network Adapters

The key to making a network adapter work correctly is to make sure it is correctly installed and configured. Although this may seem simple, it is easy to unknowingly configure a network adapter incorrectly. Sometimes this shows up right away and the card will not function at all, but other times it may be more sporadic.

Adapter Settings

One of the most difficult aspects of network cards is configuring them. Like most adapter cards that are installed in a computer, such as sound and video cards, network cards can be configured by setting some parameters. These parameters can have systemwide implications if they are not set properly. You must be sure to set their addresses so they do not conflict with any other cards in the computer. Most network cards require that you set some combination of the following parameters:

- IRQ
- I/O address
- Shared memory address
- DMA

Before you can properly adjust these settings to configure the adapter, you need to understand what each one controls.

IRQ

An *IRQ* (*interrupt request*) value is an assigned value that a device sends to the computer's processor to interrupt its processing when it needs to send some information.

An essential thing to remember here is that each device in the computer must have a unique IRQ. You must also remember that some IRQs are already in use by devices built into the main board of the computer. Table 3-1 shows the standard, or common, IRQ usage in computers. Please remember that IRQs can be changed, therefore this table may not always be accurate.

 In the real world, it is sometimes possible to let two devices share one IRQ. For the exam, IRQs should never be shared.

TABLE 3.1 Standard IRQ Usage

IRQ Number	Used By
0	System timer
1	Keyboard
2	Cascade IRQ controller or video adapter
3	COM2 & COM4
4	COM1 & COM3
5	LPT2 (second printer port) and sometimes sound card
6	Floppy disk controller
7	LPT1 (first printer port)
8	Real-time clock
9	Cascade from IRQ2
10	Unassigned (sometimes used by SCSI controllers)
11	Unassigned
12	PS/2 mouse
13	Math coprocessor
14	Primary hard drive controller (usually IDE)
15	Secondary hard drive controller, if it exists

I/O address

After a network card has interrupted the CPU with an IRQ, it needs a way to communicate with the main board. Most cards use an *input/output (I/O) address* to do this. You give the cards a set number that the software driver also knows, and they use this to communicate. Think of an I/O address like a post office mailing address. Any information sent to that address in the computer is picked up by the network card.

I/O addresses are given as *hexadecimal numbers*. You will see them written starting with "0x" or with a trailing "h," as in "300h." Some common I/O addresses are 0x280, 0x300, and 0x330. Table 3-2 shows the common I/O address usage. Again, these addresses can change, so this information may not be correct on all computers.

TABLE 3.2 I/O Address Uses

Port Number	Device
0x200	Game port
0x230	Bus mouse
0x270	LPT3
0x2F8	COM2
0x370	LPT2
0x2B0	LPT1
0x3F8	COM1

DMA

Direct memory access, or *DMA*, enables your adapter cards to work directly with the computer's memory. Normally, the CPU must be involved any time an adapter needs to move data into or out of memory. If your adapter uses a DMA channel, it can handle communications directly with memory, without the help of the CPU.

Other devices built into the computer use DMA channels, so you will need to pick a free channel. If your network card supports DMA transfers, you should enable this feature, because it could bring about a significant performance increase.

POP QUIZ **True or False?**

1. The Network layer of the OSI model handles data reliability.

2. Disaster recovery, backup strategies, and fault tolerance are all important factors to consider when planning a network's recovery.

3. All 15 IRQs are free on a computer until you put a new device in the computer.

Answers: *1. False   2. True   3. False*

Shared memory address

An option to the I/O address transfer is *shared memory addresses*. Using this method, the network card and software driver use a shared RAM address in the high memory range to communicate. The shared memory address is slower than the I/O address method, and it can be more trouble. You must be sure to block out the assigned range from any memory management software so it does not try to use that area at the same time.

Hardware Configuration

After you have decided which settings you need to adjust to configure your network card, how do you make these adjustments? Well, the answer depends on the network card in question, as well as the bus type of the card. You normally use one of the following to configure the network card.

Jumpers

Jumpers are small metal pairs of pins that stick out of the card. You change their configuration by putting small plastic covers with metal internal connectors over them, which actually completes the circuit between the two pins. A jumper with the plastic cover is considered "closed," and one without is considered "open."

DIP switches

Dual in-line package (DIP) switches are small banks of switches on the adapter card. They can be toggled so they're either open or closed, on or off, or 0 or 1. Depending on how the manufacturer phrased the settings, you could have one of those three pairs of settings.

Software configuration

The easiest way to configure a network card is with software. Network adapters using the EISA and MCA bus type are almost always configured via software. The software configuration for them is stored in the computer's CMOS. PCMCIA cards are also automatically configured via the computer's BIOS. Some also come with utilities that enable you to manually configure the card if necessary.

ISA, VESA, and PCI cards are commonly configured using software. Some of the newer cards also support Plug and Play, which allows for automatic configuration.

Interfacing the Adapter

There's a lot more to installing and configuring network adapters than simply setting up the hardware. You also have to interface the adapter with your computer.

Adapter Drivers

After making sure the card is configured correctly and working in the computer, you then need to install a driver for it into the operating system. The two standards of drivers you're most likely to see on the exam are *Network Device Interface Specification* (NDIS) and *Open Datalink Interface* (ODI).

The main purpose of these driver standards is to enable network card manufacturers to write one driver and have it support multiple operating systems. Another important feature of the ODI and NDIS standards is the capability to use more than one protocol on each network card. Before these standards existed, you could load only one driver per protocol, but with these you can load one driver and any number of protocols.

The key point to remember for the Networking Essentials exam is the purpose of ODI and NDIS network card drivers. They enable third-party vendors to easily write drivers that work with the Microsoft and Novell operating systems. They also enable you to use multiple network protocols and NICs at the same time. Remember that where functionality and purpose are concerned, NDIS is to Microsoft as ODI is to Novell.

NDIS

Network Device Interface Specification, or *NDIS*, was created by Microsoft and 3Com. It is used by most companies in the PC networking community. Several different versions of NDIS are currently being used, including:

- Version 2.0, which is the older 16-bit implementation. Mainly used by DOS and Windows 3.1 clients, it can also be used under Windows 95 if a more recent driver cannot be found.

- Version 3.0, which is the newer 32-bit implementation. This is the preferred version when using Windows 95, and is required under Windows NT (Windows NT 4.0 supports the current NDIS 4.0 standard). Some smaller revisions of the v3.0 specification have been released that enable Windows 95 and Windows NT to use the same driver, but this specification has not become popular yet.

Operating systems that use NDIS include:

- MS-DOS
- Windows for Workgroups
- Windows 95

- Windows NT Workstation
- Windows NT Server
- Artisoft LANtastic

ODI

ODI, or *Open Datalink Interface*, is Novell's answer to the driver specification question. It has many of the same features as NDIS, and serves much the same purpose.

As with NDIS, there are 16-bit and 32-bit implementations of ODI. The 16-bit implementation is used primarily on MS-DOS and Windows 3.1 workstations to connect to a Novell NetWare server. The 32-bit implementation is a newer driver used under Windows 95. This driver can completely replace the NDIS driver normally used in Windows 95. With this driver, users can connect to any type of server, not just NetWare servers.

Bus Architecture

Now, let's review bus architecture. The term *bus* refers to the connection your adapter cards have to the rest of your computer. The following sections provide a quick review of the different bus types.

ISA

The *Industry Standard Architecture* (*ISA*) bus was designed by IBM and is used in the IBM PC. Due to the need for compatible devices, IBM decided to make ISA an open standard, allowing third-party manufacturers to produce hardware without paying IBM for the use of the standard. This bus was originally designed to transfer 8 *megabits per second* (Mbps). This was done using 8-bit paths, which worked well in the 8086 and 8088 CPUs that could only handle 8 bits at once. The release of the 80286 created a need for 16-bit cards. At that time, ISA was modified to allow 8-bit or 16-bit adapters. The addition of the 16-bit adapter didn't pose a problem for people who owned the 8-bit adapters, because the 8-bit adapters fit in the 16-bit slots.

MCA

MicroChannel Architecture (MCA) operates at 16Mbps or 32Mbps and uses software to configure the resource settings. MCA was not designed to be backward compatible with ISA, which required people to buy new MCA adapters. Because IBM was the standard by which all other PCs were judged, many companies paid to use this better technology. Other manufacturers preferred to use open standards that didn't require them to pay IBM.

MicroChannel cards require what is known as a Reference Disk to be configured. This disk contains special software to help configure the card. Few MCA cards have jumpers or DIP switches to manually set configuration settings.

EISA

The *Extended Industry Standard Architecture* (EISA) bus runs at 8MHz and can transmit 32 bits at a time. While this is slightly slower than MicroChannel's speed of 10MHz, the 8MHz speed maintains compatibility with the ISA standard. EISA slots look much like ISA slots but are deeper. ISA cards can fit into EISA slots and function perfectly, but they do not go all the way into the slot. EISA cards have longer contacts that enable them to go all the way into the slot. This way, any EISA slot on a computer's main board can also be used by an ISA card.

The EISA bus also introduced another important feature, *bus mastering*. Bus mastering enables a card in a computer to operate without the main CPU being involved. For example, a disk controller can read and write to a hard disk by itself without involving the CPU. Normally, the CPU itself handles the transaction while putting other processes on hold. Bus mastering is a great help for multitasking operating systems.

EISA cards are configured using software. The manufacturer of the card usually provides a small configuration utility and a disk. All settings can be made from that utility.

VESA

The *Video Electronic Standards Association* (VESA) bus was designed for video cards. It was later used for hard drive controllers and network cards. The *VESA Local Bus*, or *VLB*, could transfer 32 bits of information at a time, and ran at speeds of up to 40MHz, depending on the system's CPU speed.

PCI

Peripheral Component Interface, or *PCI,* is a relatively new bus type. These are usually small cards, but occasionally a full-length card can be found.

PCI runs at up to 33MHz and can transfer 32 bits at a time. PCI was originally developed to help speed up graphics on newer computers. Most new PCI cards are software configurable, and usually support the new Plug and Play standard to automatically configure the card.

PCI slots are not backward compatible with any other type. They use a small, condensed connector on the main board of the computer. One advantage of PCI is that it is not tied to any specific type of computer.

PCMCIA

PCMCIA, which is an association name, not a standard name, is a new type of bus mainly for notebook and laptop computers. It stands for *Personal Computer Memory Card International Association.*

The PCMCIA v1.0 standard defines specifications for memory cards. Later, when other types of devices were needed, v2.0 of the standard was established. This enabled other devices, such as modems, disk drives, and network cards, to be used.

Network Adapter Ports

Now we'll look at connecting the adapter card to the network media. The type of connector you can use may depend on the brand of network adapter you chose or the type of network to which it is connecting. The three most common connectors are:

- **BNC connector** — BNC connectors are used in ARCNET and in thin Ethernet (10Base-2). The connector is a small, round cylinder with two small prongs on the outside that enable a connector to attach to it. A small hole for a copper wire to go into is inside the connector. Figure 3-2 shows a T connector, which has three BNC connectors on it. The T connector is used to connect the network adapter to the two pieces of coaxial cable.

Figure 3-2 *A T connector showing three BNC connectors*

- **RJ-45 connector** — The RJ-45 connector looks much like a normal telephone cable connector, but larger. It uses twisted-pair cabling with four pairs of wires. A normal telephone jack uses an RJ-11 connector, which is twisted-pair with two pairs of wires.

- **DIX or AUI connector** — These connectors are not used much anymore, but were widely used when thick Ethernet was popular. DIX/AUI is a 15-pin connector with two rows of pins. A cable attached to the NIC through this port and was attached to the thick Ethernet cable by use of a "vampire tap." The tap had to be drilled into the cable and tightened down. DIX stands for the three companies that invented it (Digital, Intel, and Xerox) and was later renamed AUI (Attachment Unit Interface).

The main use of AUI connectors today is for external transceivers. A network card with DIX and BNC connectors is shown in Figure 3-3.

DIX connector

BNC NIC connector

Figure 3-3 *Network card showing DIX and BNC connectors*

Bounded Media

Once you have the network cards installed and interfaced in your computer, you need a way to connect them to each other. The network media you use for this can be a wire, or it can be wireless. The first network media to review are wires, or *network cables*. These are referred to as *bounded media* because the signal travels through a physical media shielded on the outside (bounded) by some material.

Bounded media are made up of a central conductor (usually copper) surrounded by a jacket material. Bounded media are great for LANs because they offer high speed, good security, and low cost. Sometimes they cannot be used, however, because of distance limitations.

The type of cable you use depends on different factors. Does your building have existing cable? How many devices do you want to network? What speed do you need from your network? Which network topology (such as Ethernet, Token Ring, and so on) do you plan to use? You must consider each of these when choosing the cable type for your network. Most network protocols will run on many different cable types, unlike the older networking days when the protocol usually defined the cable.

Cables differ by the properties they have. Depending on your needs, you may opt for one cable type over another because it has some characteristics that are more important to you. For example, coaxial cable is fairly resistant to outside interference, but cannot be used for some high-speed LANs. Some of the characteristics you should look at for each cable type are:

- **Cost** — Cost can be a important consideration when deciding on a network cable. Only a few years ago, fiber-optic cable was extremely expensive, and almost no one could justify the cost to use it.

- **Installation** — Using the example above, one reason fiber-optic cable was so expensive was due to the installation. Only highly skilled technicians were capable of installing this cable correctly. Obviously, the best situation is to have someone on staff who can install the cable. If you need to get an outside contractor, the installation cost may outweigh the actual cable cost.

- **Capacity** — So you've gotten past the cost and installation issues, and now the question is, "How fast will it go?" Normally, cable speed is referred to as *bandwidth*, and is an important characteristic of a media type. Bandwidth is usually measured in *bits per second*. For example, standard Ethernet cable is usually up to 10Mbps, which is 10 megabits per second (notice the small b for bits, not B for Bytes).

- **Attenuation (maximum distance)** — Depending on what you need to network together, the maximum cable distance may also be another consideration. Attenuation will be discussed in more detail in the next section.

- **Immunity to interference** — The last property is how well the cable holds up against interference, normally *electromagnetic interference* (*EMI*). EMI could play a big part in which cable type you use, depending on the location. Suppose you needed to run a network into a manufacturing facility with a lot of heavy machinery that used electrical motors. An unshielded type of cable may not be the best choice in that situation.

Three common types of bounded media are used out in the world and are covered on the exam. They are:

- Coaxial
- Twisted-pair
- Fiber-optic

Before we review the cable types, you can take a quick lesson in electricity and some of its properties.

Electrical Properties

Installing network cable can be tricky because of the way it may react to different electrical properties. The maximum speed and distance a cable can be run are also affected by these properties. To fully understand cabling, you need to know the following electrical properties:

- **Resistance** — When electricity moves through a media it meets *resistance*. Resistance affects only the transmission of *direct current* (*DC*), and it is measured in *ohms*. When more resistance is met, more electricity is lost during transmission. The resistance causes the energy to be converted to heat. Cables with small diameters have more resistance than cables with large diameters.

- **Impedance** — The loss of energy from an *alternating current* (*AC*) is called *impedance*. Like resistance, it is measured in *ohms*. DC travels through the core of the wire, whereas AC travels on the surface.

- **Noise** — *Noise* is a serious problem for cabling, and is sometimes hard to pinpoint. Noise can be caused by *radio interference* (*RFI*) or *electromagnetic interference* (*EMI*). Many things can cause noise in a cable. Some common causes are fluorescent lights, transformers, the power company on a bad day, and pretty much anything else that creates an electrical field.

  - Noise can be easy to avoid if you plan your cable installation well. Route new cable away from lights and other EMI sources, try to use shielded cabling if you can, and ground all equipment.

- **Attenuation** — *Attenuation* is the fading of the electrical signal over a distance. The above properties all affect the rate of attenuation in a cable. Eventually, devices at the other end of a cable are unable to distinguish between the real signal and induced noise after a certain distance.

- **Cross talk** — *Cross talk* occurs when the signal from one cable is leaked to another cable by an electrical field. An electrical field is created whenever an electrical signal is sent through a wire. If two wires are close enough and do not have enough EMI protection, it is possible for the signal to leak and cause noise on the other wire.

Now you can review the types of cable that enable you to connect your networks.

Coaxial Cable

Coaxial (coax) cable is so named because it contains two conductors that are *parallel* to each other, or on the same axis. The center conductor in the cable is usually copper. The copper can be either a solid wire or a stranded material. Outside this central conductor is a nonconductive material. It is usually a white, plastic-like material, used to separate the inner conductor from the outer conductor. The outer conductor is a fine mesh made of copper. It is used to help shield the cable from electromagnetic interference (EMI). Outside the copper mesh is the final protective cover.

The actual network data travels through the center conductor in the cable. EMI interference is caught by the outer copper mesh. Coax cable should be grounded at one end to dissipate this electrical interference. Do not ground it to a computer on the network, but rather to something like a wall outlet ground.

The coax you use depends on which type of network you plan to use. The different types of coax cable vary by gauge and impedance.

Gauge is the measure of the thickness of the cable. It is measured by the *Radio-Grade measurement*, or *RG number*. The higher the RG number, the thinner the central conductor core; the lower the number, the thicker the core. Usually, the gauge list is printed on the side of the cable, somewhere on the outer material. Look at the table below to see which type of network needs which gauge of cable. The measure of resistance in the cable is called *impedance*. Just like the RG number, each different type of network uses a different resistance. The essential point to remember about impedance is that each piece of equipment attaching to the cable must use the same impedance. Again, refer to the following list to see which network type uses which impedance.

The most common coaxial standards are:

- **50-ohm RG-7 or RG-11** — Used with thick Ethernet
- **50-ohm RG-58** — Used with thin Ethernet
- **75-ohm RG-59** — Used with cable television
- **93-ohm RG-62** — Used with ARCNET

Coaxial cable is an inexpensive media to buy. It is also one of the easiest types of cable to install. It is easy to test using a multimeter, and the connector installation can be simple. Expanding a coaxial network is also easy — you can simply add a new segment of cable, as long as you have not reached the maximum distance. One of the best advantages of coaxial cable is the level of EMI interference it has. In some circumstances, such as in a factory, most other types of cables will have too much interference to operate properly.

 Each segment of coaxial cable should be terminated on both ends, and one end should be grounded. Be sure to look for this in any diagrams you see on the exam.

The main reason coaxial cable is not used anymore is due to the possibility of having to take the entire segment down because of one small problem. Should one piece of coaxial cable break, the entire segment will stop working. Connectors can also fail because they are more complicated than others, also causing the network to go down.

KNOW THIS Coaxial Cable

Characteristics:

- Low cost
- Easy to install
- Capacity usually up to 10Mbps
- Medium attenuation
- Medium immunity from EMI

Twisted-Pair Cabling

The most popular network cabling right now is twisted-pair. It is lightweight, easy to install, inexpensive, and can support many different types of networks. It can also support speeds of up to 100Mbps.

Twisted-pair cabling is made up of pairs of solid or stranded copper twisted around each other. The twists are done to reduce the vulnerability to EMI and cross talk. The number of pairs in the cable depends on the type. The copper core of the cable is usually 22-AWG or 24-AWG, as measured on the *American Wire Gauge standard.*

There are two varieties of twisted-pair cabling:

- Unshielded twisted-pair
- Shielded twisted-pair

Unshielded twisted-pair

Unshielded twisted-pair (*UTP*) is the more common of the two types. It can be either voice grade or data grade, depending on the application. UTP cable normally has an impedance of 100 ohms. UTP costs less than *shielded twisted-pair* (*STP*) and is readily available due to its many uses. There are five levels of data grade cabling:

- **Category 1:** This category is intended for use in telephone lines and low-speed data cable.

- **Category 2:** Category 2 includes cabling for lower-speed networks. These can support up to 4Mbps implementations.

- **Category 3:** This is a popular category for standard Ethernet networks. These cables support up to 16Mbps but are most often used in 10Mbps Ethernet situations.

- **Category 4:** Category 4 cable is used for longer-distance networks and higher speeds than Category 3 cable. It can support up to 20Mbps.

- **Category 5:** This cable is intended for high-performance data communications. This is the highest rating for UTP cable, and it can support up to 100Mbps. Any new installation of UTP should be using this cable rating for later upgrades.

UTP data cable consists of two or four pairs of twisted cables. Cable with two pairs uses RJ-11 connectors, and four-pair cables use RJ-45 connectors.

UTP has a good capacity. It can currently support up to 100Mbps using Category 5 cable. The most common type used is 10Mbps, usually with Category 3 cable. Should you install new cable, be sure to use Category 5 in case you ever plan to upgrade to 100Mbps. Although the idea of having 100Mbps to the desktop may sound extreme today, it won't in a few years.

With its ease of installation and high speed, why would you not use UTP? First, its distance is limited to a relatively short distance due to attenuation. Also, remember that it is unshielded, so EMI interference could be a large problem. Under normal office LAN implementations, however, these disadvantages are usually not problems.

Unshielded twisted-pair is the most common type of network cable seen today for many reasons. Because its installation routine is like that of normal telephone cable, finding someone to wire your network is easy and inexpensive. The promise of higher speeds is also another factor that makes people want to use UTP. Category 5 UTP can go as fast as 100Mbps. This gives your current 10Mbps network a real boost later, when it is needed. Probably the best characteristic of a UTP network is the fact that a single media failure brings down only one workstation. UTP networks are normally configured in a star topology, so only the "leg" of the star is affected by the failure.

Because it is unshielded, UTP cable is susceptible to electromagnetic interference. This may limit its use in environments with a lot of machinery. The maximum distance UTP can run is also shorter than other cable types.

Unshielded Twisted-Pair Cable

Characteristics of UTP:

- Cost is low, but slightly higher than coaxial
- Easy to install, especially if familiar with wiring telephone systems
- High speed capacity
- High attenuation
- Susceptible to EMI due to absence of shielding
- Distance of 100 meters

Shielded twisted-pair

Shielded twisted-pair (*STP*) is mainly used in Token Ring, which is covered in Chapter 4. It is similar to UTP but has a mesh shielding that protects it from EMI, which allows for higher transmission rates and longer distances without errors.

IBM has defined different levels for STP cable similar to the categories of UTP cable. They are:

- **Type 1:** Type 1 STP features two pairs of 22 AWG wire, with each pair foil-wrapped inside another foil sheath that has a wire braid ground.
- **Type 2:** This type includes Type 1, with four telephone pairs sheathed to the outside to allow one cable to an office for both voice and data.
- **Type 6:** This type features two pairs of stranded, shielded 26 AWG wire to be used for patch cables.
- **Type 7:** This type of STP consists of one pair of stranded, 26 AWG wire.

- **Type 9:** Two pairs of shielded 26 AWG wire, used for data, make up this type of cable.

The big disadvantage for STP cable is the cost. Because STP is almost exclusively used with IBM's Token Ring, and is not mass-produced for other uses besides data networking, it has a higher cost than UTP.

Installation of STP is also more difficult than that of UTP. STP uses a ground wire to dissipate the EMI it collects, as well as connectors that are more proprietary.

The good news is that, due to the shielding, you can have higher bandwidth rates than UTP. The bad news is that STP is used almost exclusively with Token Ring, so it normally has a bandwidth of 16Mbps.

The extra shielding does not really help the attenuation problem with twisted-pair cabling.

Shielded twisted-pair cable alleviates some disadvantages of UTP. First, it has shielding that reduces the effects of EMI. STP is also capable of speeds up to 16Mbps. This is faster than the maximum of 10Mbps for Category 3 UTP.

Although STP has some advantages over UTP, it also has disadvantages. It is more expensive than UTP and coaxial cable. Because of the extra bulk of the shielding, it is also more difficult to install. One characteristic it shares with UTP is the attenuation problem that enables it to be used only for short distances.

KNOW THIS **Shielded Twisted-Pair Cable**

Characteristics of STP:

- Medium cost
- Ease of installation is medium due to grounding and connectors
- Higher capacity than UTP
- High attenuation, but the same as UTP
- Medium immunity from EMI
- Distance is 100 meters

Fiber-Optic Cable

In a fiber-optic cable, light only moves in one direction. For a two-way communication to take place, a second connection must be made between the two devices. This is why fiber-optic cable is actually two strands of cable. Each strand is responsible for one direction of communication. A laser at one device sends pulses of light through this cable to the other device. These pulses are translated into 1s and 0s at the other end.

The light contained inside the fiber cable cannot escape. No electrical fields are created around the cable, so you could run a bundle of fiber together with no ill effects.

In the center of the fiber cable is a glass strand, or *core*. The light from the laser travels through this glass to the other device. Around the internal core is a reflective material known as *cladding*. No light escapes the glass core because of this reflective cladding. The price of fiber-optic cable has dropped substantially in the years since it was introduced, and it is becoming much more common on networks today. Most of the cost of a fiber-optic network is in the installation. At this time, the only way to learn about installation is to go to a class, which usually lasts a few days and gives you a lot of hands-on learning time.

What do you get for the high cost of installation and cable? High speeds and distances, of course. Fiber-optic cable currently has a bandwidth of over 2Gbps. And, because you can run a fiber-optic cable tens of miles, attenuation is not a problem. There is also no susceptibility to EMI because the transmission occurs through light, not electricity.

Fiber-Optic Cable

Characteristics of fiber-optic cable:

- High cost
- Very difficult to install
- Extremely high speed capabilities; current bandwidth speeds reach up to 2Gbps
- Extremely low attenuation allows for very long distances
- No EMI problems due to use of light instead of electricity

Unbounded Media

Unbounded or wireless media does not use any physical connectors between the two communicating devices. Usually, the transmission is sent through the atmosphere, but sometimes it may be just across a room. Wireless media is used when a physical obstruction or distance blocks the use of normal cable media.

The three main types of wireless media are radio wave, microwave, and infrared.

Radio Waves

Radio wave transmissions can be divided into these three categories:

- Low-power, single-frequency
- High-power, single-frequency
- Spread spectrum

Low-power, single-frequency

As the name suggests, this system transmits on one frequency and has low power output. The normal operating range on these types of devices is 20–25 meters. This is generally the cheapest wireless media type, although the price can increase if more complicated and advanced equipment is needed.

Installation can be either simple or more complex, depending on the equipment purchased. Some devices come preconfigured and are simple to install. More customized installations may need a trained technician to do the fine-tuning.

The speed of these units can vary from 1Mbps to 10Mbps, which is perfect for a small LAN. Attenuation is a problem with these devices because of the low power output that is allowed.

EMI could be a very large problem here because of other devices that operate on the same frequencies. Other equipment such as electric motors may also inadvertently produce radio frequencies in your network device's range, causing even more noise-induced problems.

Although they do not have much range, low-power, single-frequency operations do have some benefits. Imagine using them in an office where everyone has a notebook or portable computer. There would be no need for cables or other networking devices because everything would be wireless.

 Radio Waves

Characteristics of low-power, single-frequency devices:

- Cost: Low for wireless media
- Ease of Installation: Simple installation with preconfigured equipment
- Capacity: Ranges from 1Mbps to 10Mbps
- Attenuation: High attenuation which can limit range to 25 meters
- Immunity to EMI: Low

High-power, single-frequency

While similar to low-power, single-frequency systems, these devices can communicate over much larger distances. Transmissions can be either line-of-sight, for short distances, or bounced off the atmosphere for longer distances. Networks based on this technique would be useful to a mobile sales force or others who travel frequently.

Along with higher power, you get higher costs. Installation is not as easy as with the low-power units, either. This system is also susceptible to EMI.

Spread spectrum

Spread spectrum systems use several frequencies at once to provide reliable data transmissions that are resistant to interference. Using multiple frequencies ensures more secure transmissions. Direct-sequence modulation and frequency-hopping are two methods used in spread spectrum communications.

Direct-sequence modulation breaks data into chips and transmits the chips across several frequencies. The receiver knows which data to collect on the different frequencies, and assembles the data accordingly. False data can be transmitted to confuse any possible eavesdroppers. To reconstruct the data, the listener would have to know which frequencies to monitor and which data was false. Direct-sequence modulation provides 2–6Mbps transmission rates and operates in unregulated frequencies.

Frequency-hopping uses strict timing to switch frequencies. Both the sender and the receiver are set to change frequencies at a specific time. Bursts of data are sent on one frequency, and then the machines switch to another frequency for the next data burst. It is difficult for unauthorized persons to monitor these transmissions without knowing the timing scheme. (This improved security also has a high price.) Frequency-hopping networks achieve a maximum of 2Mbps transmission rates.

Microwaves

Microwaves travel at higher frequencies than radio waves and provide better throughput as a wireless network media. Microwave transmissions require that the sender be within sight of the receiver. These systems use licensed frequencies, which are more costly than radio wave systems. Microwaves are utilized on two types of communication systems:

- Terrestrial
- Satellite

Terrestrial microwave transmissions are used to transmit wireless signals across a few miles. These systems are often used to cross roads or other barriers that make cable connections difficult. Terrestrial systems require that direct parabolic antennas be pointed at each other. Relay towers can be used as repeaters to extend the distance of the transmission. These systems operate in the low gigahertz range and require licensed frequencies. Installation can be difficult because terrestrial microwave transmissions require that the antennas have a clear line of sight.

Satellite microwave transmissions are used to transmit signals throughout the world. These systems use satellites in orbit about 50,000 kilometers (km) above the earth. Satellite dishes are used to send the signal to the satellite, where it is then sent back down to the receiver's satellite. These transmissions also use directional parabolic antennas within line of sight. The large distances the signals travel can cause propagation delays. These delays vary from under a second to several seconds. These delays are roughly the same for transmissions down the street as for transmissions across the world. This equipment is expensive and quite complicated. Launching a satellite into orbit is a task beyond the capabilities of many organizations. These systems can provide average bandwidth, but lack advanced security and protection from interference. The systems can also provide a good bandwidth connection to link LANs across the world, but this comes with (literally) a hefty price.

Microwaves

Characteristics of terrestrial microwave:

- Cost: Moderate to high
- Ease of installation: Moderately difficult
- Capacity: 1–10Mbps
- Attenuation: Variable
- Immunity to EMI: Low

Characteristics of satellite microwave:

- Cost: High
- Ease of installation: Extremely difficult and complex
- Capacity: 1–10Mbps
- Attenuation: Variable
- Immunity to EMI: Low

Data Transmission

Data transmissions across the network can occur in two forms: analog or digital. *Analog* signals exist in an infinite number of values. Analog transmissions are displayed using a sine graph in which the signal slopes from one value to another; as a value increases from 0 to 1 it becomes every value along the way. *Digital* signals exist in a finite number of values. Digital transmissions are displayed using a graph in which the change from one value to another is instant; the value changes instantly from 1 to 0.

Figure 3-4 shows an example of digital and analog signals.

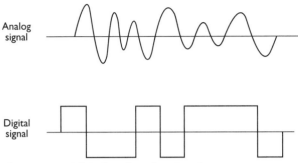

Figure 3-4 *Digital and analog signals*

Baseband transmissions

A transmission of data across network cable has limited *bandwidth,* or capacity. There are two ways of using bandwidth: baseband and broadband transmissions. *Baseband transmissions* use the entire bandwidth to transmit one signal at a time. The signals can be bidirectional. This method is frequently used in LANs, which use digital signaling to transmit data, but it can be used with analog signaling as well. Baseband transmissions have a limit of 2 km in cable length. Repeaters are often used to extend the distance. A repeater is a device that removes any distortion in the signal and retransmits it.

Broadband transmissions

Broadband transmissions use bandwidth by dividing it into channels. This enables multiple transmissions at once. Broadband transmissions are less susceptible to attenuation and can transmit farther than baseband transmissions. The drawback with this method is that transmissions can occur only in one direction. Fortunately, there are ways to overcome this. A *dual-cable configuration* uses one cable to transmit and another to receive. The *split configuration* uses the same cable but different frequencies to transmit signals in both directions. Broadband transmissions are used only by analog signals.

Baseband and broadband transmissions will be contrasted on the exam. Remember that baseband uses a single digital signal that can be transmitted bidirectionally. Broadband can send multiple analog signals at once, in only one direction.

Multiplexing

In data transmission, you must also consider multiplexing. This is a method of using a single high-bandwidth channel to transmit many lower-bandwidth channels. Many low-bandwidth channels can also be combined to provide a single high-bandwidth channel for transmitting signals. A Multiplexer/Demultiplexer (MUX) is the hardware device that allows the channels to be joined and separated. Both broadband and baseband transmissions can benefit from this technique. A commonly known use of this technique is cable TV. Many channels are sent across one cable. The channel changer on the cable box is a demultiplexer that separates the signal. The multiplexing method used depends on whether the transmission is broadband or baseband. The two types of multiplexing are:

- **Frequency-Division Multiplexing (FDM):** This method is used in broadband transmissions to transmit analog signals. The channels are on different frequencies, with an area of unused frequency ranges separating them. These unused ranges are known as *guardbands*, and they prevent interference from other channels. This is the form of multiplexing used in cable TV systems.

- **Time-Division Multiplexing (TDM):** TDM uses time slots to separate channels. Each device is given a time slot to transmit using the entire available bandwidth. This is the only technique that can be used to provide multiple channels on a baseband line.

Have You Mastered?

Now it's time to review the concepts in this chapter and apply your knowledge. These questions will test your mastery of network media.

1. Which bus type is the fastest?

☐ A. PCI
☐ B. PCMCIA
☐ C. EISA
☐ D. MCA

A. PCI allows for the fastest transfer rate and supports bus mastering. It runs at 33MHz, whereas EISA runs at 8MHz and MCA runs at 10MHz. For more information, see the "Bus Architecture" section of this chapter.

2. Which cable type can be used over the longest distance?

☐ A. UTP
☐ B. STP
☐ C. Coaxial
☐ D. Fiber-optic

D. Fiber-optic cable can be run for very long distances. Other cable types have a maximum distance measured in meters. Fiber-optic cable can extend for kilometers. See the "Bounded Media" section of this chapter for more information.

3. Which device normally uses IRQ 14?

☐ A. Serial port
☐ B. Sound card
☐ C. IDE controller
☐ D. SCSI controller

C. IRQ 14 is occupied by the primary IDE controller on most computers. For more information, see the "Adapter Settings" section of this chapter.

4. Which configuration setting is normally shown as a hexadecimal number?

☐ A. DMA channel
☐ B. I/O address
☐ C. IRQ
☐ D. Shared memory address

B. I/O addresses are represented by hexadecimal numbers such as 0x300. For more information, see the "Adapter Settings" section of this chapter.

5. Which driver specification allows third-party vendors to write protocols and services for them?

☐ A. NDIS
☐ B. Packet
☐ C. Open
☐ D. ODI

A & D. Both of these specifications allow other vendors to write software for them. See the "Adapter Drivers" section for more information.

6. **Which type of cable is best suited for environments with a lot of EMI?**

    ☐ A. UTP
    ☐ B. STP
    ☐ C. Coaxial
    ☐ D. Fiber-optic

D. Fiber-optic cable is immune to EMI. See the "Bounded Media" section of this chapter for more information.

7. **Which type of cable would enable you to have a fast LAN without spending a lot of money?**

    ☐ A. STP
    ☐ B. UTP
    ☐ C. Coaxial
    ☐ D. Fiber-optic

B. UTP cable is fairly inexpensive and can be used at 100Mbps. For more information, see the "Bounded Media" section of this chapter.

Practice Your Skills

These exercises will help you apply the material in this chapter through critical thinking.

1. Network bottleneck

EXERCISE You have just added another 50 clients to your network, and now your server seems to be acting sluggish. You run some tests on the server and find that the CPU can handle the load fine, as can the hard drive subsystem. You pinpoint the bottleneck to be in the network card. Further investigation shows a normal 16-bit ISA network adapter. Which adapter type could you replace it with to improve performance? What factors might influence your decision?

ANALYSIS The answer to the scenario depends somewhat on the type of server you have. If the server can support a PCI network card, that would be the best solution. That would increase your transfers to and from the card to the computer's CPU. The next best choice would be EISA or MCA.

2. Configuring an NIC

EXERCISE You are trying to install a network card into a computer with the following hardware: COM1, COM2, LPT1, PS/2 mouse, and an IDE hard drive controller. The NIC supports IRQs 3, 4, 5, 7, and 10. Which IRQ(s) could you use?

ANALYSIS IRQ 3 is used by COM2, and IRQ 4 is used by COM1. LPT1 would use IRQ7. This should leave IRQs 5 and 10 free. Either of these would be a good choice.

3. Choosing a cable type

EXERCISE You are consulted to install new network cabling in a building. The building turns out to be a manufacturing center with a lot of heavy equipment in it. EMI could definitely become a problem. Another requirement is the capability to connect the new wiring to the existing administration office 400 yards away. Which cable should you use? Why would you not use the other cable types?

ANALYSIS A few different cable types could be used in an area where EMI may be a problem. The deciding factor in this question is the distance. You need something that resists or is immune to EMI and can be run great distances. The only real answer for this would be fiber-optic cable.

Network
Designs

THIS CHAPTER HELPS YOU REVIEW the physical topologies and most common network types. Pay close attention to the characteristics of each, as you will surely see them again on the exam. Note the differences between the topologies and any special requirements, such as termination, for each one.

Exam Material in this Chapter

Based on Microsoft Objectives

- Select the appropriate topology for various Token Ring and Ethernet networks

Based on Author Experience

- Bus topology
- Star topology
- Ring topology
- Mesh topology
- ARCNET
- Ethernet
- Token Ring
- FDDI

Are You Prepared?

These questions help you determine whether you're prepared for exam questions on network designs or whether you need more review.

1. Which topologies can Ethernet use?

- ☐ A. Bus
- ☐ B. Star
- ☐ C. Ring
- ☐ D. Mesh

2. Which topology provides the most fault tolerance?

- ☐ A. Bus
- ☐ B. Star
- ☐ C. Ring
- ☐ D. Mesh

3. Ethernet uses which type of media access?

- ☐ A. CSMA/CD
- ☐ B. CSMA/CA
- ☐ C. Polling
- ☐ D. Token Passing

Answers:

1. A & B. Ethernet can use either star or bus, depending on the type of Ethernet used. See the "Ethernet" section.

2. D. Mesh provides the most fault tolerance due to the direct connections between all devices. See the "Physical Topologies" section.

3. A. All types of Ethernet use CSMA/CD. See the "Ethernet" section.

Physical Topologies

The way devices on the network are physically connected is known as the *topology*. Topology can include such aspects as the transmission media, adapters, and physical design of the network. Topologies specify which of these devices are used to connect systems on the network. The four main topologies are bus, star, ring, and mesh.

Bus

The *bus* topology is the simplest to install. All devices on the network are connected to one primary trunk cable, as shown in Figure 4-1. The bus topology is a passive technology that requires no special equipment to amplify or regenerate the signal, although amplification can be used to extend the signal. Bus topology is typically used with a contention network. When dealing with bus networks, it is important to pay careful attention to termination. Each end of the trunk cable needs to be properly terminated, with one end being grounded. Without termination the signal will bounce back down the cable causing collisions. Bus topologies use coaxial cable. The sections are connected with BNC connectors. T connectors are often used to connect the computer to the trunk cable. The T connector can connect the computer to two sections of cable with the bus extending in both directions. The end devices on the bus have terminators on one connector of the T.

 On the exam you will see a few diagrams of bus networks. Many times these networks are connected by things such as repeaters, bridges, or routers. Remember that each bus segment requires termination. So, if you have two bus networks connected by a repeater, each of those segments has its own termination.

Figure 4-1 *A network set up using bus topology*

Characteristics of the Bus Topology

The advantages of using bus include:

- Easy to install and configure
- Uses less cable and doesn't require expensive equipment
- Easy to extend by adding a new section of cable with a BNC connector; repeaters can be used to extend the signal range.

The disadvantages of using bus include:

- Performance degradation under heavy use
- Barrel connectors used to extend the cable lengths can weaken the signal.
- Troubleshooting a bus can be quite difficult. A problem with the cable or a workstation affects the entire network and makes it difficult to determine the location of a problem.

Star

The *star* topology uses a separate cable for each workstation, as shown in Figure 4-2. The cable connects the workstation to a central device, typically a *hub*. This configuration provides a more reliable network that is easily expanded. With the star, there is no central point of failure in the cable. If there is a problem with the cable, only the station connected to that cable is affected. There are two types of hubs, active and passive, both of which are covered in Chapter 6.

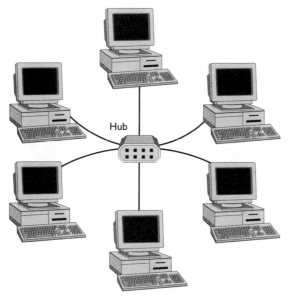

Figure 4-2 *A network set up with star topology*

Characteristics of the Star Topology

Advantages of the star topology include:

- Easy to expand
- Easier to troubleshoot than bus. If there is a problem with the workstation or cable, only that system is affected.
- Hubs can support multiple cable types allowing for a wide range of connectivity.

The disadvantages of using star include:

- The hub can be a single point of failure.
- Requires more cable than most other topologies. This can make a star network more expensive.

Ring

The ring topology looks like the bus topology with connected ends. Rings differ greatly from the bus in *function*. Ring networks provide high performance for a large number of users. Data flow on a ring network travels from computer to computer in one direction, as shown in Figure 4-3. The signal is actually retransmitted by each system when it is passed on to its neighbor. This provides a reliable signal that can travel a large network.

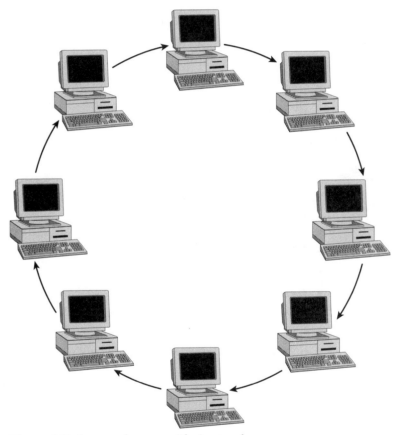

Figure 4-3 *A network set up with ring topology*

Characteristics of the Ring Topology

Advantages of using ring topology include:

- Provides an orderly network in which every device has access to the token and can transmit.

- Performs well under heavy load. The lack of collisions reduces network congestion allowing almost constant transmission of data.

The disadvantages of using ring include:

- Malfunctioning workstations and cables create problems for the entire network.

- Changes made when adding or removing a device affect the entire network.

True Or False?

1. Gateways operate at all 7 layers of the OSI model.

2. ARCNET is a new type of network.

3. Twisted pair cabling is extremely hard to install.

Answers: *1. True   2. False   3. False*

Mesh

The *mesh* topology provides the highest level of fault tolerance. A true mesh network uses separate cables to connect each device to every other device on the network, providing a straight communication path, as shown in Figure 4-4. This requires a large amount of cable and can quickly become confusing. Few mesh networks are true mesh, instead many use a *hybrid mesh* topology. These hybrids use star, ring, or bus topologies with redundant links for added fault tolerance.

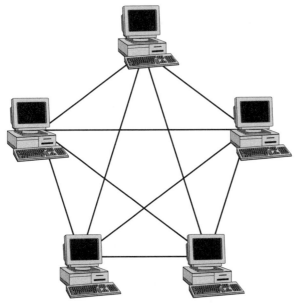

Figure 4-4 *True Mesh Network*

KNOW THIS **Characteristics of the Mesh Topology**

Advantages of using mesh include:

- Enhanced fault tolerance provided by redundant links

- Easy to troubleshoot. If there is a problem communicating with a device, simply check the connected cable and hardware.

The disadvantages of using mesh include:

- Difficult to install and maintain. The large number of connections to each device requires extensive documentation by the administrator.

- Providing redundant links can be costly due to the large amount of cable and equipment needed.

Network Types

Network types combine Physical Layer protocols with the physical topology to form the basic network. The different types of networks we review in this chapter are:

- ARCNET
- Ethernet
- Token Ring
- FDDI

ARCNET

The *ARCNET* (Attached Resource Computer Network) is the oldest network type you may see on the exam. ARCNET uses token passing in combination with a star/bus topology to transmit data at 2.5Mbps. ARCNET was designed to be a simple, inexpensive, and reliable topology. ARCNET can be a good solution for small LANs. Things to remember about ARCNET for the exam are that it can use a passive or active hub, and that you must manually configure the hardware address on each NIC card. If two NICs have duplicate addresses, you will have problems. Also, remember that any unused ports on the ARCNET hub must have terminators on them.

KNOW THIS **Characteristics of ARCNET**

Topology: Star or bus

- Cable types: RG-62, 90-ohm or 93-ohm coaxial, UTP, and fiber-optic
- Transmission speed: 2.5Mbps or 20Mbps for ARCNET Plus
- Maximum number of network nodes: 255
- Maximum number of nodes per segment: Varies

Continued

- Maximum number of segments: Varies
- Minimum distance between nodes: Varies
- Maximum network length: 20,000 feet
- Coaxial cable: 2,000 feet
- UTP cable: 400 feet
- Fiber-optic cable: 11,500 feet

Ethernet

Ethernet is the most common network. It offers support for a variety of protocols and computer platforms. Ethernet is an open network standard developed by Intel, Digital, and Xerox. Ethernet's success is due to its varied support and relatively low cost.

Packets can be sent across an Ethernet network in one of several *frame types*. These frame types are actually syntax for the messages being transmitted. If two systems are using different frame types, they're speaking different languages and they don't understand each other. IEEE developed the standards for the various frame types used across Ethernet networks. The most common are 802.3, 802.2, and Ethernet_II:

- **Ethernet_802.3** — This frame type was developed and used by NetWare for its IPX/SPX protocol before the IEEE finished developing the standard. The frame size used in 802.3 is between 64 and 1,518 bytes and includes *CRC* (cyclic redundancy check) for error checking. This frame type, which doesn't fully comply with the standards developed by IEEE, is used primarily by NetWare 2.2 and 3.11.

- **Ethernet_802.2** — This frame type differs slightly from 802.3 and is fully IEEE compliant. It contains three additional one-byte values. These values add flow control, error checking, and reliability to the previous 802.3 frame type. The packets also range from 64 to 1,518 bytes. This is the default frame type for NetWare 3.12 and 4.1.

- **Ethernet_II** — This frame type can be used by both IPX/SPX and TCP/IP. This frame type doesn't identify the length of the packet but the type. This is used to specify whether the packet is IPX/SPX or TCP/IP.

Understanding that computers using different frame types cannot communicate with each other is extremely important. You are almost guaranteed to see questions concerning this on the exam. Also, be sure to remember which frame types are the default for different versions of NetWare. There is usually an exam question concerning problems connecting to a server from one particular workstation that has to do with frame types.

There are many options for cabling on an Ethernet network. The different cable types provide for a variety of network speeds and cabling lengths. Each type has certain advantages and disadvantages. Ethernet is available in three main standards:

- 10Base-5
- 10Base-2
- 10Base-T

10Base-5

10Base-5 is the original Ethernet standard. It became known as Thick Ethernet due to the RG-8 cable used in the standard. The RG-8 cable uses external transceivers and a vampire clamp that fastens directly into the cable, which is wired in a linear bus. The transceiver then connects to a drop cable, which uses a 15-pin DIX connector to connect to the NIC in the workstation. Transceivers must be at least 8 feet apart. The coax cable must be terminated on both ends with one of the terminators providing a ground. 10Base-5 follows the 5-4-3 rule — there can be five segments with four repeaters and only three of the segments can have workstations. Figure 4-5 illustrates a 10Base-5 network.

TEST TRAP

The 5-4-3 rule may be asked about directly on the exam, but will probably be applied in a scenario. Be sure you understand how it affects the design of a network.

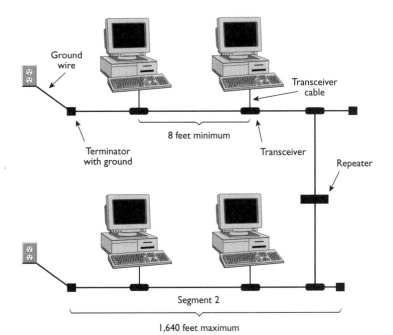

Figure 4-5 *10Base-5 network*

KNOW THIS ## Characteristics of 10Base-5

- Topology: Bus
- Media access method: CSMA/CD
- Cable types: 50-ohm Thicknet coax cable
- Transmission speed: 10Mbps

- Maximum number of network nodes: 300
- Maximum number of nodes per segment: 100
- Maximum number of segments: 5; 3 of which can have connected nodes
- Minimum distance between nodes: 2.5 meters
- Maximum network length: 2,500 meters
- Maximum segment length: 500 meters

10Base-2

10Base-2 was developed as one of the alternatives to 10Base-5 because the RG-8 cable used in 10Base-5 is rigid and difficult to work with, and also because the external transceivers were expensive. 10Base-2 standard uses RG-58 cable along with T connectors wired in a linear bus configuration. This thinner cable is much easier to work with and provides a more cost-efficient Ethernet network. The transceiver was moved onto the NIC to provide a simpler network. This, however, limits the distance the signal can travel. Another limitation is the amount of space between the trunk of the bus and the workstation. T connectors are quite small and connect the workstation directly to the trunk. 10Base-2 networks have a maximum length of 925 meters and follow the 5-4-3 rule allowing five segments, four repeaters, with three of the segments supporting as many as 30 devices, which must be 1.5 feet apart. The coax cable used is RG-58 50-ohm cable using 50-ohm terminators on each end, one of which is terminated. 10Base-2 is a simple and inexpensive solution for many small networks. Figure 4-6 shows a 10Base-2 network.

 TEST TRAP

Remember that on the exam, if you see a diagram of a 10Base-2 network and you are asked what is wrong, check termination. Make sure both ends are terminated and one is grounded.

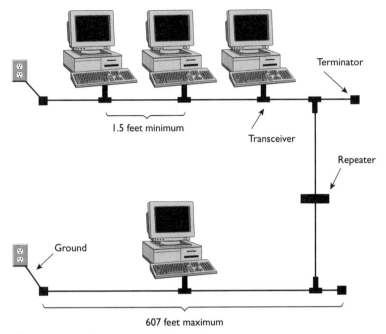

Figure 4-6 *10Base-2 network*

KNOW THIS

Characteristics of 10Base-2

- Topology: Bus
- Media access method: CSMA/CD
- Cable types: 50-ohm, RG-58 coax cable
- Transmission speed: 10Mbps
- Maximum number of network nodes: 90
- Maximum number of nodes per segment: 30
- Maximum number of segments: 5; 3 of which can have connected nodes
- Minimum distance between nodes: 0.5 meters
- Maximum network length: 925 meters
- Maximum segment length: 185 meters

10Base-T

10Base-T is quite different from the other Ethernet standards. This standard utilizes 22-AWG UTP cable with RJ-45 jacks arranged in a star configuration. This uses much more cable but also provides for a more stable and easy-to-maintain network. This configuration eliminates the single point-of-failure problem associated with the bus configuration. Each device has a separate UTP cable connecting it to the hub. The workstations must be at least 2 feet apart and no more than 328 feet from the hub. Several hubs can be connected for a larger network. 10Base-T works well for a growing network. This network standard must also follow the 5-4-3 rule, which allows for 5 segments, 4 connected hubs, and 3 populated segments with up to 512 devices. There is a limit of 1,024 total devices on the network. To overcome the problem of exceeding the 5-4-3 rule, networks can be *segmented*. In segmentation, the smaller networks are connected using bridges or routers, allowing for a large overall network. Figure 4-7 illustrates a 10Base-T network.

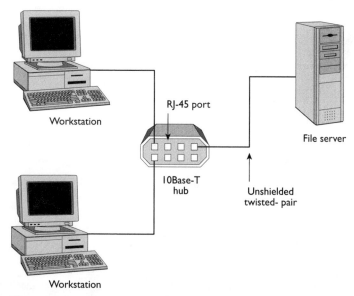

Figure 4-7 *10Base-T network*

Characteristics of 10Base-T

- Topology: Star
- Media access method: CSMA/CD
- Cable types: Categories 3-5 UTP
- Transmission speed: 10Mbps
- Maximum number of network nodes: 1,024
- Minimum number of nodes per segment: 1
- Maximum number of segments: 1,024
- Maximum distance between nodes: 2.5 meters
- Maximum network length: No maximum length
- Maximum segment length: 100 meters

POP QUIZ True Or False?

1. TCP/IP is most often used in Novell NetWare environments.

2. DIX connectors are the same as AUI connectors.

3. ODI drivers can bind to more than one protocol at a time.

Answers: *1. False   2. True   3. True*

Token Ring

Token Ring is a reliable network based on some of the best standards available. It uses token passing in a physical star configuration connected in a ring using hubs. For this reason, Token Ring holds up well under heavy network traffic. This standard was developed by IBM and was certified by the IEEE Committee as the IEEE 802.5 standard. Token Ring transmits at 1, 4, or 16Mbps using proprietary equipment. Because Token Ring uses the token-passing method of media access, it permits devices to have varying priority in accessing the network media. This can be beneficial for servers that need frequent access to the network. The IEEE 802.5 Token Ring standards allow for 250 devices, but a more practical limit is 96 stations and 12 MAUs. Token Ring is a much more expensive network than Ethernet or ARCNET.

KNOW THIS Characteristics of Token Ring

- Topology: Physical star, logical ring
- Media access method: Token passing
- Cable types: STP, UTP, and fiber-optic
- Transmission speed: 4 or 16Mbps
- Maximum number of network nodes:

  UTP: 72

  STP: 260
- Maximum number of nodes per segment: Varies according to the hub
- Maximum number of segments: 33
- Minimum distance between nodes: 2.5 meters
- Maximum network length: No maximum length
- Maximum segment length:

  UTP: 45 meters

  STP: 101 meters
- Frame size:

  4Mbps: 4k

  16Mbps: 16k

Token Ring is a bit more complex in its cabling scheme than Ethernet and ARCNET. Token Ring uses a physical star to connect systems in a logical ring. This is not as difficult to understand as it first sounds. This simply means that systems are connected to a central device using separate cables. This is called the *physical star* configuration. Inside the central device, the ports are connected in a ring. The ring configuration does have one major weakness: there is a single point of failure. If there is a break in the ring, the entire ring goes down. To help overcome this, Token Ring hubs can detect a break in the ring and disconnect that portion of the ring, enabling them to route the ring around the failed area.

One of the reasons for Token Ring's high price is the cost of the adapters. Token Ring adapters are more intelligent than other network adapters. For this reason, there are several important factors to consider when configuring Token Ring adapters. Some of the older Token Ring adapters use switches to configure the resource settings as well as the buffer size and ring speed. It is important for these items to be configured properly. If one of the settings is incorrect, the adapter won't work reliably. Newer adapters have a BIOS on-board, which stores the configuration parameters. These cards can typically handle either Plug and Play resource settings or manual resource settings. Ring speed is an important consideration. Many adapters can operate at either 4 or 16Mbps. If the adapter is configured for the wrong speed, problems may arise with that workstation as well as others on the ring.

FDDI

Fiber Distributed Data Interface, or *FDDI,* is a token-passing ring network similar to Token Ring, but running over a fiber-optic cable. Unlike Token Ring, FDDI enables several devices to transmit at once. Instead of using hubs, FDDI uses concentrators to connect devices. Because FDDI utilizes fiber-optic cable, it is capable of transmitting at the rate of 100Mbps.

FDDI uses a token-passing network over the ring, but the method used in FDDI is much different from Token Ring. FDDI permits many frames to be transmitted simultaneously. This is possible because the station that controls the token can send several frames without waiting for the previous frame to complete its journey around the ring. When one station finishes sending its frames it passes the token to the next station. The second station can begin transmitting without waiting for the frames sent by the first station to completely circle the ring. This process continues around the ring, allowing a constant stream involving several frames circulating around the ring. This provides a method of token passing that is much quicker than Token Ring.

Another way in which FDDI creates a faster, more reliable network is by utilizing two rings that run counter to one another. This provides fault tolerance on the network. If the cable is damaged, a connection is made between the two rings before and after the break, which is known as wrapping. This enables packets to loop back around the ring. This forces the packets to travel twice the distance, one trip on the first ring, another on the second, but allows the packets to reach their destination. This eliminates a single point of failure in the cable, which was a weakness in Token Ring.

There are several adapters and concentrators used in FDDI to allow for a single- or dual-ring configuration. *Class A* systems are those that are configured to connect to only one ring. *Class B* systems can be connected to both rings. Because a workstation can bring down the ring, be sure that systems connected to both rings are highly reliable.

Characteristics of FDDI

- Topology: Ring
- Media access method: Token passing
- Cable types: Fiber-optic
- Transmission speed: 100Mbps
- Maximum number of network nodes: 500
- Maximum number of nodes per segment: No maximum number of nodes per segment
- Maximum number of segments: No maximum number of segments
- Minimum distance between nodes: No minimum distance
- Maximum network length: 100km
- Maximum segment length: No maximum segment length

Fiber-optic cable was extremely expensive only a few years ago. Luckily, the price has dropped substantially in the years since and is becoming much more common on networks today. Most of the cost of a fiber-optic network is the installation. The benefits of fiber include gigabit speeds and immunity to EMI.

Have You Mastered?

Now it's time to review the concepts in this chapter and apply your
knowledge. These questions will test your mastery of network designs.

**1. Which part of a 10Base-T network is the greatest concern
considering fault tolerance?**

☐ A. Media
☐ B. Workstations
☐ C. Hub
☐ D. Connectors

C. Hubs can be a central point of failure. For more information see
the "10Base-T" section of this chapter.

**2. How many cable segments would you need for a true mesh
network with 6 devices?**

☐ A. 6
☐ B. 14
☐ C. 18
☐ D. 35

B. Diagram out a network with 6 devices, each having one connection to every other device. For more information, see the "Physical
Topologies" section of this chapter.

3. Which type of media access does ARCNET use?

- [ ] A. CSMA/CD
- [ ] B. CSMA/CA
- [ ] C. Polling
- [ ] D. Token Passing

D. ARCNET uses token passing. See the "ARCNET" section of this chapter for more information.

4. What is the maximum number of nodes you can have on an ARCNET network?

- [ ] A. 64
- [ ] B. 255
- [ ] C. 1024
- [ ] D. 128

B. You can have up to 255 devices on an ARCNET network. You can remember this because the last network ID you can manually set on an ARCNET card is 255. See the "ARCNET" section of this chapter for more information.

5. Which type of Ethernet uses vampire clamps to connect devices to the coaxial cable?

- [ ] A. 10Base-2
- [ ] B. 10Base-T
- [ ] C. 10Base-5
- [ ] D. 100Base-TX

C. 10Base-5 uses external transceivers with vampire clamps to tap into the network cable. For more information, see the "10Base-5" section of this chapter.

6. **What is the maximum number of devices on a 10Base-T segment?**

   ☐ A. 255
   ☐ B. 128
   ☐ C. 1,024
   ☐ D. 2,048

C. You can have up to 1,024 devices on a 10Base-T network segment. For more information on this, see the "10Base-T" section of this chapter.

7. **What is the default frame type for a NetWare 3.12 network?**

   ☐ A. 802.3
   ☐ B. 802.2
   ☐ C. Ethernet_II
   ☐ D. 802.5

B. The default frame type for NetWare 3.12 and 4.x is 802.2. See the "Frame Types" section of this chapter for more information.

8. **What is the frame size for a Token Ring network running at 4Mb/s?**

   ☐ A. 4K
   ☐ B. 8K
   ☐ C. 12K
   ☐ D. 16K

A. The frame size is 4K (4,096 bytes) on a 4Mb/s Token Ring LAN. For more information, see the "Token Ring" section of this chapter.

These exercises will help you apply the material in this chapter with some critical thinking.

Practice Your Skills

1. Planning network cabling

EXERCISE Your company is relocating to a new building that was prewired with Category 5 UTP cable by the previous occupants. There will initially be 150 clients and three servers on your network. The expected growth rate of the company will add twenty clients a year for the next four years. You have been asked to recommend a reliable, inexpensive network that can be easily expanded to accommodate future growth. What type of network do you recommend?

ANALYSIS By using a 10Base-T network you could leverage the existing cable at the site. Also, because this is category 5 you could later upgrade to 100 Mb/sec.

2. Troubleshooting connectivity

EXERCISE Your network uses Windows 95 clients to connect to NetWare 3.12 servers. A new workstation is having problems connecting to the servers; however, the client can access other Windows 95 clients on the network and has IPX installed. What is the most probable reason that this client cannot connect to the server?

ANALYSIS Because this is isolated to a single workstation you can rule out the server as well as a general network problem. Assuming the client has the IPX protocol installed correctly, the next most likely problem would be frame type. Make sure the client had the correct frame type selected.

3. Troubleshooting Token Ring connectivity

EXERCISE You are installing a new 16/4 Token Ring adapter in a new workstation. The network is being slowly upgraded from a 4Mbps network to a 16Mbps network. The workstation is successfully configured and tested in your lab. When delivered to the customer's office the system loses all network connectivity. The cable and port being used were working moments before on his old system. What is the most likely cause of the problem?

ANALYSIS Most likely the problem is with the speed of the network. Check to be sure the card is running at the same speed as the network. If they are different, you will not be able to talk to the network.

4. Finding a conflict

EXERCISE A workstation on your ARCNET network is having problems connecting to the network. The user is having trouble retrieving data from other systems on the network. This problem began when new workstations were added to the network. You also notice that the problem does not occur while the new part-time secretary is out of the office. What problem would cause these symptoms?

ANALYSIS The most obvious solution to this problem is a duplicate ARCNET address. This happens often on ARCNET networks, especially if addresses are not documented well. Check the two conflicting systems to see if their addresses are the same.

Network
Protocols

C HAPTER 5 GETS INTO THE WORLD of protocols and protocol stacks. This chapter will quickly review the protocol stacks and WAN protocols that are covered on the Networking Essentials exam. Be sure to remember the uses of each protocol, and when you would implement a certain protocol. Also be sure to note if the protocol stack is used primarily with a certain operating system, because that is most likely how the protocols will be used on the exam.

Exam Material in This Chapter

Based on Microsoft Objectives

- Distinguish whether SLIP or PPP is used as the communications protocol for various situations
- Select the appropriate network and transport protocol or protocols for various token-ring and Ethernet networks
- List the characteristics, requirements, and appropriate situations for WAN connection services

Based on Author Experience

- Protocol overview
- TCP/IP protocol suite
- IPX/SPX protocol suite
- Microsoft protocols
- AppleTalk
- Wide area network connections
- Public Switched Telephone Network
- SLIP & PPP
- X.25
- Frame Relay
- ISDN
- ATM

Are You Prepared?

These questions will help you determine whether you're prepared for the exam questions on network protocols or whether you need more review.

1. TCP/IP is the main protocol for which operating system?

- ☐ A. Windows 95
- ☐ B. Windows NT
- ☐ C. UNIX
- ☐ D. CP/M

2. Which of the following protocols are connectionless?

- ☐ A. IP
- ☐ B. TCP
- ☐ C. IPX
- ☐ D. SPX

3. Which two of the following make up the Data Link Layer on an IPX/SPX protocol stack?

- ☐ A. MLID
- ☐ B. VLM
- ☐ C. LSL
- ☐ D. SPX

4. Which protocol is not routable?

☐ A. IP
☐ B. IPX
☐ C. NetBEUI
☐ D. SPX

5. Each B channel on an ISDN connection has how much bandwidth?

☐ A. 28.8Kb/s
☐ B. 64Kb/s
☐ C. 128Kb/s
☐ D. 256Kb/s

Answers:

1. *C.* *UNIX was created around the TCP/IP protocol suite. For more information, see the section titled "TCP/IP."*

2. *A&C.* *Both IP and IPX are connectionless protocols that need other protocols to provide reliability. For more information, see the sections titled "TCP/IP" and "IPX/SPX."*

3. *A&C.* *In an IPX/SPX protocol stack the Data Link Layer is made up of the LSL and MLID sub-layers. See the section titled "IPX/SPX" for more information.*

4. *C.* *NetBEUI cannot be used to connect to resources across a router. For more information, see the section titled "Microsoft Protocols."*

5. *B.* *Each B channel on an ISDN connection provides 64Kb/s of data. See the section titled "Integrated Services Digital Network" for more information.*

How Protocols Work

Protocols are how computers on a network communicate. Most protocols actually consist of several protocols grouped together in a suite. One protocol usually only covers one aspect of communication between devices.

Protocols are either routable or nonroutable. Routers are used to connect LANs. One consideration in connecting LANs is the capability of protocols to work properly across the router to the different networks. A protocol with the capability to communicate across the router is known as a *routable protocol*. Routable protocols are usually more complicated than *nonroutable protocols* because they need extra layers to handle the routing features. Some protocols cannot be routed and are limited to smaller LANs. Usually, these are older protocols that were devised before networks grew as large as they are today. Although very few nonroutable protocols are left, some are still used.Besides being simpler than routable protocols, nonroutable protocols are also usually faster and provide better transfer speeds. This is due to less overhead.

Protocols can also be connectionless or connection-oriented, depending on the reliability needed. Using a *connectionless protocol* is like mailing a letter; once you give the letter to the post office to be sent, you have no real feedback as to whether it arrived safely or not. Likewise, connectionless protocols send out data across the network with no feedback as to whether the data arrived at the destination device. If you need to ensure that certain data arrives at its destination, you can use a *connection-oriented protocol*. The protocols send acknowledgments to show that data was received successfully.This is similar to receiving a delivery receipt from a package you shipped to someone.

Popular Protocol Suites

A protocol suite (or protocol stack) is a collection of protocols that work together to form a single system to handle networking devices. The purpose of a protocol suite is to handle the underlying network functions that user applications can take advantage of. Protocol suites can usually be loosely mapped to the OSI model, although some can be mapped more closely to the model than others. How well a protocol suite maps to the OSI model normally depends on when the protocol suite was developed.

TCP/IP Protocol Suite

The *TCP/IP* (*Transmission Control Protocol/Internet Protocol*) protocol suite, also known as the Internet Protocols, is a suite of industry standard protocols. The TCP/IP suite is made up of many protocols, not just TCP and IP, and has a broad feature set due to its large number of open standard protocols. TCP/IP has also evolved over the years, and today it is the main protocol used on the worldwide Internet (due to its being included in the UNIX operating system, which was the main operating system for early users of the Internet).

Every host on a TCP/IP network is given an *IP address*. This address is a unique 4-byte address in dotted notation — for example, 56.88.1.231. IP addresses are handed out by a single organization, called InterNIC, so each computer has its own unique address; however, organizations should request their IP addresses from the Internet provider to which they are connecting.

TCP/IP and the OSI model

The original designs for TCP/IP were started long before the OSI model was developed; instead of OSI's seven-layer model, TCP/IP was based on a DoD model with four layers. The four layers can be loosely matched to the OSI model in the following ways:

- **Network Access layer** — This layer corresponds to the Physical Layer and Data Link Layer of the OSI model. When TCP/IP was developed, it was made to use existing standards for these two layers so it could work with protocols such as Ethernet and Token Ring. Over the years, TCP/IP has been shown to run over almost any type of network connection from FDDI to radio wave.

- **Internet layer** — This layer of the DoD model roughly matches up with the Network Layer of the OSI model.

Both of these layers are responsible for moving data to other devices on the network. Internet Protocol (IP) is mainly responsible for this job.

- **Host-to-Host layer** — This one is similar to the Transport Layer of the OSI model. The job of both of these layers is to communicate between peers on the network. As a result, almost all devices on a TCP/IP network are considered hosts, whether they're a workstation, a server, or a network-attached printer.

- **Process/Application layer** — This fourth layer does the same job as the top three layers of the OSI model, which is to provide network services.

Figure 5-1 shows how the TCP/IP protocol suite relates to the OSI model.

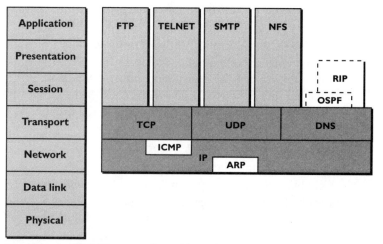

Figure 5-1 *TCP/IP protocols and how they correspond to the OSI model*

What's in the TCP/IP suite?

The Internet Protocols are made up of a lot more than just TCP and IP, although these are the main two protocols. Let's review the major protocols in the TCP/IP suite:

- **Internet Protocol (IP)** — A connectionless protocol that sits in the Network Layer level of the OSI model. The job of IP is to address and route packets accordingly through the network. An IP header is attached to each packet (also referred to as a *datagram*) and includes the source address, destination address, and other information used by the receiving host. Another job of IP is to fragment and reassemble packets that were split up in transit.

- **Internet Control Message Protocol (ICMP)** — Protocol that provides error reporting for IP. Because IP is connectionless, and no error checking is happening, it cannot detect when an error occurs on the network. It is up to ICMP to report errors back to the host that sent the IP packet.

- **Routing Information Protocol (RIP) and Open Shortest Path First (OSPF)** — Two routing protocols in the Internet Protocol suite. RIP, similar to NetWare's RIP, uses the number of routers (hops) between the originating computer and the destination to decide the best way to route a packet. OSPF uses much more information than just the number of hops to make a decision. Usually, OSPF is configured to figure in the hop count, the speed of the connection between the hops, and the load balancing to calculate the best way to route packets.

- **Transmission Control Protocol (TCP)** — A connection-oriented protocol that corresponds to the Transport Layer of the OSI model. TCP opens and maintains a connection between two communicating hosts on a network. When an IP packet is sent between them, a TCP header that contains flow control, sequencing, and error checking is added to the packet. Each virtual connection to a host is given a port number so datagrams being sent to the host go to the correct virtual connection.

- **User Datagram Protocol (UDP)** — A connectionless transport protocol that is used when the overhead of TCP is not needed. UDP is responsible only for transporting datagrams. UDP also uses port numbers similar to TCP, except that they do not correspond to a virtual connection, but rather to a process on the other host. For example, a datagram may be sent to a port number of 53 to a remote host. Because UDP is connectionless, there is no virtual connection setup, but a process on the remote host is "listening" on port 53.

- **Address Resolution Protocol (ARP)** — Suppose a computer needs to communicate with another computer on a network. The source computer has the IP address of the destination computer, but not the MAC address that is needed to communicate at the Physical Layer of the OSI model. ARP handles the conversion of the address by sending out a discovery packet.

- **Domain Name System (DNS)** — The system that converts user-friendly names such as http://www.idgbooks.com to the correct IP address. DNS is a distributed database hierarchy maintained by different organizations. A number of main DNS servers point clients to the more specific servers at each company.

- **File Transfer Protocol (FTP)** — The file-sharing protocol most commonly used in a TCP/IP environment. This protocol enables users to remotely log on to other computers on a network and browse, download, and upload files. One of the main reasons FTP is still very popular is that it is platform independent.

- **Simple Mail Transfer Protocol (SMTP)** — This protocol is responsible for making sure that e-mail is delivered. SMTP handles only the delivery of mail to servers and between servers. It does not handle the delivery to the final e-mail client application.

- **Dynamic Host Configuration Protocol (DHCP)** — This protocol takes over the job of assigning addresses and configuring computers on the network when your network becomes large. Instead of configuring each device on the network manually, the administrator does it once for the entire network on the DHCP server. The DHCP server is given a range of IP addresses to hand out to network devices. The range of IP addresses is also configured for the network on which they will be given out. When a computer comes online to the network, it sends out a DHCP request. The nearest DHCP server responds with all the information to set up TCP/IP on the new client.

For the Networking Essentials exam, know that DHCP is responsible for automatic IP addressing. Questions may present a scenario where an administrator needs an easier way to manage network addressing and configuration. Be aware that DHCP can provide all configuration settings — not just an IP address, but also a subnet mask, default gateway, and so on.

- **Telnet** — This protocol enables a user to remotely log on to another computer and run applications. The computer that the user is physically working on effectively becomes a dumb terminal — no processing is done on that computer, it is simply used for display. Telnet clients are available for almost every operating system on the market today. Windows 95 and Windows NT come with a Telnet client right out of the box.

True or False?

1. The Transport Layer of the OSI model provides unreliable data communications.

2. DHCP is used to automatically assign IPX addresses.

3. Repeaters use CRC checks on packets so that they only forward "good" packets.

Answers: *1. False 2. False 3. False*

IPX/SPX Protocol Suite

The *IPX/SPX* protocol suite was developed and maintained by Novell, Inc. Like TCP/IP, the name comes from the two main protocols in the suite, IPX and SPX, even though there are many other protocols in the suite.

The Microsoft version of the IPX/SPX suite is called NetWare Link (NWLink). You may see this on the exam and should know it refers to the IPX/SPX protocols.

The IPX/SPX suite is relatively new, whereas TCP/IP is extremely old in the world of computers and networking. Because IPX/SPX was created around the time the OSI model was conceived, it can be easily mapped to this model. You will learn the individual protocols by OSI model layer. Figure 5-2 shows how each of the IPX/SPX protocols compares to the OSI model.

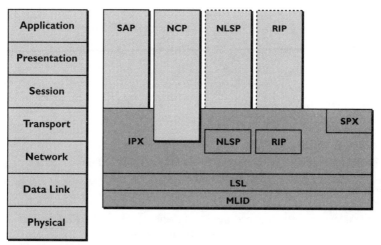

Figure 5-2 *IPX/SPX and the OSI model*

Lower-layer protocols in the IPX/SPX suite

The layers discussed in this section correspond to the Data Link Layer of the OSI model. There are no protocols in the Physical Layer of the IPX/SPX suite because it can use any popular physical network type, such as Ethernet, Token Ring, or FDDI. The protocols that work at the Data Link Layer are responsible for media access and interfacing to the network card. There are two protocols in this layer:

- **Multiple Link Interface Driver (MLID)** — This protocol is concerned with media access. Remember from previous chapters that media access is the arbitration method devices use to decide who can transmit on the media. MLID is a network interface board driver specification — the piece of software that makes the network card in a computer work. Such drivers are written to a certain specification called the Open Datalink Interface (ODI) specification. The ODI spec was written by Novell to enable third-party vendors to create network card drivers that would work with their NetWare operating system. Each network card requires a separate MLID driver.

- **Link Support Layer (LSL)** — This protocol functions as the interface between MLID and the upper-layer protocols. The Link Support Layer is responsible for making sure data goes to the correct upper-layer protocols, should multiple protocol stacks be loaded.

Middle IPX/SPX suite protocols

The middle protocols in the IPX/SPX suite map to the Network Layer and the Transport Layer of the OSI model. They are responsible both for transferring data between devices on the network and for some routing functionality. The protocols in this layer include:

- **Internetwork Packet Exchange (IPX)** — This protocol corresponds to the Network Layer of the OSI model. IPX is responsible for connectionless data service. It handles the routing of data across an internetwork as well as the logical network addressing. An IPX address is a combination of the physical MAC address on the network card and a logically assigned network address. IPX also uses socket numbers to successfully deliver data to the correct upper-layer process on the destination device. Socket numbers are the IPX/SPX equivalent of TCP/IP port numbers.

- **Sequenced Packet Exchange (SPX)** — This protocol also corresponds to the Network Layer and makes up for the inherent unreliability of IPX. Whereas IPX is a connectionless datagram protocol, SPX is connection oriented, with sequencing and error control. SPX rides on top of IPX to add this extra functionality, in a similar way that TCP rides on top of IP in the TCP/IP suite. SPX is mainly used when a connection is made across an internetwork device such as a router, or to a print server to service a printing request. SPX uses acknowledgments to ensure delivery, whereas IPX does not.

- **Routing Information Protocol (RIP)** — One protocol IPX can use to decide the best route through an internetwork is the RIP. RIP is a very simple routing protocol that uses the distance vector method to calculate hop count (basically, it just counts the number of times a piece of data crosses a router before reaching its destination), and then chooses the route with the least number of hops.

- **NetWare Link Services Protocol (NLSP)** — This protocol is a more advanced routing protocol than RIP. Instead of using a simple distance vector scheme, it uses a link state routing mechanism to choose the best route. In a link state routing protocol, the best route is chosen using more information than just hop count. Factors such as latency and speed of the links between the internetwork devices come into the picture.

Upper-layer IPX/SPX protocols

The two upper-layer protocols in the IPX/SPX suite for use with NetWare cover multiple layers of the OSI model. These two protocols are:

- **NetWare Core Protocol (NCP)** — This is the "language" spoken between a NetWare client and a server. This protocol handles most network services, including file services, printing, file locking, resource access, and synchronization. NCP functions at four layers of the OSI model:

  - **Transport layer** — Connection services with segment sequencing, error control, and flow control
  - **Session layer** — Session control
  - **Presentation layer** — Character translation
  - **Application layer** — Application and service interface to the end-user application

  NCP is a high-level language built into NetWare, and is used inside any lower-level protocol that accesses the server. This way, you can use NCP whether your clients and servers are using IPX/SPX or TCP/IP — though it is most often used with IPX/SPX. Developers can use NCP to make requests and send replies between a client and a server. The commands are grouped into requests and replies. The NCP commands are mainly concerned with file, directory, and printer access.

- **Service Access Protocol (SAP)** — Servers using the IPX/SPX protocol are so easy to set up and maintain, thanks to the Service Access Protocol (SAP). Each computer sharing a resource on the network sends out an SAP packet containing information about the resource and where it is located. These packets are sent out at a set interval. Although the SAP feature is very useful and makes the network easy to configure, it can also become a problem. While enabling clients to find servers without having to manually configure every client for each server, the SAP packets can quickly overrun a large network. Steps must be taken to filter out the excessive SAP packets and keep them down to a manageable level.

Microsoft Protocols

Microsoft network operating systems can use many different protocols to function. This contrasts with many network systems that require a set suite of protocols. Although Microsoft can use many standard protocol suites, there are some protocols that Microsoft uses almost exclusively. These are NetBEUI, NetBIOS, and Server Message Block.

- **NetBEUI (NetBIOS Extended User Interface)** — A small, very fast protocol used in Microsoft networks. It has some advantages and some disadvantages that must be considered for its use. The main advantage of NetBEUI is speed and ease of configuration. NetBEUI is one of the fastest (if not *the* fastest) protocols you can use to share files. Configuration is simple because all that is needed is a computer name — no network or logical addresses are required.

KNOW THIS NetBEUI is a small, fast, nonroutable protocol used in small Microsoft workgroup networks.

- **NetBIOS (Network Basic Input/Output System)** — Originally, the NetBIOS protocol and NetBEUI were considered the same protocol, but that is no longer the case. NetBIOS has been "separated" from NetBEUI and is now a distinct Session Layer protocol that can be used on top of other Transport Layer protocols.

  NetBIOS was originally developed by IBM and acts as an interface for applications to the network. It was made so that developers could easily use this interface to write network-aware applications. NetBIOS is still very prominent today, even without NetBEUI. Most Microsoft systems use NetBIOS commands for communications. Most file sharing and administration done on Microsoft networks uses the NetBIOS interface on top of TCP/IP or IPX/SPX.

- **Server Message Block (SMB)** — A Presentation Layer protocol used by Microsoft networking software to communicate. Once a communication channel has been established with a protocol such as TCP/IP, a NetBIOS session is made between the devices. The SMB commands flow over this NetBIOS session. SMB is similar in function to Novell's NCP protocol — that is, it provides the communication and commands between the client and server to handle resource requests and replies.

POP QUIZ **True or False?**

1. The IEEE 802.3 standard deals with Ethernet.
2. The OSI model has 6 layers.
3. PPP was designed before SLIP.

Answers: *1. True   2. False   3. False*

The AppleTalk Protocol Suite

AppleTalk was developed by Apple Computers for use with its Macintosh brand of computers. AppleTalk is a large suite of protocols that make up a networking system that is easy to configure and use. Originally designed with the company's LocalTalk cabling architecture in mind, AppleTalk has expanded to support other network types such as Ethernet and Token Ring.

The original AppleTalk specification greatly limited the size and type of network on which it could run. Its design was meant for use in a small workgroup type of environment, not large enterprise-wide networking. Later, Apple revised the specification in 1989 to allow for larger, more robust networks. The second version, named Phase 2, allowed the use of other network protocol suites, such as TCP/IP.

Original AppleTalk networks could not be internetworked because of the address space used. Phase 2 added support for a network address, along with a node ID to allow for larger networks.

AppleTalk is very modular and can be mapped to the OSI model quite easily.

You won't get any in-depth questions on AppleTalk during the exam. Just know that it is used exclusively by Apple for its workgroup networks.

Data Link Control

Data Link Control (DLC) is a nonroutable data transfer protocol designed for connecting terminals to mainframe computers. It is also popularly used to connect networked computers with Hewlett-Packard network printers. It is not a full protocol suite and cannot be used for normal client/server interaction. Specifically, you could not use DLC to share files.

For the exam, the most important thing to remember about DLC is that it is mainly used for Hewlett-Packard network printers, and that it cannot be used for data communications.

Wide Area Network Protocols

The protocols we just reviewed involve clients talking to servers, usually over a LAN. However, suppose your company just merged with another that had a remote office in another state. You need technology to handle the moving of data across these WAN connections. In this section I discuss the currently popular technologies used by companies to send data across WANs. Before I do that, however, let's look at WAN connection types (see Chapter 2).

Connection Types

The best WAN connection would simply be one long wire between sites. This would give you unrestricted, dedicated bandwidth. The main problems with this are, of course, cost and feasibility. Instead of having a dedicated cable, companies buy or lease connections from some sort of service provider. Leased connections can take two different forms: dedicated or switched.

Dedicated connections

In a dedicated connection, you have full use of the connection as if it were a physical cable. The difference is that the service provider owns and manages the "cable." No one else can use the line you have leased. The cost of a dedicated connection is usually high. You pay the same amount whether you use the bandwidth or not.

Switched connections

Switched connections enable several people to use a connection at once. Switched connections take special hardware to manage the connections, but give you the benefit of lower cost for the connection.

Another advantage of switched connections is that you are normally charged only for the bandwidth used, not the total capable bandwidth. A drawback to this is that bandwidth could be limited due to the possible number of people sharing the connection.

Popular WAN Protocols

Now let's review the WAN protocols that enable you to route data over a large internetwork. These protocols do not replace the upper-layer protocol suites such as IPX/SPX or TCP/IP; they carry these protocols through the internetwork so they may deliver the data. In this section we'll review the following:

- Public switched telephone network
- SLIP and PPP
- X.25

- Frame Relay
- ISDN
- ATM

Public switched telephone network

The *public switched telephone network* (*PSTN*) has been around for a long time and is a very popular way to move data across an internetwork. You may also hear this referred to as "POTS," or "plain old telephone system." In the United States, the PSTN is handled by Regional Bell Operating Companies (RBOC) and other long-distance providers.

When the local telephone company installs the telephone lines to your office, they bring the connection to the demarc point. The *demarc point* is the spot where the phone company connects to your location. Usually, it is an outside box from which the interior phone lines run. Anything beyond the demarc point is your responsibility. Most often, businesses will contract the same phone company to handle all inside wiring, but that wiring is still not the phone company's responsibility.

The local telephone company is responsible for all communications between your demarc point and their local central office (CO). The connection between the CO and your demarc point is known as the *local loop*. This local loop is usually made up of UTP cable or, if you are lucky, fiber-optic cable. The central offices are then connected to each other through high-capacity trunk lines. Long-distance carriers also tie into this large network of COs to offer long-distance service.

Calls made over the PSTN use circuit switching. The call travels over a dedicated wire to the CO, but once there, a switched circuit is set up to the CO to which the call is destined. Once the call is completed, the circuit is torn down.

Using the PSTN, you can get several different connection types. They include:

- **Dial-up connections** — This is the simplest and most common connection over the PSTN. You make one of these connections each time you call up your Internet provider. Using a normal modem, speeds can reach up to 56Kbps (but usually don't, due to imperfect local loop conditions).

- **Dedicated leased lines** — Dedicated leased lines are a step up from a normal dial-up connection. Leased lines are either analog or digital. Analog leased lines are simply dial-up connections that are connected all the time. They use standard modems at each end, and are susceptible to the same speed-limiting problems that normal dial-up connections are prone to. These lines are somewhat expensive, but because they are dedicated, they can usually be tuned and cleaned up to provide higher speeds than normal telephone lines. Digital leased lines are faster than analog lines. Their speeds can range from 2Kbps all the way to 56Kbps. Because of digital transmission, they are less susceptible to interference and can truly reach the 56Kbps speeds. They also are not as error-prone as analog lines.

- **Switched-56** — This is the answer to the high cost of a dedicated leased line connection. Switched-56 provides 56Kbps speeds over a switched connection, not a dedicated connection. Users are charged only for the time that is used, not for when the connection sits unused. A different CSU/DSU is used than with a standard dedicated 56Kbps line.

- **T-carrier system** — When you need bandwidth larger than what 56Kbps connections provide, another option is available. Originally designed in the 1960s to handle multiple voice calls at once, the *T-carrier system* is now used in data communications. The T-carrier system uses devices called *multiplexers*, or *MUXes*, to combine multiple communications into one. At the other end, another MUX separates the different communications.

  The basic T-carrier system is a *T1*. A T1 is composed of twenty-four 64Kbps channels that can be combined for a total bandwidth of 1.544Mbps. One outstanding feature of this system is that the channels can be split so that some are used for voice traffic and some for data. These 64Kbps channels are called *Digital Signal Level 0* (DS-0) signals. A full T1 line is also known as a *DS-1*, or in Europe an *E-1*. Table 5-1 shows the different T-carrier lines available.

TABLE 5.1 T-Carrier Systems

Digital Signal	Carrier	Speed (Mbps)	Channels
DS-0	N/A	0.064 (64 Kbps)	1
DS-1	T1	1.544	24
DS-2	T2	6.312	96
DS-3	T3	44.736	672
DS-4	T4	274.760	4032

SLIP and PPP

Serial Line Internet Protocol (*SLIP*) is an older protocol used to handle TCP/IP traffic over a dial-up or other serial connection. SLIP is a Physical Layer protocol that doesn't provide error checking, relying on the hardware (such as modem error checking) to handle this. It also supports only the transmission of one protocol, TCP/IP.

A later version of SLIP, called *Compressed SLIP* (*CSLIP*), became available. Although the name says "compressed," this protocol actually just reduces the amount of information in the headers, and does not compress the transmission. *Point-to-Point Protocol* (*PPP*) is much more robust than its earlier cousin, SLIP. PPP provides a Physical Layer and Data Link Layer functionality that fixes many problems with SLIP. Basically, your modem is transformed into a network card, as far as upper-level protocols are concerned.

At the Data Link Layer, PPP provides error checking to ensure the accurate delivery of the frames it sends and receives. PPP also keeps a Logical Link Control communication between the two connect devices by using the Link Control Protocol (LCP).

Besides being less prone to errors, PPP also enables you to use almost any protocol you want over the link. TCP/IP, IPX/SPX, NetBEUI, and AppleTalk can all be sent over the modem connection. PPP also supports the dynamic configuration of the dialed-in computer. Unlike SLIP, where your addresses and other information have to be hard-coded ahead of time, PPP enables the client computer to receive its information from the host it dials into.

Most Internet dial-up connections today are made using PPP over modem or ISDN.

Remember that Windows NT can dial out to a SLIP or a PPP host. However, Windows NT can only act as a PPP host — it cannot let SLIP clients dial into it.

X.25

X.25 was developed in 1974 by the CCITT as a Network Layer packet-switching protocol. It specifies how internetwork devices connect over a packet-switched network, giving users an alternative to dedicated connections.

X.25 consists of three levels that can be mapped to the bottom three layers of the OSI model:

- **Level 1 (X.21)** — Physical layer protocol that defines rules for connectivity and data transmission standards

- **Level 2 (LAPB)** — Provides Data Link Layer connection-oriented data transmission using the Link Access Procedures Balanced (LAPB) protocol

- **Level 3 (X.25)** — Defines how packets are sent between Data Terminal Equipment (DTE) and Data Circuit-Terminating Equipment (DCE). X.25 relies on other protocols for switching and routing functionality.

X.25 was developed before the PSTN was as error-free as it is today. For this reason, it has a high-error control system built in, and is kept fairly low-speed (the maximum speed of an X.25 network is 64Kbps).

The physical connection of an X.25 network requires that you lease a line to the switched network through an X.25 provider. A hardware Packet Assembler/Disassembler (PAD) is needed to handle the packet switching.

X.25 is no longer a good choice when building an internetwork. Other technologies such as Frame Relay and ATM make more sense today.

Frame Relay

Frame Relay is based on X.25, but has less overhead. As technology increased, the need for tight error control was diminished. Frame Relay took the features of X.25 and stripped out the error control and accounting. The assumption is that most connections now are made over fiber-optic cable, which provides an extremely low error rate.

Unlike X.25, which had dynamic routed packets, frame relay uses Permanent Virtual Circuits (PVC) to establish connections ahead of time. Packets can now have just the PVC number attached to them and be sent through the frame relay network. With the removal of the error control and the use of PVCs, Frame Relay can reach speeds of 1.544Mbps.

A notable feature of Frame Relay is its capability to guarantee bandwidth, and then occasionally exceed that amount when needed. When you have a Frame Relay connection installed, you determine your Committed Information Rate (CIR). This becomes your guaranteed bandwidth. You may also occasionally exceed that bandwidth limit if your provider's network is capable of delivering it.

Frame Relay is an economical choice for the bandwidth received — so, not surprisingly, it's a very popular WAN protocol right now.

Integrated Services Digital Network

Integrated Services Digital Network (ISDN) has been around for a number of years, but has just recently become affordable. ISDN enables you to send voice, data, and video over normal copper telephone lines by sending digital signals instead of analog signals. ISDN uses 64Kbps channels, called *B channels*, for data transfer. It also has a 16K channel, called the *D channel*, for call setup and control information. It is also possible to send X.25 data over the D channel.

There are two types of ISDN:

- **Basic Rate Interface (BRI)** — BRI is geared toward home users and small offices. It consists of two B channels and one D channel, for a total data bandwidth of 128 Kbps. Each B channel can be used separately. You could use one for data while the other is handling a voice call.

- **Primary Rate Interface (PRI)** — PRI is mainly for larger organizations that need high bandwidth connections. It provides twenty-three B channels and one D channel for a capacity of 1.544Mbps, the same as a T1 line. Again, the B channels can be used either for voice or data.

ISDN was not originally designed to be set up as a continuous connection service, but rather a fast dial-up service. Depending on your location, ISDN service may be billed by the minute or at a flat-rate pricing.

The physical connection is through standard telephone lines. An ISDN adapter (sometimes called an ISDN modem) is required to dial in or out.

Asynchronous Transfer Mode

Asynchronous Transfer Mode (ATM) is a packet-switching technology aimed at real-time applications, such as voice and video over data lines. ATM uses a different type of switching called *cell switching*. It uses a fixed packet size of only 53 bytes, 5 of which is header information. Each of these 53-byte packets are called *cells*. With the use of fixed-size packets, routing and switching can be done much faster by the networking hardware. Speeds of ATM can reach 622Mbps!

ATM uses switches to move the cells quickly across a network. When a connection needs to be made to a distant device over ATM, a virtual connection is set up through the switches. As you may have guessed, 5 bytes of header on a cell is not enough to define the source and destination. To set up a connection, a special cell is sent through the network to the remote device. This path is recorded by the switches along the way and is given a connection number. For the duration of the virtual connection, the cells only need this connection number in the header to designate their path through the network.

ATM hardware is still very expensive and complicated. As it becomes more popular, the price will drop, and others will be able to enjoy its speed.

Have You Mastered?

Now it's time to review the concepts in this chapter and apply your knowledge. These questions will test your mastery of network protocols.

1. Which protocol in the TCP/IP suite is used for error reporting?

☐ A. OSPF
☐ B. IGRP
☐ C. ICMP
☐ D. SMTP

C. ICMP is used to report back messages and errors to a host in a TCP/IP network. See the "TCP/IP" section of this chapter.

2. Which protocol in the IPX/SPX suite is used for routing?

☐ A. NLSP
☐ B. ODI
☐ C. SPX
☐ D. SAP

A. NLSP is a link state routing protocol. See the "IPX/SPX" section of this chapter.

3. **Which protocol is used for dial-up when multiple transport protocols are needed?**

  ☐ A. SLIP
  ☐ B. ATM
  ☐ C. PPP
  ☐ D. Frame Relay

C. Only PPP enables you to dial up a remote host and then use multiple transport protocols. See the "PPP" section of this chapter for more information.

4. **Frame Relay is based on which older protocol?**

  ☐ A. X.25
  ☐ B. ATM
  ☐ C. Leased lines
  ☐ D. Switched-56K

A. Frame Relay is an optimized version of X.25. See the "Frame Relay" section of this chapter.

5. **ISDN uses what kind of cable?**

  ☐ A. Fiber
  ☐ B. Coaxial
  ☐ C. Phone cable
  ☐ D. STP

C. A big feature of ISDN is that it runs over normal phone lines. See the "ISDN" section of this chapter for more information.

Practice Your Skills

These exercises will help you apply the material in this chapter through critical thinking.

1. Expanding the network

EXERCISE You administrate a network that currently has NetBEUI as its primary protocol. Your company is expanding and will soon be moving to a large office building with multiple floors. You have decided to split up your network with internetworking devices to handle the increased volume. Should you change your protocol choice? What protocol(s) could you possibly change to? Why?

ANALYSIS NetBEUI begins to break down on anything but the smallest of networks. Because you are spreading out and starting to use internetworking devices such as routers, a better choice would be TCP/IP. TCP/IP would enable you to continue growing far in the future, and would give you better use of your network resources.

2. New network printer

EXERCISE A new Hewlett-Packard printer was just connected to your LAN. What changes must be made to the clients to enable them to print to it?

ANALYSIS HP network printers use DLC to print. You would need to install this on each workstation that needs to be able to print.

3. Remote connectivity

EXERCISE Your company has recently decided to allow remote access for users who travel. A limited number of IP addresses is available, so the company has decided to assign the numbers dynamically to users when they are connected. Users will also need to use NetBEUI to access their printers remotely. Which protocol would users need to access the network?

ANALYSIS You would need to use PPP for the dial-in users. PPP enables you to use multiple protocols over the one connection. SLIP only supports TCP/IP.

Connecting Networks

WELCOME TO CHAPTER 6! This small chapter covers the different devices that can be used on a network. The key points to remember in this chapter are the function of the device, of course, and the layer of the OSI model at which they operate. You can be sure you'll get an exam question about one of these and the OSI model!

Exam Material in this Chapter

Based on Microsoft Objectives

- Define the communication devices that communicate at each level of the OSI model
- Select the appropriate connectivity devices for various Token Ring and Ethernet networks

Based on Author Experience

- Repeaters
- Bridges
- Ethernet hubs
- Routers
- Gateways

Are You Prepared?

These questions will help you determine whether you're prepared for questions on connecting networks or whether you need more review.

1. Which device is used simply to extend the range of a network?

- ☐ A. Bridge
- ☐ B. Repeater
- ☐ C. Router
- ☐ D. Gateway

2. Bridges filter on what type of address?

- ☐ A. MAC address
- ☐ B. IP address
- ☐ C. Network address
- ☐ D. IPX address

3. Routers operate at which layer of the OSI model?

- ☐ A. Data Link
- ☐ B. Transport
- ☐ C. Physical
- ☐ D. Network

Answers:

1. B.   Repeaters extend the range of a network by simply
        regenerating the electrical signal. See the "Repeaters"
        section for more information.

2. A.   Bridges use the MAC, or physical, address to filter
        data. See the "Bridges" section for more information.

3. D.   Since routers are responsible for routing data across
        the network, they must operate at the Network Layer.
        For more information, see the "Routers" section.

LAN Connectivity Devices

When your LAN reaches its limit on distance or number of nodes that you can have on a segment, you may turn to hardware devices such as repeaters, bridges, or hubs to extend your network and allow for expansion.

Repeaters

One of the easiest devices you can use to extend the distance of a network is a repeater. Repeaters work at the Physical Layer to regenerate the electrical signal on the network media. At this layer, they do not understand things such as protocols, packet addresses, or anything concerning the data they carry. They simply understand the electrical signal of 1's and 0's. The signal is read in as the binary 1's and 0's and retransmitted as the 1's and 0's so the noise in the signal can be cleaned out. Repeaters send and receive data at the speed of the network, but signal regeneration does take a small amount of time.

 Keep this in mind! Repeaters can connect two networks with different cable types, but only if they are the same type of network, such as Ethernet or Token Ring.

Most network types have a limit to the number of repeaters that can be used to connect segments. In Ethernet, this rule is called the *5-4-3 rule.* With this rule, you may have a total of five Ethernet segments, four repeaters, and three populated segments. The extra two segments that cannot be populated are used for distance to reach other locations. Figure 6-1 illustrates the 5-4-3 rule. Any more segments or repeaters would cause timing problems and would affect the collision detection used by Ethernet.

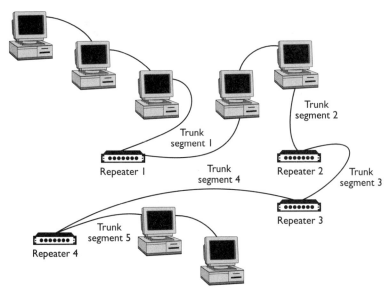

Figure 6-1 *5-4-3 rule*

KNOW THIS **Repeaters**

Advantages of repeaters:

- Repeaters easily extend the length of a network.
- They require no processing overhead, so very little, if any, performance degradation occurs.
- You can connect segments from the same network types that use different types of cable.

Repeaters do have some disadvantages. Because they simply pass data through with no intelligence, they cannot be used to segment traffic on a network.

Disadvantages of repeaters:

- Repeaters cannot be used to connect segments of different network types.

- They cannot be used to segment traffic on a network to reduce congestion.
- Many types of networks have limits on the number of repeaters that can be used at once.

Bridges

Whereas repeaters do not filter the traffic they pass, bridges do. Bridges work at the Data Link Layer of the OSI model, and like repeaters, they attach two different network segments and pass data. Unlike repeaters, bridges filter the data and decide whether it needs to be passed. Suppose you have a workstation and a server on one side of a bridge that are communicating. The data they are sending does not need to pass through the bridge. The bridge knows this and blocks the traffic.

If you use bridging, be sure to think about its placement on the network. If all clients access the same server and you put the bridge between the server and the clients, you will get no benefit. Place the bridge for maximum effectiveness. The optimum situation would be to block about seventy percent of the traffic from coming to the segmented LAN.

 True or False?

1. You use a Time Domain Reflectometer to locate bad NIC cards.
2. Repeaters can be used to isolate broadcast storms.
3. Share-level security uses a single password to secure a resource.

Answers: *1. False   2. False   3. True*

 Remember that bridges pass data by using MAC addresses, not logical addresses such as TCP/IP or IPX/SPX addresses.

Bridges

Advantages of bridges:

- Bridges extend network segments by connecting them together to make one logical network.
- They segment traffic between networks by filtering data if it does not need to pass.
- Like repeaters, they can connect similar network types with different cabling.
- Special translational bridges can connect different network types together.

Disadvantages of bridges:

- Bridges process information about the data they receive, which can slow performance.
- Bridges pass all broadcasts.
- They cost more than repeaters due to extra intelligence.

Ethernet Hubs

Ethernet hubs are simply multiport repeaters for UTP cable. Hubs range in size from four ports up to several hundred ports, and are specific to the network type. You can only have up to four hubs between any two points on a network to follow the 5-4-3 rule.

Some hubs are just repeaters; they work the same way and follow the same rules. Some hubs have the intelligence of a bridge built in; these hubs are called *switches*.

There are two types of hubs: *passive* and *active*. *Passive hubs* provide no signal regeneration. They are simply cables connected together so that a signal is broken out to other nodes without regeneration. These are not used often today because of the loss of cable length that is allowed. *Active hubs* act as repeaters and regenerate the data signal to all ports. They have no real intelligence to tell whether the signal needs to go to all ports, so the signal is blindly repeated.

Ethernet Hubs

Advantages of hubs:

- Almost no configuration is needed.
- Active hubs can extend maximum network media distance.
- No processing is done at the hub to slow down performance.

Disadvantages of hubs:

- Passive hubs can greatly limit maximum media distance.
- Hubs have no intelligence to filter traffic, so all data is sent out all ports whether it is needed or not.
- Because hubs can act as repeaters, networks using them must follow the same rules as with repeaters.

Internetworking Devices

Now that we've reviewed how to extend and expand the capacity of a LAN, let's look at the devices used to connect LANs. Several pieces of hardware enable you to connect LANs, including:

- Routers
- Brouters
- Gateways

Table 6.1 shows how these devices relate to the OSI model.

TABLE 6.1	How Internetworking Devices Relate to the OSI Model
Device	**OSI Layer**
Repeater	Physical
Bridge	Data Link
Router	Network
Gateway	All seven layers

The information in Table 6.1 is the most important information contained in this chapter. There are always questions on the exam asking at which layer a certain device operates. Be sure to know them for the exam.

Routers

Routers are used to connect complicated networks with many segments. They do more than just filter traffic; they make intelligent decisions on the path of the data. Routers can use either MAC addresses or administratively assigned logical addresses (such as IP addresses) to handle data routing. This enables you to segment your network into *subnets*. A subnet is a network connected to another network via a router. Figure 6-2 shows a network divided into subnets using routers. Routers operate at the Network Layer of the OSI model.

Bridging routers, or *brouters*, offer the best of both worlds between bridges and routers. Remember that some protocols are nonroutable, such as NetBEUI. What if your network consisted of NetBEUI traffic and TCP/IP traffic? In this scenario, you could use a brouter to route the TCP/IP and to bridge the NetBEUI traffic.

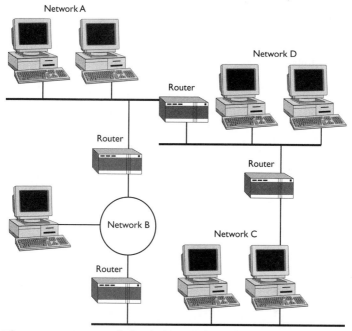

Figure 6-2 *A network divided into subnets by routers*

 Routers

Advantages of routers:

- They use the highest level of intelligence to route data accordingly.
- They can also act as a bridge to handle nonroutable protocols such as NetBEUI.

Disadvantages of routers:

- Higher level of intelligence takes more processing time, which can affect performance.
- Routers are very complicated, which makes installation and maintenance difficult.

Gateways

Gateways can operate at all seven layers of the OSI model. Their function is to perform any necessary conversion of protocols between networks. Gateways are customized and designed to perform a specific function, and are used on a case-by-case basis. Gateways may do anything from converting protocols to converting application data. There is no limit.

One use of a gateway is for e-mail. Most large companies upgrade their e-mail system at one time or another. During the upgrade process, there will normally be two e-mail systems, the original system and the new system, running at once. Users will still need to mail others on the old system after they are upgraded. To accomplish this, you can install an e-mail gateway between the two systems until the migration to the new system is finished. This gateway would be written just to connect the two specific mail systems together.

POP QUIZ True or False?

1. Domains use centralized security, whereas workgroups do not.

2. ISDN connections have a maximum bandwidth of 56K.

3. Modems are an inexpensive way to link networks.

Answers: *1. True   2. False   3. True*

Have You Mastered?

Now it's time to review the concepts in this chapter and apply your knowledge. These questions will test your mastery of connecting networks.

1. Which device operates at the Physical Layer of the OSI model?

- ☐ A. Bridge
- ☐ B. Repeater
- ☐ C. Router
- ☐ D. Modem

B. Because repeaters only regenerate the signal on the network media, they operate at the Physical Layer. For more information, see the "Repeaters" section of this chapter.

2. Bridges work at which layer of the OSI model?

- ☐ A. Data Link
- ☐ B. Segmentation
- ☐ C. Network
- ☐ D. Physical

A. Bridges use the MAC address to filter data. This information is passed at the Data Link Layer. For more information, see the "Bridges" section of this chapter.

3. Which type of hub regenerates signals as it splits them?

☐ A. Passive
☐ B. Powered
☐ C. Active
☐ D. Closed

C. Active hubs act as repeaters and regenerate the signal, enabling the network to have a longer distance. See the "Ethernet Hubs" section of this chapter for more information.

4. Routers use what type of address to make decisions?

☐ A. Network
☐ B. MAC
☐ C. Physical
☐ D. Device ID

A. Routers are responsible for getting data to the correct network segment. They do this by making decisions based on the network address of the destination device. See the "Routers" section of this chapter for more information.

5. Which device would you use to connect two networks that use different protocols?

☐ A. Router
☐ B. Bridge
☐ C. Hub
☐ D. Gateway

D. By using a gateway, you could connect these dissimilar networks. Some popular gateways connect IPX networks to TCP/IP networks. For more information, read the "Gateways" section of this chapter.

Practice Your Skills

These exercises will help you apply the material in this chapter through critical thinking.

1. Extending the network

EXERCISE   You are in charge of an Ethernet network that uses the bus topology. You are currently close to the maximum number of client workstations allowed on a single segment. Which network device would be the best choice to extend your network? What if your main protocol was TCP/IP?

ANALYSIS   For a normal Ethernet network, you could simply use a bridge to extend the segment. This would also help filter traffic. If the network primarily uses TCP/IP, a better solution may be a router.

2. Connecting distant LANs

EXERCISE   You have decided to connect the network used by the HR department in your company to the network used by Accounting. HR has a thinnet Ethernet network using coaxial cable, and Accounting is using a 10Base-T Ethernet network running over UTP cable. The signal is not currently strong enough to cover the distance effectively. What device would you use to connect the networks?

ANALYSIS A repeater would easily solve this problem. It would extend the cable the distance needed, and can connect 10Base-T and coaxial networks because they both use Ethernet.

3. Adding a protocol

EXERCISE Your network is currently 100% TCP/IP. A new application requires that the users install the NetBEUI protocol. What changes to your network devices would be needed to accommodate this new application?

ANALYSIS You would need to add NetBEUI to each work-station. If your network uses routers, then you must also enable bridging on the routers, or else they will not pass the NetBEUI traffic.

Administration

T HIS CHAPTER REVIEWS the different administration tasks and concepts you will see on the exam. Pay attention to the differences between domains and workgroups, account types, and security models. These are the main points you will see on the exam.

Exam Material in this Chapter

Based on Microsoft Objectives

- Compare user-level security with access permission assigned to a shared directory on a server
- Choose an administrative plan to meet specified needs, including performance management, account management, and security
- Choose a disaster recovery plan for various situations
- Implement a NetBIOS naming scheme for all computers on a given network

Based on Author Experience

- Workgroup
- Domain
- User account
- Group
- Share-level security
- User-level security
- Auditing
- Backups
- RAID
- UPS

Are You Prepared?

These questions will help you determine whether you're prepared for exam questions on network administration, or whether you need more review.

1. Which of the following is not a domain component?

- ☐ A. Primary domain controller
- ☐ B. Backup domain controller
- ☐ C. Windows NT Server
- ☐ D. Workgroup

2. Which of the following uses share-level security?

- ☐ A. Windows 95
- ☐ B. Windows NT Server
- ☐ C. Windows NT Workstation
- ☐ D. Novell NetWare

3. Which RAID level provides disk mirroring?

- ☐ A. RAID 0
- ☐ B. RAID 1
- ☐ C. RAID 3
- ☐ D. RAID 5

Answers:

1. *D.* *Workgroups are not a domain component. See section titled "Microsoft Networks."*

2. *A.* *Windows 95 uses share-level security. User-level security is available only when a Windows 95 computer logs into a domain or a NetWare server. See section titled "Security Types."*

3. *B.* *RAID 1 provides for disk mirroring and disk duplexing. See section titled "Redundant Systems."*

User and Security Administration

Installation and configuration of the network is just the beginning of the job for the network administrator. Once the network is in place, many maintenance tasks are involved in network administration. Users come and go, and new network resources are added involving network reconfiguration. The foundation for security and administration starts with the Microsoft networking models, which include workgroups and domains.

Microsoft Networks

Microsoft networks come in two forms: workgroups and domains. When a computer is configured for networking, a computer name must be supplied, along with a workgroup or domain name. It is important to maintain a standard naming scheme. Standardizing the naming scheme can make it much easier to locate network resources. Workgroups and domains should be given names that identify either location or function (a combination can also be used). One example of this is to name all workgroups according to department: for example, ACCOUNTING, MARKETING, and HR. Inside the workgroups, you need naming standards to specify each machine.

Workgroups help organize computers in a peer-based network according to department or function. There can be a large number of workgroups on a network. Each computer can be a member of one workgroup. When users on a Microsoft network browse the network, they first see all the computers in their workgroup that have sharing enabled. They can then browse the entire network to see a list of workgroups on the network. Each workgroup is browsable. Any computer can join a workgroup by simply specifying the workgroup name. A server is not required in a workgroup but can be present. Workgroups require that each user manage his or her own resources and users. Microsoft Windows 95, Windows for Workgroups, and Windows NT Server and Workstation are capable of joining a workgroup.

Although you can employ user-level security in workgroups and share-level security in domains, this is not usually the case on the exam. When you see a domain, think user-level security, and vice versa for workgroups.

Domains are server-based networks that provide a higher level of security and central administration than is available with workgroups. The *primary domain controller*, or *PDC*, is a Windows NT server that validates accounts as users log on to the network. *Backup domain controllers*, or *BDCs*, are also Windows NT servers, and can assist with logons if the PDC is unavailable. A user must have an account on the domain before he can log on to it. Once a user logs on to the domain, network resources are granted based on user rights and permissions assigned to that account.

A domain provides a central database of users and groups, which can be granted rights to resources throughout the domain. Domains provide centralized administration and accounts for the network. Windows 95, Windows for Workgroups, and Windows NT Server and Workstation are capable of joining a domain.

 Workgroups and Domains

Workgroups have the following characteristics:

- Peer-based networks
- No central administration
- Used to organize resources

Domains have the following characteristics:

- Require a Windows NT server to function as a PDC
- Provide central administration of users and resources
- More secure; require an account to log on to the network

Users

Anyone who accesses resources on a network needs a *user account*. User accounts identify the user to the network, and it allows rights to be granted to that specific user. User accounts can be created and administered for one computer or for an entire domain. Domains make it easier to maintain proper user accounts throughout the network. User Manager for Domains is a utility in the Administrative Tools program group that is provided with Microsoft Windows NT Server to manage user accounts for the domain. Non-domain user accounts are managed with User Manager on Windows NT Server and Workstation.

When an account is created on any Windows NT computer, it is assigned a number that identifies it. This number is called a *SID*, or *security identifier*. SIDs are very large numbers that theoretically should be unique in the universe. All rights given to the user are identified with that account number. When an account is deleted, the number is lost. If a new account is created, even with the same user name, then a new number, or SID, is assigned. This means an account cannot be re-created if it is deleted. Instead, the new user account will need to be assigned the necessary permissions.

POP QUIZ True or False?

1. Most protocol stacks match the OSI model almost exactly.
2. Auditing is enabled in Security Manager.
3. Repeaters help alleviate network bottlenecks.

Answers: *1. False   2. False   3. False*

Creating user accounts

There are some rules to keep in mind when creating user accounts. In Windows NT, a user account can be up to twenty characters using any combination of letters, numbers, and symbols except for: /, \, :, ;, |, =, +, *, <, and >. The following list shows the standard information needed to create a user:

- **User name** — Short name that signifies the user (for example, nashwj). This is the name that the person sitting at the client computer will use to log on to the network.

- **Password** — Password that provides security for the user account.

- **Full name** — Full name is usually needed for an account for informational purposes.

- **Description** — Description usually contains information pertaining to the user's role in the company.

- **Home directory** — The *home directory* is a private directory on the server, to which users normally save their work.

- **Login scripts** — Script name that is executed upon the user's logging in. This normally sets up the network environment for the user and attaches the scripts to resources.

These options may not all be available in every network operating system. Other options, such as the times at which a user is allowed to log in, or which computers they are allowed to log in from, may also be available.

Most network operating systems have a graphical utility to add and manage users. In Windows NT, this is User Manager for Domains, and with NetWare, it is SysCon or NWAdmin.

Special accounts

Network operating systems usually come with at least a few special accounts that are created when the software is installed. The first account is usually some sort of administrator account. In Windows NT, the administrative account is known as *Administrator*. Under NetWare, the account is *Supervisor* or *Admin*, and in UNIX it is *root*. Normally, this user cannot be deleted and should have a very good password assigned to it that contains numbers and symbols. The password should be changed often, but should not be forgotten. Generally, these accounts have the capability to:

- Start the network
- Set the security parameters
- Create other accounts

Another account created automatically by Windows NT is the *Guest* account. This enables you to share resources to users on your network who may not be authenticated through a user account. By default, the Guest account is disabled under Windows NT Server and enabled under Windows NT Workstation.

Passwords

The network is only as secure as the user's password. That is why users must carefully choose their passwords. Users should follow some basic rules when deciding on a password. These are:

- Do not use obvious passwords such as your birth date, spouse's name, children's name, or the type of car you have.

- Memorize your password. Do not write it down, and especially do not write it on a sticky note and stick it to your monitor.

- Be sure to change your password often in case someone does compromise your account.

Also, as mentioned earlier, policies can be used to help manage passwords. They can be used to control password length, duration, and uniqueness. Data with a higher sensitivity level requires a higher level of password control. Users may be forced to change their passwords often. This decreases the likelihood of an unauthorized user gaining access to a password. Forcing users to log on to change their password also helps prevent an unauthorized user from gaining access to the system. Windows 95 computers do not require that a user know the correct user name and password to gain access to the system. Windows 95 is a less secure operating system that allows anyone to type a new user name and password to gain access to the system (users can also simply cancel the logon screen). This enables any user to gain access to data stored on the system. The security requirements of the data can dictate which operating system is used. Windows NT requires the correct user name and password before a user can access the system.

The account policy editor in User Manager enables you to set these policies.

Group Accounts

A group is a special account that contains other accounts. With a group, you only need to make one change to affect hundreds or thousands of users. Almost every network operating system supports these type of accounts. Groups can be used to:

- Grant access rights to resources such as files and printers
- Give users the capability to perform system functions such as backups, reboots, and changing configuration settings
- Simplify communications by cutting down on the number of messages or broadcasts that must be sent across the network

Types of groups

Windows NT has four different types of groups: local groups, global groups, special groups, and built-in groups.

- **Local groups** — These groups are created and stored on a local computer's security database. They are used to group users together on a single server or domain, and cannot be shared with other servers or domains.
- **Global groups** — These groups enable you to share group information between domains and servers. In a network that uses Windows NT and domains, these groups enable you to assign rights to users in other domains by simply giving the rights to the group, not to each user individually.
- **Special groups** — This type of group is used by Windows NT to handle users dynamically. Two examples of these special groups are the *Interactive group* and the *Network group*. Administrators cannot control the membership of these groups; Windows NT does it automatically. The Interactive group is composed of users who are physically working on the computer's console. The Network group's members use the computer's resources from across the network.

- **Built-in groups** — Windows NT, NetWare, and most other network operating systems have some groups that are automatically created when the software is installed. Some examples of groups in Windows NT include:

  - **Administrators** — This group includes network administrators with full rights to the server.

  - **Operator-type groups** — These groups grant the members system functions such as the capability to back up and restore data.

  - **System groups** — These groups are used by Windows NT to manage data. The Replicator group is used to help replicate data between servers on the network.

Security Types

Two main types of security are available for use on the network. The type of security you use depends largely on the type of network and on the operating system. Workgroups depend on share-level security, whereas domains employ user-level security.

Share-level security involves assigning a password to resources shared on the network. All a user needs to access the resource is the password. The same resource can be shared with different permissions and different passwords. The level of access to the resource depends on which password one uses to access it. This enables the resource to be shared as read-only, and the password for this share is given to the users who need to view the resource. The resource can then be shared as full-access. The users who use the password assigned to the full-access share can delete, change, and read the data. This enables the data to be shared with different levels of access for a variety of users on the network. This method of security can be difficult to maintain. Users may have to remember several passwords to access all the resources they need to perform their jobs.

Most networks share data with user-level security. User-level security requires the proper user name and password to access a resource. When resources are shared, permission is granted to certain users or groups of users. Only those user accounts can access the resource. Microsoft Windows NT Server and Workstation employ user-level security when in workgroups and domains. When the computers are in a domain, accounts from the PDC can be granted access to shared resources. In addition, a local accounts database can be used in a workgroup. User-level security can be used on a computer running Windows 95 when it is member of a domain or is configured as a client to a NetWare server. User-level security not only provides a higher level of security, it can also allow a wide variety of permissions. A Windows 95 computer using share-level security has only two options: read and full control. User-level security provides options to read, write, add, change, delete, and so on. The added security and flexibility make user-level security the preferred method for networks with more than ten computers.

Security

Be sure to know the differences between the two levels of security for the exam:

- *Share-level security* relies only on a single password to access a resource, and it is used in workgroups.

- *User-level security* requires a user name and password to log on to the resource. User-level security is used in domains, especially Windows 95 computers in a domain and Windows NT workstations and servers in a workgroup or domain.

Auditing

Auditing helps you track events on your network to ensure security. This can include events such as users logging on and off the system, access to files and/or directories, as well as system reboots.

Audit logs can be a great tool to help administrators identify unauthorized access, as well as simple security mistakes the administrator may have overlooked. Common events that can be audited are:

- Success and failure of user logons and logoffs
- Connections to network resources such as disk shares and printers
- System reboots
- Password changes

- Opening, closing, or changing of a file
- Any permission changes or user rights changes
- User or group accounts that are created or deleted

Windows NT and NetWare support auditing, and Windows NT provides the Event Viewer to show the audit log.

Enabling Auditing

Auditing is enabled through User Manager, and the results are seen using Event Viewer.

In Windows NT, auditing is enabled through User Manager for Domains. This is done by choosing Policies from the menu bar, and then selecting Audit from the menu. Select the Audit These Events option to enable auditing. To view the logs, you must use Event Viewer from the Administrative Tools group in Windows NT.

True or False?

1. MAC addresses on network cards are unique to the manufacturer only.
2. Performance Monitor can be used to decode protocol information on a network.
3. Fiber-optic cable is one of the most difficult types of media to install.

Answers: *1. False   2. False   3. True*

Safeguarding Data

Data saved on the servers often takes months or years to obtain and is impossible to replace, so you must take measures to safeguard it against threats. Threats to network data can vary. Therefore, it is extremely important to have disaster recovery plans in place to safeguard the data. Methods that make your network fault-tolerant include data backups, redundant data, and uninterruptible power supplies.

Backups

Tape drives, recordable CD-ROM drives, and other removable disk drives can be used to back up and archive data. These devices enable you to back up certain files, directories, or entire disk drives, depending on what data is most critical and how often it changes. You can back up remote data and data saved on other systems across the network.

A number of methods are used for backing up data, and most effective backup plans employ several of these methods. The methods used vary according to the amount of data that needs to be saved and the amount of time you want to spend backing up and restoring data. Methods include:

- **Full backup** — A full backup is used to back up all selected files. This process marks the files as archived.

- **Incremental backup** — Incremental backups are used to back up selected files that have been changed since the last backup. The files are then marked as archived.

- **Differential backup** — Differential backups are used to back up selected files that have changed since the last backup. This method does not mark files as archived.

- **Copy** — Copying backs up selected files without marking them as archived.

- **Daily copy** — Daily copying backs up selected files that have changed during the day without marking them as archived.

Redundant Systems

Another fault-tolerant system that can be used in combination with backups is *redundancy*. With redundancy, data is duplicated or spread across drives. Redundant systems can help quickly restore the system in case of a device failure. Several types of redundancy are used in today's networks. *Redundant arrays of inexpensive disks* (*RAID*) provide for several levels of redundancy with varying levels of fault tolerance. RAIDs use a combination of hard drives to provide a higher level of fault tolerance or to provide greater speed when accessing data on the drive. The levels of RAID listed below are the most commonly used today. They also happen to be the levels Windows NT Server supports in software.

RAID 0

RAID 0 uses disk striping. Striping divides data into 64K blocks and spreads the blocks across each drive or partition. All the devices combine to create one logical device. This does not provide fault tolerance because the data is not duplicated. If one device fails, all data is lost. The amount of storage space used is 100%. Figure 7-1 illustrates disk striping.

RAID 0 does provide a few benefits. Small partitions can be combined to form one logical device. In addition, disk access rates are increased if multiple disk controllers are used. This enables several devices to read and write data simultaneously. Microsoft Windows NT is capable of configuring RAID 0 through Disk Administrator.

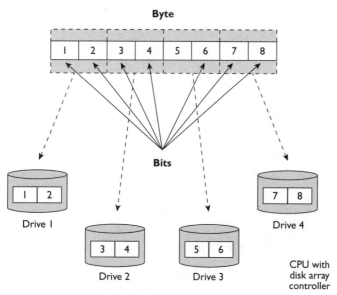

Figure 7-1 *Disk striping*

RAID 1

RAID 1 uses *disk mirroring*. Disk mirroring duplicates all data and partitions to a separate physical disk. This provides two full copies of the system and all data. If one drive fails, the duplicate can be used in its place. This provides quick restoration of the system without restoring several backups. The weakness of disk mirroring is that both drives use the same controller. If the controller fails, then both copies of the data are unusable. Figure 7-2 illustrates disk mirroring.

RAID 1 can also use *disk duplexing*. Disk duplexing is simple disk mirroring with separate controllers. This provides a higher level of fault tolerance. Microsoft Windows NT comes with the software necessary to create a mirror set. Figure 7-3 illustrates disk duplexing.

The drawback of disk mirroring and duplexing is the cost. The duplicate drive provides no extra storage space. Duplexing is more expensive because of the extra controller that is used. Usable storage space versus storage space purchased is 50 percent. Due to the cost of mirroring and duplexing, RAID 1 is rarely used for all disks in the server; it is used primarily for system disks.

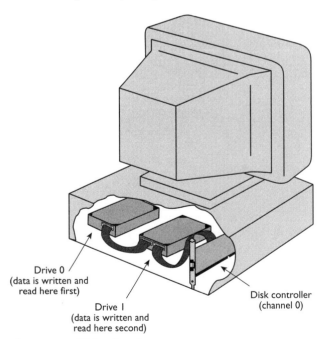

Drive 0
(data is written and
read here first)

Drive I
(data is written and
read here second)

Disk controller
(channel 0)

Figure 7-2 *Disk mirroring*

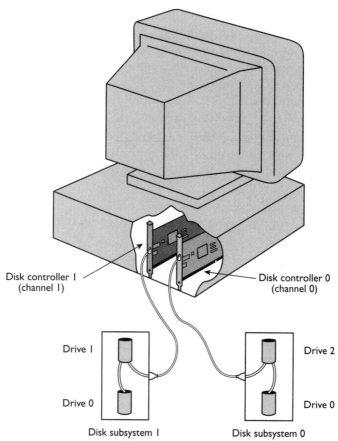

Figure 7-3 *Disk duplexing*

RAID 5

After RAID 1, the next type of RAID configuration that is commonly used is RAID 5. RAID 2, 3, and 4 are simply variations that are not normally used because of their limitations. RAID 5 uses disk striping with parity. Data blocks are striped to several disks with a parity stripe written in varying locations. The data and parity are always written on different disks. The parity stripe contains information that can be used to reconstruct data. RAID 5 can combine between 3 and 32 drives in an array. Because the parity is spread across several disks, if any one disk goes down, it can be replaced and the data can be reconstructed. The level of fault tolerance this provides often makes it worth the amount of disk space lost to parity. RAID 5 can be controlled through special hardware or software. Windows NT contains Disk Administrator, which is capable of configuring software RAID 5. This is currently the preferred redundancy system.

Figure 7-4 illustrates RAID 5.

 Remember that you cannot use RAID 5 on the drive where Windows NT is stored.

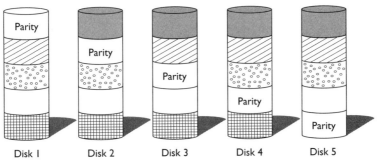

| Disk I | Disk 2 | Disk 3 | Disk 4 | Disk 5 |

Figure 7-4 *RAID 5*

Uninterruptible Power Supplies

An *uninterruptible power supply* (*UPS*) can be used to safeguard against power outages. An UPS is a battery that operates between the power outlet and the computer. The size of the battery varies, and it is important to purchase a UPS powerful enough to support the equipment that is attached.

The UPS sends valuable information such as power conditions and available battery life to the computer. In case of a power failure, the UPS can alert the user and the system when battery life is low. This allows the computer to go through an orderly shutdown, writing data to the disks and avoiding corrupt data.

Some operating systems such as Windows NT include software that is capable of communicating with the UPS. There is also third-party software available that can communicate with UPSs over a serial connection, providing greater functionality.

Performance

Monitoring performance of the network and servers alerts you to trends in the network and possible problems. Performance monitoring involves monitoring the performance of systems as well as performance of the network. Components monitored on computers include memory usage, CPU utilization, and available disk space.

When monitoring the network, pay attention to the amount of bandwidth that's being used. You can also detect which segments of the network have the highest utilization. This helps you effectively segment and maintain the network. Packet loss alerts you to possible problems with cables, connectors, or other equipment. By monitoring the network, you learn which areas need upgrades, and where there may be failing components.

Some network operating systems such as Windows NT include performance-monitoring software. Also, many third-party software products are available to aid in performance monitoring. The Simple Network Management Protocol can be a very useful tool for doing performance monitoring on your network. Most network devices now include SNMP as a support protocol. With a good SNMP management software system, you can obtain almost any statistical information you desire.

Have You Mastered?

Now it's time to review the concepts in this chapter and apply your knowledge. These questions will test your mastery of network administration.

1. Which of the following best describes a workgroup?

- ☐ A. A server-based network that uses groupings to provide a high level of security
- ☐ B. A peer-based network that provides a loose grouping of computers
- ☐ C. A network managed by a server that determines user access
- ☐ D. A grouping of user accounts

B. A workgroup is a loose grouping of computers in a peer-based network. See the "Workstation" section of this chapter.

2. Which built-in group contains accounts that have full rights to the server?

- ☐ A. Administrator group
- ☐ B. Operator-type group
- ☐ C. User group
- ☐ D. System group

A. The administrators group contains the accounts that have full access to the server. See the "Special Accounts" section of this chapter.

3. Which of the following is a valid user name?

☐ A. a+j
☐ B. a&j
☐ C. a:j
☐ D. a*j

B. The /, \, :, ;, |, =, +, *, <, and > symbols are not allowed in user names. See the "Creating User Accounts" section of this chapter.

4. Which access level is not allowed with share-level security?

☐ A. None
☐ B. Read
☐ C. Write
☐ D. Full

C. The only access available in share-level security is Read and Full. No access is given if the resource is not shared. See the "Security Types" section of this chapter.

5. Which type of backup is used to back up files that have changed since the last backup, and doesn't reset the archive bit?

☐ A. Full backup
☐ B. Copy
☐ C. Incremental backup
☐ D. Differential backup

D. A differential backup will back up files that changed since the last backup, and doesn't reset the archive bit. See the "Backups" section of this chapter.

Practice Your Skills

These exercises will help you apply the material in this chapter through critical thinking.

1. Security planning

EXERCISE You are the administrator of a small company network that is migrating to Microsoft networking products. Your users typically work on documents for which they maintain and control security. You also do not currently have a central file server. Would you choose to implement workgroups or domains? Why?

ANALYSIS The best solution would be a workgroup. Workgroups enable users to operate in a peer-to-peer manner, and unlike domains, they do not require a dedicated server.

2. Windows NT administration

EXERCISE Create a user account under Windows NT for yourself. Make sure your password must be changed at next logon and that it never expires. Next, make yourself a member of the Administrators group so you can change the configuration of your computer.

ANALYSIS Using User Manager, select User and then New User. Fill out the information as needed. Next, double-click the Administrators group from the main User Manager window and add your new account as a member.

3. Monitoring users

EXERCISE You are suspicious that a user has gained access to the account files on your network. You need to find a way to catch the user and document the information for your report to management. Which Windows NT feature could you use?

ANALYSIS You would use auditing. You can enable this through User Manager, and then you must choose which objects to audit. The results can be seen in the Event Viewer.

4. Security considerations

EXERCISE You have just installed a Microsoft network using workgroups. Which type of security will you use on the Windows NT Workstation computers in the workgroup? Why would you choose this type?

ANALYSIS The easiest way to secure information would be to use share-level security. This would enable each user in the workgroup to manage his or her own security on his or her workstation. Technically, you could use user-level security, but each user would need an account on every other workstation he or she needs to access. This would quickly become too difficult to manage.

Troubleshooting

HIS FINAL CHAPTER COVERS troubleshooting. While troubleshooting is a difficult issue to teach and grasp from a book, this chapter reviews the basics of troubleshooting, the Microsoft way. The important points in this chapter are the fundamental ideas and general information. You may be quizzed on where to go to find help, or how to begin solving a problem.

Exam Material in this Chapter

Based on Microsoft Objectives

- Identify common errors associated with components required for communications
- Diagnose and resolve common connectivity problems with cards, cables, and related hardware
- Resolve broadcast storms
- Identify and resolve network performance problems

Based on Author Experience

- Network adapters
- Digital volt meter
- Time-domain reflectometer
- Advanced cable tester
- Oscilloscopes
- Network monitors
- Protocol analyzer
- Network protocols
- Broadcast storm
- Microsoft TechNet
- Microsoft Knowledge Base

Are You Prepared?

These questions will help you determine whether you're prepared for questions on network troubleshooting or whether you need more review.

1. Which device is used to detect the location of a break in a segment of network cable?

☐ A. Digital volt meter
☐ B. Time Domain Reflectometer
☐ C. Oscilloscopes
☐ D. Network monitors

2. Which of the following can cause a broadcast storm?

☐ A. Disconnected router
☐ B. Unplugged computer
☐ C. Cable break
☐ D. Malfunctioning bridge

3. Which of the following is not a possible cause of a malfunctioning network adapter?

☐ A. IRQ conflict
☐ B. Incorrect transceiver setting
☐ C. Incorrect speed setting
☐ D. Incorrect gateway setting

Answers:

1. B. Time domain reflectometers can detect the location of a break in network cable. See the "Time-domain reflectometers" section of this chapter.

2. D. Broadcast storms can be caused by a malfunctioning bridge. See the "Broadcast Storms" section of this chapter.

3. D. An incorrect gateway setting does not cause a network adapter to malfunction. Data may not be delivered to the appropriate recipient but the adapter will still function properly. See the "Client Hardware Troubleshooting" section of this chapter.

Troubleshooting Basics

Everyone has his own method of troubleshooting. Some methods, however, are better than others. For the Networking Essentials exam you should be familiar with the Microsoft approach to troubleshooting problems. Microsoft recommends a structured approach for troubleshooting, which involves the following five steps:

- **Set the problem's priority** — Priority can be a big issue when it comes to resolving a network problem. Everyone wants his or her computer fixed right away. You have to prioritize problems based on things such as the time necessary to fix the problem, importance, and who has the problem.

- **Collect information** — Once you have decided which problem to concentrate on, you must then collect information to help isolate the trouble. If you have a baseline performance chart for your network — and you should — you can use it to compare against the current network operations. The key question to ask when a problem arises on a network is "What changed?" About 99 percent of the time something was added, removed, or reconfigured prior to the problem starting.

- **Determine possible causes** — At this point, you should be starting to determine the source of the problem. You may not know the exact problem but instead have a small list of possible causes. The next step is to try out your possible causes.

- **Isolate the cause** — Now, try your most likely solution to see if it fixes the problem.

- **Study the results** — Carefully study the results for each fix you try. See if the problem was fixed or changed in any way. Even if a solution does not fix the problem entirely, it may help you further pinpoint the real issue. If you run out of ideas, you may need to start back at collecting information to see if you overlooked anything.

POP QUIZ **True Or False?**

1. User-level security enables you to set permissions with more detail than share-level security.
2. Most computers support AppleTalk networking.
3. Most wireless media is very high speed.

Answers: *1. True   2. False   3. False*

Client Hardware Troubleshooting

It is common for the client hardware to become faulty and cause errors. The good news is that it is usually easy to pinpoint the exact issue and resolve it.

If only one workstation on your network is affected by a problem, odds are the problem is at the workstation itself. While sometimes frustrating, as all the other workstations on your network are functioning normally, this can make the job easier because the problem is already isolated. Some places where common workstation problems occur are:

- Network adapters
- Protocol configuration
- Application configuration

The most common workstation-related network problem involves the network adapters. Problems occur when adapters are incorrectly configured or when adapters malfunction.

Network adapter configuration

When configuring a network adapter, you must be sure that the settings, such as IRQ, I/O address, and shared memory range are unused by anything else in the computer. One sign of a conflict with another device is that the other device doesn't function either. A device that is conflicting with another may also seem erratic. The careful eye may notice that the troubled network adapter card does not function when another device, such as a scanner or modem, is being used. The simple solution to this problem is to change one of the conflicting devices to another unused setting.

When checking the configuration of a network card, also pay close attention to the transceiver type that is selected. A common problem with a computer that cannot make a connection to a server is that its transceiver type setting is wrong. For example, it may be set to use the AUI port when you should be using the UTP port.

Malfunctioning network adapter

It is generally easy to spot a malfunctioning network adapter because most have diagnostic LEDs on the back to help you diagnose problems. Two common lights are the link light and the data transmission light. The link light shows that the network card has made a connection to a hub (or, as in the case of Token Ring, a MAU). If you see the link light is not illuminated, you may need to check the network card, cable, or sometimes the port on the hub. The data transmission light shows when, and if, data is being sent and received by the network card.

Network Troubleshooting

Once you've determined that a problem is with the network, and not isolated to one workstation, the number of possible causes of the problem increases greatly. Thankfully, several hardware devices exist to help you find the problem. Also, some common problems are easily solved, and I discuss those in the following section.

The Right Tool for the Job

There are a number of hardware devices that can help you pinpoint your problem on the network. Some of the most common ones are:

- Digital volt meters
- Time-domain reflectometers
- Advanced cable testers

- Oscilloscopes
- Network monitors
- Protocol analyzers

For the exam, be sure to know exactly when and why to use a particular hardware troubleshooting device.

Digital volt meters

The *digital volt meter* (DVM) is a basic electronic measuring device. Although this is typically used to check the amount of voltage going through a circuit, it can help you pinpoint certain types of cable problems. For instance, you can use a DVM to check for continuity on a network cable, to see if there are any breaks in the physical media. By connecting the DVM to the ground mesh and the central core, you can check for a short in the cable, which may cause disturbances in the communications.

Time-domain reflectometers

While a DVM can only tell you if a break exists in the cable, a *time-domain reflectometer* (TDR) can tell you exactly where the break occurred. The TDR uses a sonar-like pulse that is sent down the cable. The signal bounces back from a break in the cable. The TDR calculates the time that the signal took to go down the cable and back, and then computes the distance.

TDRs are great to use when a new network is being installed and also after the installation, when a break can be hard to troubleshoot.

Advanced cable testers

Advanced cable testers work beyond the lower levels of the OSI model to give you real insight into how your network is functioning. They can display all sorts of information, including the following:

- Frame counts
- Congestion errors
- Network utilization

- Late collisions
- CRC errors
- Network-level statistics
- Protocol statistics
- Information concerning which applications are using the network

By using these statistics, you can watch for network errors, such as collisions caused by excessive cable length or congestion errors due to an overloaded network. Normally, problems resulting from these statistics are segment- or network-wide and affect all users.

Oscilloscopes

Oscilloscopes are used to show voltage over time. While used frequently in diagnosing problems with electrical equipment, they can also test for faulty network cable. Oscilloscopes can be used to check for

- Shorts
- Crimps in the cable
- Breaks in the cable
- Attenuation

Network monitors

Network monitors are software programs that track and show information about a network. They can generate reports showing utilization, errors, and overall traffic patterns on your network — reports that are very beneficial, as they show your network growth over time. By watching the growth, you can predict when problems may arise and take proactive steps to avoid them.

 Don't get network monitors confused with protocol analyzers. Network monitors are used over a longer period of time to track trends and growth. Windows NT's Performance Monitor can act as a network monitor.

Protocol analyzers

Protocol analyzers can do the job of network monitors and much more. A protocol analyzer often proves to be an important tool when debugging problems on a network. Also called *network analyzers* or *sniffers*, protocol analyzers can be hardware only or a combination of hardware and software. They collect information by examining all data going across the network and decoding the information for display.

Make sure you remember that Microsoft supplies a protocol analyzer with Windows NT Server and Systems Management Server. This is called *Network Monitor* and you may see it on the exam.

Some problems that protocol analyzers can find are

- Bad network cards
- Cable problems
- Bottlenecks
- Configuration errors in protocols

Protocol analyzers are excellent tools for finding most problems on a network. They can look at the network packet by packet and tell you exactly what is being transmitted. You may even use them to debug network applications by looking at the "conversation" going on.

Some popular protocol analyzers are Network General's *Sniffer*, Hewlett-Packards's *Network Advisor*, Novell's *LANalyzer*, and Microsoft's *Network Monitor* that ships with System Management Server.

Many common protocol analyzers run on a normal workstation computer. They use the workstation's network hardware to access and monitor the network. The correct choice of network card is important in the computer that will be running the protocol analyzer software, as the network card must function in what is called *promiscuous mode*. Normally, the MAC address on a network frame header is checked at the Data Link layer. If the MAC address is found to be different from the computer that is reading it, it is discarded. A network card running in promiscuous mode passes all frames up to the higher-level processes, whether the frame was intended for it or not.

Most Token Ring network cards cannot run in promiscuous mode. This is common with cards that have an IBM chipset. Special Token Ring cards can be bought that do permit promiscuous mode operation.

Common Network Problems and Solutions

Some fairly common problems don't require the use of the aforementioned hardware devices. Be sure to check for these potential problems before you waste a lot of time.

Cable problems

Many problems you will encounter will be Physical layer problems having to do with cables. Common cable problems include

- A break in the cable
- A cable short
- A faulty connector

Cable should be one of the first things checked when troubleshooting a network problem. It could be as simple as a piece of thinnet Ethernet cable getting disconnected, which would take down the entire LAN segment.

The first step in working with a cable problem is to make sure that it is, in fact, a cable issue. The easiest way to check is by attaching a notebook computer to the LAN over the questionable cable.

The next step is to ask if anyone has moved equipment or furniture recently. Many times cables are broken when being moved or having things moved on top of them.

If the network uses a bus topology, you can use a terminator to segment the network in half and start isolating the faulty cable. While this may cause disruption to the other users, it can quickly solve the problem.

Network adapters

It is rare for a network adapter to suddenly quit working. The more usual situation is that a new piece of hardware was added to the computer. The first step should be to check for conflicting IRQs, I/O addresses, and shared memory ranges. You can check the link lights and data transmission lights on the network card to see if the card is talking to the hub or the rest of the network.

Network adapter drivers can cause many problems should they become corrupted or replaced by a wrong version. The simple solution is to reinstall the drivers. An easy way to totally reconfigure the network under Windows 95 is to remove the network card from the Network Properties menu, and then reboot the system. When the computer comes back up, you can manually re-add the card.

Incorrect protocol settings can keep a workstation from attaching to a network server. The most common solution involves checking the frame type; this mainly occurs with IPX/SPX. Be sure you are using the same frame type on your workstations as you do on your servers.

Also check your IP address, subnet mask, and default gateway (typically a router functions as the gateway between subnets). An incorrect setting on any of these can keep your workstation from participating on the network.

Network protocols

Protocols can be especially hard to troubleshoot. They are designed to overcome any network problems that arise. Sometimes you may not know network problems, such as a faulty connector, exist until the protocol slows down and users start complaining. Some questions to ask at this point are:

- If the computer receives an error while connected to the LAN, does the computer function offline?
- Has the traffic on this part of the network increased substantially?
- Is there any connection between the devices that are getting the error?

To further troubleshoot protocols, other tools (such as a protocol analyzer or network monitor) may be needed.

Network traffic congestion

Network congestion is usually noticed by users, though it should not be. A good network administrator has a protocol analyzer or other sort of network monitor tracking the network traffic trends. Congestion should be cleared up before it is a problem.

Once you have decided to head off the congestion problem, you can use several hardware devices to help. Bridges can be used to filter traffic, and routers can split the network into logical segments.

Broadcast storms

Broadcast storms are a condition where there are so many broadcasts, the entire network slows down. Remember that broadcasts are read by every device on the network, so not only is network access slow, but the computers will be slow as well. Broadcast storms can be caused by several conditions. A bad network adapter can send out infinite numbers of broadcasts for no reason. This condition is called *jabber*. Malfunctioning or badly planned bridges can also cause broadcast storms.

Most routers do not pass broadcasts, so they can provide some level of protection. The best bet is to find the offending device by the use of a protocol analyzer and remove it.

KNOW THIS

Remember for the exam that bridges are used to stop broadcast storms.

Network-intensive applications

Use of new applications may contribute to new congestion problems. A new breed of applications, known as *push applications*, can cause a lot of network traffic. These applications constantly receive information from a server and provide real-time information, such as news, stock quotes, sports scores, and so on.

Another problem to watch out for on your network is gamers. Many popular games now support playing against other people over a network. The only real solution to this problem is to ban the applications. Some of the new push applications are utilizing special server software that caches information and sends it to the client so each client does not receive the same data over and over.

Power problems

Most problems having to do with power can be solved with an uninterruptible power supply (UPS). Fluctuations and power surges can all be handled by a good UPS.

Most UPS systems also come with software that shuts down your server if there is a total power failure. This enables your applications running on the server to be shut down gracefully, so as not to lose any data.

POP QUIZ **True Or False?**

1. Novell's IPX protocol suite is used primarily on the Internet.
2. Performance Monitor can be used to track network trends, such as utilization and errors.
3. I/O Address 0x300h is normally used by the IDE controller.

Answers: *1. False   2. True   3. False*

Troubleshooting Resources

There are times when a problem may be extremely hard to pinpoint and solve. When this occurs, you may need to turn to outside resources to help you through the process. Luckily, there are some excellent resources for any problem that a network engineer or administrator may run into, some of which are:

• **Microsoft download library** — A quick way to get file updates for Microsoft products is through its download library. The download library is available by dialing into Microsoft's electronic bulletin board system.

- **Microsoft TechNet** — TechNet is a subscription-based service. With this service, you receive a CD containing all sorts of documents and file updates each month to help you with any problems you encounter with Microsoft products. There are excellent articles, white papers, and documents to help with planning, engineering, troubleshooting, and deployment.

- **Microsoft Knowledge Base** — This is the next best resource, after TechNet. It contains many articles describing problems having to do with any of Microsoft's applications and resolutions. These articles are written by developers and support engineers from within Microsoft. A copy of this Knowledge Base is sent to you on TechNet (though it is not as up-to-date).

- **Vendor support Web sites** — Almost every vendor in the networking field now has a support site on the Internet. Normally, these can be reached by going to `http://www.company_name.com`.

- **Newsgroups** — Newsgroups can be a good way to reach a large number of people who may be able to help you find the answer to a problem. Quite often, someone has had the same problem as you, and the answer to your question is already there.

  There are many Microsoft-specific newsgroups as well. They usually start with `microsoft.public.product_name`.

- **Online services, such as MSN and CompuServe** — Online services can be a good source for technical information. Though not as important as they once were due to the number of companies with excellent Web sites, they can still be your best bet for information.

- **Publications** — There are many publications that deal with the networking industry. A lot of them can be had for free. Some publications are done weekly and others are done monthly. Some good examples of publications are *LAN Times*, *LAN Magazine*, *Windows NT Magazine*, *Communications Week*, *InfoWorld*, and *PC Week*.

Have You Mastered?

Now it's time to review the concepts in this chapter and apply your knowledge. These questions test your mastery of network troubleshooting.

1. Which device can detect protocol configuration errors?

- ☐ A. Digital volt meters
- ☐ B. Time-domain reflectometer
- ☐ C. Oscilloscopes
- ☐ D. Protocol analyzers

D. Protocol analyzers can be used to detect protocol configuration errors. This is the only device in the list that can decode the protocols and see exactly what data is being sent. See the "Protocol Analyzers" section of this chapter for more information.

2. Which of the following is a software program that can track information, such as utilization and errors?

- ☐ A. Digital volt meter
- ☐ B. Time-domain reflectometer
- ☐ C. Network monitor
- ☐ D. Oscilloscopes

C. Network monitors are actually software programs that gather information about network utilization, errors, and so on. They can keep this information for long periods of time and show trends.

The other devices are used for finding networking problems. See the "Network Monitors" section of this chapter.

3. Which of the following is an example of an incorrect protocol setting?

☐ A. IRQ conflict
☐ B. Incorrect frame type
☐ C. Incorrect transceiver type
☐ D. Incorrect speed setting

B. An incorrect frame type setting is an incorrect protocol setting for the IPX/SPX protocol. The other answers are incorrect hardware settings. See the "Common Network Problems and Solutions" section of this chapter.

4. Which of the following is not a troubleshooting resource?

☐ A. TechNet
☐ B. Knowledge Base
☐ C. Newsgroups
☐ D. Training & Certification

D. The Training & Certification Web site has information on Microsoft certifications but contains no information on troubleshooting Microsoft products. The other three answers are excellent sources for information and help. See the Troubleshooting Resources section.

Practice Your Skills

These exercises will help you apply the material in this chapter through critical thinking.

1. Detecting conflicts

EXERCISE A user on your network is complaining that every time she uses her modem her serial mouse freezes. What is the likely cause of the problem?

ANALYSIS This is most likely an IRQ conflict, especially if the user has a serial mouse. Remember that COM1 and COM3 both use IRQ 4, while COM2 and COM4 both use IRQ 3. If a user has a mouse on COM1 and a modem on COM2, this could lead to trouble.

2. Troubleshooting physical connections

EXERCISE A user suddenly began having problems connecting to the network after redecorating his office. When his workstation is plugged into the Ethernet cable in his neighbor's office, it works properly. What would you suspect as the problem and what equipment could be used to verify the problem and locate its exact location?

ANALYSIS Most likely a cable was broken during the move. The best tool would be a time domain reflectometer to see exactly where the break occurred.

3. Locating answers to problems

EXERCISE A Windows NT computer is returning a specific error code when the messenger service fails to start. You can find no information about this specific error code in Windows NT Help or in your copy of the Resource Kit. Which resources would you use next to discover the meaning of the error code?

ANALYSIS You could check either the Microsoft Knowledge Base on the Internet or in TechNet.

4. Configuring TCP/IP

EXERCISE A user on the network is complaining about her new workstation. She can access resources that are on her floor but not those on the floor above her. The floors are separated by a router. TCP/IP is the only protocol installed on the network, and no other user is experiencing problems. What is the most likely cause of her problem?

ANALYSIS She most likely has an incorrect setting for her default gateway. This would cause traffic to be sent incorrectly when destined for another network.

Appendix

Adding Services to Your Network

THIS APPENDIX IS NOT REQUIRED READING to prepare for the Networking Essentials exam. It will walk you through adding some simple but effective network services to a small LAN — either a small-office LAN you are building or your own personal network at home. The solutions given below use the easiest and most inexpensive methods available so that you may enjoy these services on the smallest of LANs.

This appendix covers the addition of many useful services to your network. These services supplement the file sharing that is inherent in almost all network systems.

The following network services are covered:

- Network printing
- Network faxing
- Sharing CD-ROMs

- Internet access
- Telecommuting

Some of these services are built into your network operating system, while others require third-party products.

Network Printing

The first network service I will discuss is probably the most popular. This section will cover the installation, maintenance, and management of network printers, print servers, and queues. If you are not familiar with any of these terms, don't be scared. They will be covered soon! The first thing to understand is the difference between local and network printing.

Printing Terminology

Before I can really begin to discuss printing, I need to cover the terms you will encounter when reading about network printing. One problem with network printing terminology is that the meanings sometimes change depending on the network software used.

The printing terms to know are:

- Print job
- Print queue
- Print server
- Printer

When a user chooses to print a document or graphic, the data is sent across the network to the server and stored there in a file. The file includes the document or graphic data to be printed as well as any formatting or commands that need to be sent to the printer. The size of the document does not matter; it is all held in that one file. This request and data is referred to as a print job.

The queue is the area on the print server (or workstation, if printing is local) where the print job is stored. Under Novell NetWare, this is by default a directory on the SYS volume under the SYSTEM directory. Microsoft's Windows NT uses the SYSTEM32\SPOOL directory.

Occasionally, a print job will be corrupted and you may need to clear out the spool directory.

A print server services print queues. The print server process takes print jobs from the queue and sends them to the physical print device.

So you thought you knew what a printer was? You may not. Depending on which network operating system you use, the term printer may describe a software object or the physical printer that puts words to paper. Under NetWare and most other operating systems, the term printer refers to the physical device. When using Windows NT, the term server refers to the object that users connect to. The physical printer is called the print device. This is important to remember when setting up Windows NT printing.

Local Versus Network Printing

Before networks were common, printers were attached directly to the computers that needed them. Printing was a simple task. An application would send the data to be printed to the printer port on the computer, which would in turn send it through the cable to the printer. This process was easy to set up and easy to troubleshoot if something went wrong.

Networked printing can complicate this procedure. Printing directly to a network printer can be similar to the stand alone procedure, but when the network is client-server the process can be complex. The application must send the print request to the network requester software. The network requester software then "talks" through the network to the server. The server accepts the data to be printed and places it in a print queue where it stays until the physical printer is ready for it. Many things can go wrong in this process, and it can sometimes be hard to track down the exact problem.

While network printing provides the advantage of enabling all of your users to print to shared printers, it can have some disadvantages to users and network administrators. Some users may not trust the network to handle their print requests. Hearing a printer start up and print their document as soon as they give the command can be reassuring. As a network administrator, you will find that printing is an extremely important, and sometimes personal, service for your users. Network printing is also harder to set up than local printing. It is very easy to just attach a printer to a personal computer and configure it to print. Sometimes setting up printers off a server can be a hassle — and time-consuming.

Advantages of network printing

There are many more advantages to network printing than there are disadvantages, however. The main advantages are:

- Reduction in number of printers required
- Print spooling
- Improved print management and security
- Flexibility

Reduction in number of printers required Probably the most compelling reason to use network printing is the reduction in the number of printers needed. If you use conventional local printing, each user who needs to print must have his or her own personal printer. This scenario can be very expensive and hard to maintain. Each user may have a different configuration, or a user may have different requirements that require a special printer. Why buy five expensive color printers for a department when everyone could share one?

Print spooling Print spooling enables a user to continue working while the printer does its job. If an application sends data directly to a printer, the computer must wait until that job is completed before it can enable the user to move on. If the document is large or a graphic is complex, the user may be forced to wait for a lengthy amount of time.

Print spooling is the process of storing the print job data in a temporary location while it is being printed. Once the entire print job is put into that temporary location, the computer and user can continue working on other tasks. The printer can print the job whenever it needs to or is available. Print spooling does not speed up the printing process, but it does enable the user to continue working.

Most new operating systems support spooling on local printing. MS-DOS uses RAM to spool the data. Windows and Windows NT use files on the local hard disk to store the data. Network printing has even better spooling than local printing. When a network printing user spools the print job, it goes to the file server. Being low on local hard disk space is a very common problem that can cause local printing to fail. This happens much less often with network printing since servers normally have abundant disk space.

If a user is trying to print a large or complex job to a network printer, he or she can log off the workstation without waiting for the job to finish. Since the spooled information is on the server, the local workstation is no longer needed. This also helps if the printer is offline or out of paper, since the job will get printed as soon as the problem is remedied.

Improved printer management and security Printer management is also easier with networked printing. Most printer configuration changes can be done from one computer instead of on each individual workstation.

Printer security is usually simple to administer with network printing. Access to the networked printers is controlled by the user's own login. The network administrator can define the different levels of access. For example, most users will simply be given the right to send print jobs to the printers while others may be allowed to administer the printers.

Flexibility Network printing provides for greater flexibility and options. For example, you may set up a separate print queue that is only serviced after business hours. Users can still send data to the queue at any time, but it will only be printed at night. This enables users to send very large jobs that would tie up the printer for a long time and have them printed at off-peak hours. You may also give print queues higher priorities for different users. If you only have one printer, you can have it service multiple queues. One of those queues could have a high priority and only be accessible by Vice Presidents. This way their jobs get printed first.

Printer Interfaces

There are several different ways to attach printers to computers. The interface is used to transmit data to, and sometimes from, the printer. Some interfaces simply require the user to plug in a cable, while others may need an administrator to configure it for that particular network. The three main types of printer interfaces are:

- Parallel
- Serial or RS-232

- Network interface

The following sections will cover each of these interfaces in detail.

Parallel interfaces

The parallel printer interface is the most commonly used connection today. The original parallel interfaces were unidirectional. They could only send data to a printer; they could not send any information back to the printer. This was not a major problem for printers at that time, but it has become a problem recently. Printers today need the capability of sending back error and information messages to the computer and the printing application. The bidirectional parallel port has also been used for other peripherals. SCSI adapters that plug into the parallel port are common now, as are Ethernet cards.

Parallel ports are also quicker than serial ports at transmitting data. This is due to the way that they function. As the name implies, the data is sent in parallel, eight bits at a time instead of a single bit at a time. Each data path has a separate physical wire in the cable to use. Bidirectional parallel ports have a total of sixteen wires for data transfer.

The one peculiar thing about the parallel interface is its physical connectors. The connector on the workstation or client device is different than the one on the printer. The computer interface is a 25-pin female connector. Table A.1 shows the pin-outs for the workstation connector.

TABLE A.1 25-Pin Parallel Pin-outs

Pin	Signal
1	Strobe
2	Data Bit 0
3	Data Bit 1
4	Data Bit 2
5	Data Bit 3
6	Data Bit 4

Pin	Signal
7	Data Bit 5
8	Data Bit 6
9	Data Bit 7
10	Acknowledge
11	Busy
12	Paper End
13	Select
14	Auto Feed
15	Error
16	Initialize Printer
17	Select Input
18	Data Bit 0 Return
19	Data Bit 1 Return
20	Data Bit 2 Return
21	Data Bit 3 Return
22	Data Bit 4 Return
23	Data Bit 5 Return
24	Data Bit 6 Return
25	Data Bit 7 Return

If you have ever seen an external SCSI-1 connector, then you have seen the 36-connector parallel connector for printers. A company named Centronics originally designed it, and the connector is now named after it. Table A.2 shows the Centronics connector pin-outs.

TABLE A.2 Centronics Pin-outs

Pin	Signal
1	Strobe
2	Data Bit 0
3	Data Bit 1
4	Data Bit 2
5	Data Bit 3
6	Data Bit 4
7	Data Bit 5
8	Data Bit 6
9	Data Bit 7
10	Acknowledge
11	Busy
12	Paper Out
13	Select
14	Auto Feed
15	Ground
19–30	Ground
31	Initialize
32	Fault
33	Ground
34	Select

Most computers have a limit of three parallel ports. Each parallel port uses an input/output (I/O) address, and two use an interrupt request (IRQ). Table A.3 shows the resources each uses. Parallel ports are referred to as LPT (line printer) ports on MS-DOS computers.

TABLE A.3 Parallel Port Resources		
Parallel Port	**I/O Address**	**IRQ**
LPT1	3BCh	7
LPT2	378h	5
LPT3	278h	None

Serial or RS-232

The serial port interface is also known as the RS-232 interface. The serial interface sends data one bit at a time. It also uses start and stop bits to handle the flow of information. For this reason it is referred to as an asynchronous interface. Because computers transmit data in parallel, serial ports require that the data be converted. This conversion is done using a universal asynchronous receiver/transmitter chip also known as a UART chip. This chip is also responsible for converting serial data to parallel form. Data sent across a serial port uses start and stop bits. These bits are used to signal when a data byte begins and ends. Parity can also be used for error checking to ensure data reliability. Due to the overhead caused by the translation of data from parallel to serial form, serial communications are slower than parallel. The benefit of parallel over serial connections is the distance allowed. Serial cables can have greater cable lengths with no loss of signal. Table A.4 shows a standard transmission of data across a serial port. This is a typical transmission that occurs with every byte that is transmitted.

TABLE A.4	
Bits Transmitted	**Purpose**
111111111	Mark bits that are sent continuously when no transmission is occurring
0	Start bit that signals the beginning of a transmission
10101001	Byte that is transmitted. The length can vary but is usually either 7 or 8
11	End bits that mark the end of a transmission

The physical serial interface is either a 25-pin connector or a smaller, 9-pin connector. Table A.5 shows the pin-outs of the 25-pin connector.

TABLE A.5 25-pin Serial Port Pin-outs

Pin	Signal	Abbreviation
1	Chassis/Frame Ground	GND
2	Transmitted Data	TX or TD
3	Receive Data	RX or RD
4	Request to Send	RTS
5	Clear to Send	CTS
6	Data Set Ready	DSR
7	Signal Ground	GND
8	Data Carrier Detect	DCD or CD
9	Transmit +	TD+
10	Unused	
11	Transmit -	TD-
12–17	Unused	
18	Receive +	RD+
19	Unused	
20	Data Terminal Ready	DTR
21	Unused	
22	Ring Indicator	RI
23	Unused	
24	Unused	
25	Receive -	RD-

TABLE A.6 9-pin Serial Port Pin-outs

Pin	Signal	Abbreviation
1	Data Carrier Detect	DCD
2	Receive Data	RD
3	Transmit Data	TD
4	Data Terminal Ready	DTR
5	Signal Ground	GND
6	Data Set Ready	DSR
7	Request to Send	RTS
8	Clear to Send	CTS
9	Ring Indicator	RI

Most computers can use four serial, or COM, ports. If more than two ports are used, then IRQs must be shared. It is important to be cautious when configuring ports to share IRQs. If two devices attempt to use the same IRQ simultaneously, problems could occur causing one or both of the devices to fail. This problem has caused a problem for many people that use a serial mouse and an external modem. When the modem is initialized, the mouse freezes. Table A.7 shows the resources used by each serial port.

TABLE A.7 Parallel Port Resources

Parallel Port	I/O Address	IRQ
COM1	3F8h	4
COM2	2F8h	3
COM3	3E8H	4
COM4	2E8H	3

Network interface

Printers can also be connected directly to the network using a network interface. The network interface is really just a network adapter designed for printers. These come with a variety of connector types to enable the printer to be easily connected to the existing network.

The network interface also provides for the configuration of a number of protocols to enable the printer to function with computers on the network. The network interface cards have a processor and RAM; they receive data from the network and pass it on to the printing device. Software from another computer is used to configure the network interface. This provides more flexibility in installation and configuration. The printer can be configured and utilized by any computer on the network. This also enables the printer to be connected using the network cable, which is capable of greater speeds than parallel or serial cables.

The adapter and software are often proprietary to the type of printer being used. One of the most commonly known devices is the Hewlett-Packard Jet Direct card.

Setting Up Network Printing

Setting up network printing can be either simple or complicated, depending on the network operating system and how you perform your setup. I will discuss adding printing in NetWare and Windows NT environments.

NetWare

There are clearly many options for configuring printers and queues in NetWare. The print server services the print queue, and each printer must have a corresponding queue. The queue can exist on the print server and on other file servers throughout the network. There can be a one-to-one relationship between queues and printer as well as a many-to-one relationship. It is possible for multiple printers to share a single queue, and multiple queues can be configured for only one printer. Each printer must be set up individually and pointed to the appropriate queue.

NetWare print servers As I said earlier, a print server is a process that takes print jobs from a queue and sends them to a physical printer.

NetWare supports running the print server process a few different ways. The server can be run on any one of the following devices:

- File server
- Dedicated workstation
- Nondedicated workstation
- Dedicated print server devices

If you have a small network, the easiest way to add printing functionality is to load the printer server process, `Pserver.nlm`, on the NetWare file server. To do this you can simply hook the printer to the file server computer's serial or parallel interface ports. Under NetWare 3.12 the `Pserver.nlm` can support up to sixteen printers, with five of them directly on the file server. NetWare 4's `Pserver.nlm` can handle up to 255 printers, with up to seven of them directly connected to the file server.

Loading the print server on the file server can make things much simpler, but at a cost. Parallel ports are very CPU intensive and can greatly hinder the file server if they are used often. Physical location can also be a problem. Most often the file server is not readily accessible by end users, but if you have a printer attached to it they must be able to get to that.

A solution to the location problem may be a dedicated workstation as print server. All you need to do for this is to connect a printer to the computer, and run Pserver.exe. This file can support up to sixteen printers with five of them connected directly to the workstation. Another great feature of this setup is that you do not incur any performance penalties. You also do not need a large computer to act as a print server.

NetWare 4.1 does not support dedicated print servers. You can use them only on NetWare 3 networks.

The next type of print server that NetWare supports is the nondedicated workstation print server. This setup is supported under NetWare 3 and 4. The appeal of a nondedicated setup is that any computer on your LAN can act as a print server. All you need to do is attach a printer to the computer and load either `Rprinter.exe` for NetWare 3 or `Nprinter.exe` for NetWare 4. These two files enable the `Pserver.nlm` process on the file server to access and use the local printer on the workstation. This setup is good because you can put a printer anywhere it is needed, but at the cost of a performance penalty on that workstation.

The final type of print server is quickly becoming the most popular. Many printer manufacturers are putting the print server functionality directly in the printer, or offering small boxes that act as a print server. Intel was one of the first to offer small print server boxes. They enable you to attach four printers to the box and not be required to use any of your workstations. These devices enable `Pserver.nlm` to connect to them and use the attached printers. They enable you to put printers anywhere that you have a LAN cable.

The print server configuration you use depends on a few different considerations. The first is performance. Serial and parallel ports are much slower than printers connected directly to the LAN. A LAN-attached printer also frees up the CPU time on your workstations and servers. Cost is, of course, a consideration. Small, dedicated workstations used to be the choice since they could be built inexpensively. But now that small, print server boxes are getting cheaper, they have all but replaced these dedicated boxes.

The best type of print server to use is one of the new small print server boxes directly connected to the LAN. Most new printers have these built in. If you add a large amount of memory to your printer to help it buffer the print jobs, you can get a fast, easy to maintain, and fairly inexpensive solution.

Configuring print servers in a NetWare environment

Configuring print servers in NetWare is fairly simple. You need to set up the connections between the print server(s) and print queue(s). In NetWare, you set up print servers and print queues, and then connect them. As you will learn, this is handled behind the scenes in Windows NT.

PCONSOLE is used to manage and configure printers in NetWare. The options available in PCONSOLE vary in NetWare version 3.x and 4.x. Table A.8 covers the options shown under NetWare 3.x.

TABLE A.8 PCONSOLE in NetWare 3.X

Option	Function
Change Current File Server	Used to change the default print server and attach additional file servers. This provides management of multiple queues and servers in one session.

Option	Function
Print Queue Information	Brings up a list of defined queues which may be examined or deleted and provides for the creation of new queues.
Print Server Information	Brings up a list of defined print servers which may be examined or deleted and provides for the creation of new servers.

The options available under PCONSOLE in NetWare 4.x vary somewhat. These options are shown in Table A.9:

TABLE A.9 PCONSOLE in NetWare 4.X

Option	Function
Print Queues	Brings up a list of the print queues which may be examined or deleted and provides for the creation of new queues.
Printers	Brings up a list of the printers which may be examined or deleted and provides for the creation of new printers.
Print Servers	Brings up a list of the print servers which may be examined or deleted and provides for the creation of new print servers.
Quick Setup	Provides for the easy creation of new printers and print servers. There may be some customization required afterwards.
Change Context	Used to change your default NDS context; provides for the management of queues and print servers in more than one NDS context.

The options in NetWare 3.x and 4.x function in much the same way. Many of the options in PCONSOLE, especially the Print Servers and Print Queue options, involve working with objects. The objects can be managed using the keys listed in Table A.10.

TABLE A.10 Keys used in PCONSOLE

Key	Function
Insert	Creates a new object
Delete	Deletes an object
F5	Tags object; used when deleting multiple objects
F3	Renames an object
Enter	Edits an existing object

Creating print components Now that you have covered the tools used to create network printing components in NetWare, look at the process of creating these components.

To create Print Server using PCONSOLE, follow these steps:

1. Select Printer Servers in NetWare 4.x or Print Server Information in NetWare 3.x.
2. Press Insert.
3. Name the server.

Once the print server has been created, a printer needs to be configured. The process for configuring the printer varies under NetWare 3.x and 4.x.

To define printers under NetWare 3.x, follow these steps:

1. Highlight the printer name under Print Server Information in PCONSOLE and press Enter.
2. Select the Print Server Configuration option; up to sixteen printers can be configured per server.
3. Highlight a slot and press Enter.
4. Name the printer.
5. Choose the type field and select the appropriate printer type. Available options include local parallel, local serial, remote parallel, remote serial, and so on.

6. Select the appropriate resources used by the printer port; when using a serial port, you must also choose the appropriate settings for parity, stop bits, data bits, and so on.

7. Pressing the ESC key exits the configuration utility and prompts to save the values.

NetWare 4.x handles printers as objects and therefore requires a different configuration method. To configure a printer under NetWare 4.X, follow these steps:

1. Select the Printers option in PCONSOLE.

2. Using the Insert key, enter the name of the printer.

3. Highlight the printer name and press Enter.

4. Choose the corresponding print server from the list.

5. Select the correct printer type.

6. Edit the resources field to show the resources used by the printer port.

Once the print server has been created and defined, it is necessary to assign the appropriate print queue to the printer.

To assign the appropriate print queue to the printer, follow these steps:

1. In PCONSOLE, choose the configuration menu for the print server.

2. Select the Queues Serviced by Printer option.

3. Choose the appropriate printer.

4. Press the Insert key to see a list of queues.

5. Select the queue that the printer will utilize.

6. If you wish, change the priority of the queue.

7. Press Enter to save the configuration.

Windows NT

Network printing is installed and managed in a much different way. Any printer installed on Windows NT can easily be shared to other users on the network. Wizards are used to guide users through the process of installing and configuring the printer. NT enables several print devices to be configured and shared as one printer. This is known as printer pooling and provides for easy expansion of network printing capabilities. You do not need to worry about making queues and printers and print servers, and then connecting them together. All of this is handled by Windows NT.

Printer folder Printers are configured in Windows NT in the Printers folder. To configure a printer in the Printers folder, follow these steps:

1. From the Start button choose Settings and Printers. Double-click the Add Printers icon to activate the Add Printer Wizard.

2. You will be prompted as to whether the printer is to be connected as a Network Printer or to My Computer. When configuring a print server, click the radio button next to My Computer.

3. Click Next. You will be prompted to specify the port used by the printer. Ports can be added and configured using the buttons in this section. There is also a checkbox used for specifying whether printers will be pooled. If you are pooling printers, you can select multiple ports for each of the connected devices.

4. Click Next. You are prompted to choose the appropriate printer driver. Windows NT comes with drivers for many printers, and there is also an option to add a driver not included with NT. Clicking the Have Disk button leads to a prompt for the location of the printer driver.

5. Click Next. You are prompted to name the printer and to decide whether you want the printer to be the default printer for the computer.

6. Click Next. You will be prompted to determine whether the printer is shared or used strictly as a local printer. If you select the radio button next to Shared, you are prompted for a share name for the printer. You can then choose the operating systems that will print to the printer.

7. Click Next. You will be prompted to print a test page. This test page is used to confirm that the printer has been installed correctly and is working properly. The driver for the printer is then installed. If you have elected to enable other operating systems to print to the device, there will be prompts for the

location of the drivers for the corresponding print drivers for the operating system.

Managing printers Once the printer has been installed, it can then be managed in the Printers folder. The Printers folder contains the Add Printer icon and icons for all printers that have been installed on the computer. Right-clicking the icon for the printer brings up a menu which can be used to manage the printer.

The Properties option on the menu contains several tabbed pages used to configure the printer.

Table A.11 lists the options from the property page.

TABLE A.11 Property Page Options

Tab	Function
General	Used to specify comments and a physical location of the printer. The printer driver is specified here. The Separator Page, Print Processor, and Print Test Page options are set here.
Ports	Used to specify the port used by the print device and whether printer pooling is enabled. Ports are added, deleted, and configured here.
Scheduling	Used to specify when the printer is available, the priority of the printer, and how spooled documents are printed. These options are used to produce more efficient printing.
Sharing	Used to specify whether the printer is shared on the network, the share name, and the operating systems which can print to the printer.
Security	Used to set permissions and auditing for the printer.
Processing	Used to set the show status option.
Help	Used for getting help with printing problems.
About	Shows the driver version installed.

Print queues Double-clicking the printers icon in the Printers folder
shows the documents present in the printer's queue. The printer queue
is created automatically when the printer is installed in NT. Properties
of the documents are also displayed. Printing can be paused in this
window. Documents can be deleted or jobs can be restarted. This
enables a document that is causing a problem and hanging the queue to
be deleted without affecting other documents waiting to be printed.

Connecting to a shared printer Connecting to a shared printer
from a Windows NT computer is also very easy. The easiest way to do
this is from the Add Printer Wizard again. You can connect to printers
shared from Windows NT, Windows 95, or NetWare servers this way.
To connect to a shared printer, follow these steps:

1. Double-click the My Computer icon from the desktop.
2. Double-click the Printers folder.
3. Double-click the Add Printers icon.
4. When the Printer Wizard appears, choose Network Printer Server.
5. Click Next. You will see a browse window.
6. Your browse window may not be as complicated as the one
   shown. Navigate through the browse window until you find the
   computer that is sharing the printer you need.
7. When you find the computer you are looking for, click it to
   show its shared printers.
8. Highlight the printer you want to connect to and click OK.
9. You will be prompted to make this new printer the default
   printer.
10. Make your selection and click OK.
11. You will see the final screen telling you that you are done
    adding the printer. Click Finish.

Once you have selected the printer to connect to, you may be
prompted to install a driver for it depending on what operating system
is hosting the driver. If the printer is being shared from a Windows NT
computer, you can most likely use the driver on the print server. If the
printer is shared from a Windows 95 computer, you will need to install
a driver.

Windows 95

Setting up shared printers under Windows 95 is very similar to doing it under Windows NT. Once you configure the printer locally, it is just a matter of a few steps to share it to the entire network. To configure a shared printer under Windows 98, follow these steps:

1. Double-click the My Computer icon on your desktop.

2. Double-click the Printers folder. You will see a window.

3. Double-click the Add Printer icon. You will see the Add Printer Wizard start up.

4. Click Next. You will be prompted for the type of connect.

5. Choose Local Printer and click Next. You will see the printers list.

6. Choose the manufacturer and model of the printer you want to install and click OK. You will see a list of ports.

7. Choose the port to which the printer you want to install is connected. Click Next.

8. You will be prompted for the printer name. Enter the name you want the printer known as. Click Next.

9. You will be prompted to print a test page. If you want to, and it is always a good idea, choose Yes.

10. Click Finish to install the printer.

Connecting to a network printer through Windows 95 is also easy. Again, you use the Add Printer Wizard to do the job. To connect to a printer shared from Windows 95, Windows NT, or NetWare, follow these steps:

1. Double-click the My Computer icon on your desktop.

2. Double-click the Printers folder.

3. Double-click the Add Printer icon. You will see the Add Printer Wizard welcome screen.

4. Click Next. Choose Network Printer.

5. Click Next. You will be prompted for the location of the shared printer. The easiest way to do this is to click the Browse button and search for the printer.

6. If you clicked the browse button, you will see a browse window.

7. Navigate through the network and find the computer that is sharing the printer you need.

8. Once you have found the computer, click it to show all of the shared printers it has. You will see them listed.

9. Once you have chosen the printer you want, click OK. The queue name for the printer will be put into the blank.

10. If you will need to print from MS-DOS applications under Windows 95, answer Yes to that question, and click Next. If you don't need to print from MS-DOS applications, skip to Step 13.

11. In the window that appears, click the Capture Printer Port button.

12. You will be prompted to specify the port you want to capture. Any information sent to this port by an application will actually be sent to the network printer. Choose the port you want to capture and click OK.

13. Click Next. You will see a list of printers that you can install.

14. Choose the printer driver that corresponds to the type of printer you are connecting to.

15. Click Next. In the window that appears, enter a name for the printer, then select whether you want the printer to be set as default or not.

16. Click Next. You will be prompted to print a test page. It is usually a good idea to print a test page. Choose whether to or not, and click Finish.

Increasing Printing Speed

When network printing is too slow and causes a problem for the users (not to mention a headache for the administrator), it may become necessary to optimize or upgrade network printing. There are several options to increase printing speed on the network.

Optimizing network printing

Network printing can be optimized to provide for faster printing with existing equipment. One way to handle this is to use printing priorities. Printers can be set with a variety of priorities to accommodate groups of users that require quicker printing of their documents. Users can print to the device configured with the higher priority, and their documents will print first. This technique can also be used to print long documents that aren't needed immediately. These documents can be printed to a device with a lower priority and printed when other documents aren't waiting.

Spooling of documents can be used to optimize network printing, as well. If the printer is configured to print spooled documents first, the documents that are spooled quickest will be printed quickest. Configuring printing so that printing occurs as soon as the first page is spooled also decreases printing time.

Upgrading network printing

If optimization has been done and printer speeds are still too slow, upgrades to the network printing system may be required. There are several options for upgrading the printing system.

Memory upgrades can increase printer performance. The increased memory will help the printer process and print the jobs quicker. When planning a memory upgrade, consult your printer documentation. It is important to know how much memory the printer can hold and how much is currently installed.

Installation of a network interface is another way to improve printer performance. Moving the printer to the network media provides a faster path to the printer and removes bottlenecks that can occur at the print server. Network interfaces also enable the printer to communicate using a variety of protocols, which can enable a wide range of users to connect to the printer.

Printer pooling can also be used to upgrade network printing. Also, a new printer can be installed and configured to use the same print queue as an existing printer. Two printers provide load balancing and improve printing speeds.

Sometimes the best way to upgrade the printing process is to buy a better printer. Newer printers are much quicker than their older counterparts and can handle options that some older printers cannot. New printers are more likely to be color capable and have a built-in network interface. If a specialized page size is required, a new printer may be required to print on that page size. The old printer can still be utilized on the network, but a new printer can handle more of the printing load.

Printer Maintenance

Different printer types require different types of maintenance. Cleaning is a big part of maintenance. Printing with ink and toner can be a messy job, and it's important that the printer be carefully cleaned and maintained to ensure a long life. The following guidelines should be used along with the printer documentation to determine the best cleaning method and components needed for your particular printer. When encountering problems with printers, it is important to make sure that the components have been properly cleaned and maintained. You can also use your printer documentation for troubleshooting tips. To better understand cleaning and maintenance, you must first understand how the printer functions. This can help with troubleshooting printing problems, as well.

Laser printers

Laser printers use heat and pressure to fuse the toner powder onto your paper to print. The following is an overview of the laser printer print process:

1. An electric current is carried across a wire, known as the primary corona wire, and places a static electric charge on a photosensitive drum called the electrophotostatic (EP-S) drum.

2. A laser beam casts light on the image areas of the EP-S drum. This changes the electric charge on the area.

3. The drum is rotated, and the charged image areas pick up the toner particles.

4. A sheet of paper passes over the transfer corona wire which puts an electric charge on the paper. The paper and the drum now have an opposite charge.

5. This difference in charge causes the paper to pick up the toner particles from the drum.

6. High temperatures and pressure in the fusing unit then fuse the toner to the paper.

These components can be replaced individually in some of the older printers and are combined in the newer printers. The combined equipment provides for smaller printers, but at the cost of maintenance. Now instead of just replacing a drum, you may end up replacing a lot more, which will cost more.

The high temperatures and pressure used in laser printers affect what media can be passed through it. Anything that melts can do damage to the laser printer. As a guideline, you should follow these rules:

- Do not use anything with adhesives. Use only labels specially made for laser printers.
- Do not use thermal paper.
- Do not use carbon paper.
- Do not use envelopes with transparent windows.
- Double check with your printer manufacturer to make sure that transparencies are OK.

Routine maintenance After using your laser printer for a while, the stray toner particles and pieces of paper that gather in the printer may cause problems. You should carefully clean the laser printer from time to time. Your printer documentation should have information on how to clean your specific printer.

Be careful when working with laser printers since they can be very hot. Unplug the printer in advance before cleaning it to give it time to cool.

At a minimum, you should occasionally open the printer and blow out any toner dust that you see.

Troubleshooting laser printers Normally, laser printers will print thousands of pages without a single problem. But with that heavy a workload, anything can break. Table A.12 lists many common problems you may find with your laser printer, as well as common solutions.

TABLE A.12 Common Laser Printer Problems and Solutions

Problem	Solutions
Inconsistent vertical shading	Remove the toner cartridge from the printer and shake it from side to side to evenly distribute the toner.
Light printing	Clean the corona wire. You may also need to adjust the darkness level on your printer. Replace toner cartridge.
Blurred vertical lines	Replace the fuser roller cleaning pad.
Faded blotches and spots	Clean the transfer corona wire.
Fading across the page	Clean the transfer corona wire.
Streaks and marks on the leading edge of the paper	Clean the paper separator and any other paper guides in the printer.
Page is totally black.	Replace the primary corona wire. Check the printer drum.

Dot matrix printers

Most people are familiar with dot matrix printers. They print on paper by using small pins to push ink onto paper from a ribbon. Most print heads have either nine or twenty-four pins on them. The more pins they use, the more detail they can print. Since dot matrix printers are fairly simple, maintenance and troubleshooting are easy.

Routine maintenance Normally, all it takes to clean a dot matrix printer is a damp cloth. Just wipe off the outside and inside of the printer to remove any dust or pieces of paper. If there is a lot of dust, you can use a small vacuum cleaner to get it out.

Occasionally you will need to clean the print head of the printer. Usually you can tell it is time to do this because your print outs are starting to look smudged. First, you must remove the print head. You need to check your printer documentation on how to do this. Next, clean the small pins with a cotton swab and alcohol.

Common dot matrix problems and solutions Table A.13 lists
the most common problems associated with dot matrix printers, as
well as their solutions.

TABLE A.13 Common Dot Matrix Problems and Solutions

Problem	Solution
Light print out	Check your ribbon to see if it is jammed or needs to be replaced. If that is not the problem, adjust the print head so it is closer to the paper.
Smudged characters	Check to see if your ribbon is twisted. You may need to move the print head away from the paper. Also check to see if the print head needs to be cleaned.
Paper jam	Adjust the tractor pull mechanism to make sure that the paper is held tight, but not too tight.
Incomplete characters	Clean or replace the print head.
Overlapping lines of text	Check for paper jams.

Ink-jet printers

A new and popular type of printer, especially for home and small
offices, is the ink-jet printer. Ink-jet printers use liquid ink to print.
They can do black and white or color. They use small nozzles to
"squirt" the ink onto the paper. Most new ink-jet printers are self-
cleaning as long as they are used properly. Problems can arise if power
is removed from the printer without it shutting down. This can leave
the print head and liquid ink exposed to air, which lets it dry.

Routine maintenance As stated above, if you do not let the printer
shut itself down properly, ink can dry out and damage the print head. If
this happens you may be able to use a built-in head cleaning routine.
Check your printer documentation to see if you have this option. Other
than that, the only real maintenance is to occasionally open up the
printer and wipe it out with a damp cloth.

If you plan to store the printer for a long time, consider putting an empty ink cartridge in it instead of a full one.

Network Faxing

The next logical step for many people is from printing to faxing. Luckily, if your network uses Windows 95, you can add shared faxing very easily. Included with Windows 95 is a faxing feature that lets you fax documents with your fax modem as easily as you print them. But— and this may be new to you— the faxing software in Windows 95 also allows you to share this capability with other network users. To start the process, you first need to install the fax software for Windows 95. To install the fax software for Windows 95, follow these steps:

1. Click Start, then Settings, and then Control Panel.
2. Double-click the Add/Remove Programs icon.
3. Click the Windows Setup tab.
4. Scroll down and find the Microsoft Fax box. Check the box and click OK.

Once the fax software has been installed, you may notice a small difference on your computer. If you open the Printers folder again, you will see that a new printer has been added.

Now that the fax software is installed, it must be configured. While you can do this manually through the Mail and Fax icon in Control Panel, it is easier to do with a wizard. To invoke the wizard, all we need to do is try and use the new fax software.

To configure the fax software with the wizard, follow these steps:

1. Open WordPad by clicking Start, then Run, typing in WordPad, and pressing Enter. From WordPad, click File, then Print. Choose Microsoft Fax as your printer.
2. The Inbox Setup Wizard will start.
3. Choose the Modem connected to my computer option and click Next.
4. If you do not have a modem driver installed in Windows 95, you will see the Modem Wizard start. If you already have a modem

installed, choose the modem you want to use, click Next, and go to Step 6.

5. Click Next to have Windows 95 detect your modem.

6. Once you have completed the modem wizard process, another window will appear.

7. Choose whether you want the modem to receive every call or only receive calls manually.

8. Click Next.

9. Enter your information into the blanks and click Next.

Your fax software is now installed. To use it you will need to open the Inbox application on your desktop. You can use this software anytime by just "printing" to the fax device.

Next, you need to make sure that you can share printers.

To share a printer, follow these steps:

1. Double-click the Network icon from Control Panel.

2. Click the File and Print Sharing button. A window will appear.

3. Check the I want to be able to allow others to print to my printer(s) checkbox. Click OK.

4. Click OK again. (You may be required to reboot.)

Now, the next step is to share that fax with other network users.

To share a fax, follow these steps:

1. Open Control Panel.

2. Double-click on the Mail and Fax icon.

3. You should see a list of services.

4. Highlight the Fax service and click Properties.

5. Click the modem tab.

6. Check the Let other people on the network use my modem to send faxes box.

7. If you want to set a password or other security, click the Properties button.

8. Click OK.

9. Click OK again.

Your fax is now shared on the network. Only one more series of steps to go. These show you how to connect to the shared fax server from across the network.

To connect to a shared fax server, follow these steps:

1. Go to the workstation computer, and install the fax software as shown above. Then start the configuration wizard by printing to the fax device.

2. When the Inbox Setup Wizard starts, choose Network fax service or other type of device.

3. Click Next. You will see the Add a Fax window.

4. Choose network fax server and click Next.

5. A window will appear. In the path field, enter **\\COMPUTERNAME\fax**. COMPUTERNAME is the name of the computer you installed the fax modem on.

6. Enter the name and click Next. A window will appear.

7. Choose the path that you just entered in the previous window. Click Next.

8. Enter your information into the next screen and click Next.

Like a local fax modem device, you print to the fax device in your printing listing. The fax software handles routing your fax through the network and out your fax modem.

Sharing CD-ROMs

"Floppy disk? What's that?" With the advance of CD-ROMs into the computing community, it won't be long until you hear those words. CD-ROMs enable you to easily store large amounts of data in a small physical medium that lasts for many years. With these great features, it is no wonder people want access to CD-ROMs on a network.

Sharing one CD-ROM on a network is pretty simple. You can do that easily with Windows 95 or Windows NT. But what if you want a lot of CD-ROMs available? Before going over the different ways to share CD-ROM media, first look at the hardware you will need.

CD-ROM Drive Characteristics

When you go to buy a CD-ROM drive or tower, you will see many different pieces of information concerning them. Exactly what does all this mean to you? It all depends on what you will be using the CD-ROM to store. Most of the specifications you hear concern the speed of the drive. When shopping for CD-ROM hardware pay close attention to the following characteristics:

- Speed
- Access time
- Buffer space
- Interface
- External or internal configuration
- Installation
- CD handling

The following sections discuss each of these different characteristics. Recommending what you should shop for is difficult, however, since this technology is changing so quickly that any recommendations would quickly be obsolete.

Speed

How fast will it go? Originally, CD-ROM drives could transfer data from the CD-ROM to the computer at speeds up to 150 kilobytes (K) per second. These drives are known as single-speed CD-ROM drives. Long gone are the days of everyone having a single-speed drive. New drives are many times faster than these older ones.

The speed at which the CD-ROM can get data from the CD to the computer is known as the data transfer speed. These are measured in multiples of 150K per second. For example, you may see a drive that says it is a quad-speed drive, or 4X. This means that it can transfer four times as much data in the same amount of time as an original single-speed CD-ROM.

Access time

The next consideration in deciding on a CD-ROM is its access time. Access time is the amount of time it takes the laser of the drive to reach the location where the data is stored on the CD-ROM. This time also includes the delay when the drive has to decide where the data is stored. The lower the access time, the better the CD-ROM will handle requests from different users accessing different data on the CD-ROM.

Access times are getting faster all the time. Currently, a very good access time would be less than 150ms. This number may fluctuate depending upon where the data is stored on the CD-ROM. If the data is on the outside edge of the CD-ROM, the laser takes longer to get to it.

Buffer space

Most CD-ROM drives now have a buffer. Most low-end CD-ROMs have either 64K or 128K of memory on the drive. High-speed drives have as much as 1024K, or 1 megabyte. If data is held in the buffer and the CPU needs it, sending it from that buffer is much quicker than getting it from the CD-ROM.

Interface

CD-ROMs normally use one of three types of interfaces. These are:

- EIDE
- SCSI
- Proprietary

These interfaces can play a large role in your hardware decision buy, especially if you want to share a large number of CD-ROMs from one computer.

EIDE Enhanced Integrated Device Electronics (EIDE) is a relatively new standard for CD-ROMs. Hard drives have been using IDE for many years. EIDE is the cheapest type of interface for CD-ROMs. Most home-level CD-ROM drives use this interface. The main problem with EIDE CD-ROMs is a limit of EIDE itself. You can only put two, or sometimes four, drives in one computer.

SCSI The Small Computer Systems Interface (SCSI) has been around for many years. Normally, SCSI is only used in large workstations or servers. It is much more expensive than EIDE, but it also has many more features and enhancements.

First, SCSI can handle from seven to fifteen devices on each controller. You can put multiple controllers in one controller. If you use SCSI CD-ROM drives, you can easily build a large CD-ROM server.

Next, SCSI is very fast. The new ultra-wide SCSI supports up to 40MB per second. New CD-ROM drives are starting to support this standard. While one CD-ROM may not be able to use all of this bandwidth, fifteen at one time can use the extra breathing room.

Proprietary While proprietary interfaces were very common in the early days of CD-ROM drives, they are much less so now. Proprietary interfaces usually limit you to one or two CD-ROM drives per computer, and they were known to hinder performance. Stay away from proprietary controllers and drives.

External or internal placement

Most CD-ROM drives can either be put into the computer or reside in a case that sits outside the PC. The two types of drives have no functional differences.

Internal drives are very common in home computers and as single drives in servers to handle software installation. Adding an internal EIDE drive is easy.

Most often, external drives use the SCSI interface since it is easy to implement. EIDE was made for internal hard drives and is much harder to implement for external devices. External placement makes more sense if you plan to use many drives. It would be next to impossible to find a computer case that would accommodate the maximum number of drives you could use with a SCSI interface, while it is very easy to chain seven or fifteen external drives.

External drives give you the advantage of disk space, and you can add an external CD-ROM to almost any computer. But the external device does use space on your desk! External drives also cost about $100 more than internal drives.

Installation

Most new CD-ROM drives are very easy to install. For EIDE drives, you usually need to set only one jumper. SCSI drives are slightly harder to install since they have other settings that need to be addressed. Windows NT and Windows 95 support EIDE and SCSI CD-ROMs right out of the box. NetWare supports SCSI CD-ROMs with the addition of a few NetWare Loadable Modules (NLMs).

CD handling

CD-ROM drives handle discs in two different ways. Some drives use a plastic case, called a caddy, into which you insert the disc; you then insert the caddy into the drive. The advantage of this setup is that it lets you leave the discs in the caddy so that they are not damaged. This may be a good idea in a network environment where other people may handle your discs.

The alternative to caddies is a drive that extends out a tray into which you place the disc. This keeps you from having to worry about caddies, but at the cost of an exposed disc.

Connecting CD-ROM Drives to a Network

CD-ROMs on a network function the same as those in a small PC. The difference is that the drives are set up to share data. In most cases you want to share many discs at one time. If you want to share just one disc, any PC with a CD-ROM drive can do this using peer-to-peer networking software. To handle large amounts of data, you would usually choose one of two devices. You would use either a jukebox or a CD tower.

Jukebox

CD-ROM jukeboxes are similar to the jukeboxes that play 45s. A CD-ROM jukebox has one or more CD-ROM drives and a library of CDs to choose from. Depending on what data the user requests, the jukebox chooses the appropriate disc from its library and puts it in a drive.

Jukeboxes are cheaper than towers, but at the cost of performance. If you have many users trying to access different data at the same time, the jukebox will spend more time shuffling discs than it will sending out data. Nowadays, you most often see small jukeboxes used in personal computers as CD-ROM changers.

Tower

The best solution to sharing large amounts of CD-ROM data on a network is a CD-ROM tower. A CD tower has many drives in one case. Each CD-ROM you want to share has its own drive. This allows the tower to read and send out data from any CD-ROM at any time.

Almost all CD-ROM towers use SCSI as their back-plane interface. This enables them to support many drives at one time. The use of SCSI also makes it easy to connect these towers to computers. Just plug the tower into your server's SCSI port, load the correct driver, and you're set.

New, smarter towers are becoming very common. These are stand alone boxes that do not need to be connected to a computer. They are connected directly to a network. To use these you normally need to load some special software on your network server that lets the CD-ROMs appear as if they are shared from the server, even though they are not.

Internet Access

A connection to the Internet is quickly becoming a requirement for networks today. The main problem is getting that connection. This section shows you how to add an Internet connection to a small network. Large networks can afford to get a direct connection using a high-speed, dedicated connection. Normally, small networks can only afford a single dial-up connection.

The method described in this chapter requires a third-party utility to connect your LAN to the Internet. This product is called WinGate and is available at http://www.wingate.net. WinGate is shareware and therefore may require you to pay the author if you continue to use it. Luckily, the authors have been kind enough to let you have a single computer license for free. This means that you can let one other computer connect to the Internet through WinGate for free.

WinGate and How It Works

WinGate is a very simple and cost-effective way to add Internet access to a small network. With WinGate you need only a dial-up connection to the Internet. In addition, you will need only one IP address for the computer that is dialing up to the Internet, rather than one for every computer that will connect to the Internet.

WinGate functions as a proxy server. A proxy server does not allow client computers to directly connect to the Internet through them. Instead, the client computer connects to the proxy, and the proxy then connects to the resource on the Internet. This way only one computer is actually connecting to the Internet, and you do not need extra IP addresses or special Internet accounts. One thing that you cannot do with a proxy is to allow other computers on the Internet to connect to computers on your LAN. Computers on the Internet do not know how to reach your LAN workstations, since all connections are actually made by the computer running WinGate.

Most Internet applications work through a proxy. The following is a list of the most common ones:

- WWW
- FTP
- Telnet
- IRC
- RealAudio/RealVideo
- Mail
- News

As you can see, almost any application you may want is supported. The main applications that do not work are games. Games normally use the UDP protocol instead of the TCP protocol. A UDP connection normally comes from the server (the computer hosting a game) and not the client. As you saw earlier, a computer on the Internet cannot connect to a computer on your LAN.

Finding an Internet Provider

Before you can connect to the Internet, you need to find an Internet service provider, or ISP. ISPs are companies that handle connecting people to the Internet. Some ISPs connect large companies to the Internet while others handle small offices and single users. Choosing a good ISP is the key to making a good Internet connection.

Here are a few key points to think of when shopping for Internet providers:

- Bandwidth: Most Internet providers today support 56Kbps or faster modems. If your network has five or fewer users, 56Kbps may meet your needs.

- Reliability: If your company will use the Internet connection heavily, you need to make sure your ISP is reliable. Some ISPs provide service level agreements (SLA) to show how reliable the connection will be.

- Growth: If you company grows, your Internet connection will most likely grow as well. Make sure the ISP you choose can handle your future growth. Eventually you may want to upgrade your connection or have your ISP host a web server for you. Make sure the ISP can handle what you plan.

To find your area ISPs, you can check local computer trade papers, or the newspaper. Some ISPs are nationwide and cover a large area. They are larger than local ISPs, so it may be hard to get customized or personal service, but they are normally very reliable and offer better technical support.

Choosing Your Connection

Before you start looking for an Internet service provider, you should have a good idea of the type of connection you will need. The connection you need depends on how you plan to use the Internet. Since I am discussing small LANs here, I will focus on dial-up and ISDN connections. Large companies may have their own dedicated high-bandwidth connections, which are more complex than those discussed in this chapter.

Dialing in to the Internet

If your network is very small, you may be able to use a dial-up Internet connection with a modem. This connection is usually adequate to serve up to four or five people. Depending on whether you plan to use this connection twenty-four hours a day or only on demand, it may be a very inexpensive solution.

Most ISPs now provide unlimited dial-up accounts for less than $30 per month. These are not intended to be connected twenty-four hours per day, seven days per week. If you need to connect to the Internet only occasionally, this may work for you. You can configure the WinGate computer to dial up when a computer attempts to connect to the Internet, and then hang up after a set amount of idle time passes.

If you need higher speed than a modem can provide, you may need a dial-up ISDN account. As you learned in Chapter 5, Integrated Services Digital Network allows for high-speed connections over normal telephone lines. With an ISDN connection, you can connect to the Internet at 128Kbps. Unlike the current 56Kbps modems, ISDN provides speeds of 128Kbps in both directions, not just when downloading to your LAN. Dial-up ISDN accounts are becoming more common for use with ISPs. Before, the only way you could connect to an ISP with ISDN was with an expensive dedicated connection. An ISDN connection can easily handle ten to twenty users.

Dedicating the Connection

If your Internet connection needs to be available any time, you need a dedicated connection. Dedicated Internet connections are more expensive than dial-up connections, costing anywhere from $150 up. Dedicated connections can use either modems or ISDN, depending on what you need and want to spend.

The first step to adding an Internet connection to your LAN is to add the TCP/IP protocol to your workstations.

Planning Your Network

Before you run off to install the TCP/IP protocol on your network, you should plan ahead. Before you start planning, you need to have some information about your ISP account. At a minimum, you will need the

IP address of your DNS server. I said above that you only needed one IP address, which is for the computer that will run WinGate. This is half-true; you will only need one registered IP address. All of the computers on your network will need IPs, but you can choose which ones they will be since they will only be used between the computer running WinGate and the other computers on your LAN.

Luckily, there is a range of IP addresses set aside for this purpose. You can use the entire 192.168.0.0 range of IP addresses for your LAN. I suggest using 192.168.0.1 for your WinGate computer and the rest for your workstations. The subnet mask to use with this range is 255.255.255.0.

To help you with the administration of the IP addresses, you could make a HOSTS file to map these addresses to computer names. Below is a sample of our HOSTS file.

```
192.168.0.1   ANGIE
192.168.0.2   Jason
192.168.0.3   Win95-CD
192.168.0.4   NT_Server
```

This HOSTS file lets me type in the computer name instead of the IP address if I need to do any testing. Check with your operating system to see where you need to store the HOSTS file.

Adding TCP/IP to Your Computers

Computers on the Internet use the TCP/IP protocol. Therefore, you will need to make sure any computer that needs Internet access supports this protocol. Most popular operating systems now come with TCP/IP. You just need to install the protocol and configure it. The following sections walk you through installing TCP/IP.

Installing TCP/IP on Windows 95

Windows 95 is shipped with a TCP/IP stack included. You just need to install it. Before you do that, you may want to make sure someone hasn't installed it for you.

To check if TCP/IP is installed, follow these steps:

1. Open Control Panel by clicking Start_Settings_Control Panel.

2. Double-click the Network icon.

3. You will see a list of installed network options. If TCP/IP is installed, you do not need to install it again.

If TCP/IP is not installed, you will need to install it now. To install TCP/IP, follow these steps:

1. Click Start_Settings_Control Panel.

2. Click the Network icon.

3. When you see the Network window, click the Add button.

4. Select Protocol.

5. Choose Microsoft from the Manufacturers list.

6. Select TCP/IP from the Protocols list. Click OK.

The TCP/IP protocol is now installed. To configure TCP/IP for your network, follow these steps:

1. Highlight the TCP/IP protocol in the Installing Components list.

2. Click Properties.

3. Click the IP Address tab.

4. In the IP Address fields, enter the address you have chosen for this computer.

5. In the subnet mask field, enter 255.255.255.0.

6. Click the DNS Configuration tab.

7. Choose the Enable DNS option.

8. In the DNS Search Order field, add the IP address of the computer that will run the WinGate software.

9. Click OK.

10. You should see the Installed Components list again. Click OK. (You may be required to reboot the computer.)

Once you have installed and configured TCP/IP on the workstation and rebooted, you should test it. To do this, you may want to ping the computer that is running WinGate. To do this, open an MS-DOS prompt and type ping 192.168.0.1 (assuming that the WinGate computer is using the 192.168.0.1 IP address).

Installing TCP/IP on Windows NT

Microsoft also included a TCP/IP stack in its Windows NT operating system. The installation and configuration process is the same on Windows NT Workstation as it is on Windows NT Server.

To add TCP/IP, follow these steps:

1. Click Start_Settings_Control Panel.
2. Double-click the Network icon.
3. Click the Protocols tab.
4. Click Add.
5. Choose TCP/IP Protocol from the list and click OK.
6. When you return to the Network properties window, click OK.
7. The network bindings will be recalculated. You may need to configure TCP/IP now.

Now that TCP/IP has been installed, you will need to configure it. To configure TCP/IP, follow these steps:

1. Click the Protocols tab.
2. Highlight the TCP/IP protocol.
3. Click Properties.
4. Choose the Specify IP Address option.
5. In the IP Address field, enter the IP you have chosen for this computer.
6. In the Subnet Mask field, enter 255.255.255.0.
7. Click the DNS tab.
8. Click the Add button.
9. Enter the IP address of the computer that will run WinGate.
10. Click OK.
11. Click OK again at the Network properties window. (You may be required to reboot.)

Now that you have installed TCP/IP on your workstations, you can install and configure WinGate.

Installing and Configuring WinGate

The first step in installing WinGate is to get it. Go to http://www.
wingate.net and download the correct version for your operating
system. It will run on either Windows 95 or Windows NT.

At the time of this writing, the current version of WinGate was 2.0e.
These instructions were written for that version.

To install and configure WinGate, follow these steps:

1. Once you have downloaded the WinGate software and
unzipped it, you can install it. From Windows Explorer, click
the Wg2ent.exe file. You will see the "Welcome to WinGate 2.0"
screen.

2. Click the Install WinGate 2.0e for Windows NT (or Windows 95),
then click Next. You will see the Select Installation Directory
window.

3. If you want to use the default directory, click Next. You will see
the license window.

4. Leave the fields blank and click Next. You will see the Basic
Services window.

5. Normally, you would leave all of the choices checked. If you do
not want to support a particular service, uncheck it now. Click
Next. You will see the Mail Settings window.

6. In the SMTP Relay Server field, put the IP address or name of
your ISPs SMTP host. Click Next. You will see the News and
IRC Settings window.

7. In the News field, put the news server IP address or name that
you received from your ISP. In the IRC server field, put the
name of the IRC server you wish to use. If you are unsure of an
IRC server, you may try irc.nol.net. Click Next. You will see the
DNS Settings window.

8. In the DNS Server field, put the IP address of your ISP's DNS
server. Click Next. You will see the Cache Settings window.

9. WinGate uses a cache manager to cache frequently accessed
Web pages. You choose the settings you want on this screen.
Choose the amount of space you want to set aside for caching
and click Next. You will see the WinGate Client Utility window.

10. Enter the name and IP address of the computer you are installing WinGate on. Click Next. You will see the Begin Installation window.

11. If you do not need to go back and correct any settings you have made so far, click the Begin button to install WinGate. When the install has finished you will see the Installation Complete window.

12. Click Finish.

13. Now that WinGate has been installed, you need to configure it just a little bit more before you can use it. To do this, click Start_Programs_WinGate 2.0, and choose GateKeeper. GateKeeper will prompt you for a login.

14. Press Enter to log in with a blank password. You will be asked if you want to continue without a password. Click OK. After you log in you will be required to create a password.

15. Leave the Old Password field blank, and enter a password that you choose in the other two fields. Then click OK. Once you have changed the password, you will be shown the main GateKeeper screen.

By default, you can manage the WinGate computer with GateKeeper only from the computer it is running on. If you want to manage WinGate from another computer you must enable this feature. To manage WinGate from another computer, follow these steps:

1. Click the + (plus) symbol next to the Services option in the right window pane. It will expand.

2. Double-click the Remote Control Service option. A window will appear.

3. Uncheck the Bind to specific interface option.

4. Click OK.

Now that WinGate has been installed and configured, you will need to set up your client applications to use the new proxy.

Configuring Client Applications

Almost any application that your network clients might use can be configured to use the proxy. If your application does not have support for a proxy server built in, you can possibly use what is known as a SOCKS client. Next, I will cover the following applications and how to configure them for the proxy:

- FTP
- Telnet
- WWW
- News
- Mail
- RealAudio
- IRC
- SOCKS client

FTP

Like most clients you will find, the way to configure your FTP client may depend on who made it. As an example, we will cover configuring a popular client, WS_FTP, as well as doing command line FTPs through the proxy.

WS_FTP WS_FTP is a well-known shareware FTP client that uses a graphical interface. It also supports many different types of network proxies.

You can obtain the free trial version of WS_FTP from http:\\www.ipswitch.com.

To configure WS_FTP to use WinGate, follow these steps:

1. When you load WS_FTP you will see a window appear.
2. Create a new connection by clicking New.
3. Enter all relevant information for the connection that you are creating.
4. Click the Firewall tab. A window will appear.
5. Click the Use Firewall box.

6. In the Host Name field, enter the IP address of the computer running WinGate.

7. Make sure that the USER with no logon option is selected.

8. After you have made your selections, click OK.

9. Click the Save button to save your connection.

Once you have configured the connection, test it by connecting to the server.

Command-line FTP Even though graphical utilities are usually preferred to command-line programs, you may one day need to use the command-line FTP. Changing the command-line FTP to use the proxy is simple.

To change the command-line FTP to use the proxy, follow these steps:

1. Open FTP by clicking Start, Run, and then typing FTP IP_OF_WINGATE_COMPUTER.

2. You will see the FTP program.

3. Normally, at the User prompt you would enter your user name, or anonymous, to the server. But since you have only connected to the WinGate computer and not the actual server, you cannot do this. At the User prompt, enter `anonymous@ftp.microsoft.com`. User name is the name you want to log in as, and server name is the FTP site to which you want to connect. Press Enter.

4. The connection to `ftp.microsoft.com` is shown as anonymous.

5. At the password prompt, enter your password (or e-mail address for anonymous) just like you normally would. Press Enter. You are now connected to the FTP site just as you would normally be.

Telnet

Using Telnet with WinGate is also easy.

To connect with Telnet, follow these steps:

1. Open your Telnet application. For this example we will use the normal Windows Telnet.

2. Click Connect, then Remote System. A window will appear.

3. In the Host Name field, enter the IP address of the computer running WinGate.

4. Click OK.

5. You will see the WinGate prompt.

6. At the WinGate prompt, type in the host name to which you want to connect.

7. Press Enter. You will be connected just as you would without WinGate.

WWW

Almost all Web browsers support the use of a proxy server. For this example we will use the version of Microsoft Internet Explorer included on the CD-ROM in this book.

For information on installing Microsoft Internet Explorer, refer to Appendix F.

You have two choices of proxy types when using Internet Explorer. You can either use an HTTP proxy or a SOCKS proxy. The steps below show you how to configure these settings.

To configure Internet Explorer for a HTTP proxy or a SOCKS proxy:

1. Open up Internet Explorer.

2. Click View_Internet Options.

3. You will see a window appear.

4. Click the Connection tab.

5. Check the box that says Access the Internet using a proxy server.

6. Click the Advanced button.

7. The window that appears lets you choose many different types of proxy servers.

8. You can either use the HTTP proxy or the SOCKS proxy. To enable the SOCKS proxy, put the IP address of the WinGate computer in the Socks field.

9. To use the HTTP proxy, enter the IP address of the computer running WinGate in the HTTP field. Then check the Use the same proxy server for all protocols box.

10. Click OK.

News

Configuring news clients could not be easier. All you need to do is enter the IP address of the WinGate server in the news client where you would normally put the IP address of the news server. When the client connects to WinGate, it will automatically be rerouted to the news server you defined. The following steps are for use with Outlook Express, which is included with Internet Explorer version 4.0.

To configure news clients with Outlook Express, follow these steps:

1. Open Outlook Express.
2. Click Tools_Accounts.
3. You will see a list of accounts in the window that appears.
4. Click the News tab.
5. To set up an account to use WinGate, click Add, and then News.
6. You will see the first window in the wizard to create a news account.
7. In the Display name field, enter the name to use to post a message.
8. Click Next.
9. Next, you will be prompted for your e-mail address so that others can reply to your posts. Enter this and click Next.
10. The next screen prompts you for your news server address.
11. Enter the IP address of the computer running WinGate.
12. Click Next.
13. Enter the account name you want to be shown for this account. Enter anything you want.
14. Click Next.
15. The next window will prompt you for a connection type.
16. Choose Connect using my local area network, and click Next. You will be shown the final window in the wizard.
17. Click Finish.
18. Click Close.

Mail

Mail configuration depends on the software you use. The following steps are for use with Outlook Express. Installation on other clients just requires changing the SMTP server and/or POP mail server address(es). In either case, just change the addresses to the IP of the WinGate computer.

To configure mail clients using Outlook Express, follow these steps:

1. Open Outlook Express.
2. Click Tools_Accounts. You will be presented with a list of all current accounts.
3. Click the Mail tab.
4. Click Add, and then Mail.
5. In the Display name field, enter the name you want others to see when you send an e-mail.
6. Click Next.
7. Next, you will be prompted for your e-mail address so that others can reply to your messages. Enter this and click Next.
8. You will be prompted for the e-mail server names. For both the POP Mail and SMTP servers, enter the IP address of the computer running WinGate.
9. Click Next.
10. You will then see a window requesting mail account information. Enter the information given to you by your Internet provider. Click Next.
11. Next, enter the friendly name for this account. This is used inside of Outlook Express only.
12. Click Next.
13. Next, choose Connect using my local area network and click Next.
14. Click Finish.
15. Click Close.

RealAudio

RealAudio is a new application that is quickly becoming popular on the Internet. It is used to send stereo sound over the Internet.

The RealAudio client can be obtained from `http://www.realaudio.com`.

RealAudio can support two different proxy servers. If the RealAudio site you are connecting to supports sending out the data over HTTP, you can use a normal HTTP, or Web, proxy. The problem is that many sites do not yet support this method and therefore you must use a RealAudio only proxy. Luckily, WinGate has supported RealAudio for a long time now.

To configure RealAudio to the WinGate proxy, follow these steps:

1. Load the RealAudio client.

2. Click View, then Preferences. A window will appear.

3. Click the Proxy tab.

4. In the RealAudio proxy field, enter the IP address of the computer running WinGate.

5. Click OK.

IRC

Internet Relay Chat, or IRC, is a chat protocol commonly used on the Internet. There are many IRC clients out now, but only a few that support a proxy server. For the steps below, we will use the PiRCH client.

You can obtain the latest version of PiRCH at `http://www.bcpl.lib.md.us/~frappa/pirch.html`. This is the client I use at home, and it has functioned very well with WinGate.

You can support IRC users on your network two different ways with WinGate. One way uses what is known as a port mapping connection, while the other uses the SOCKS proxy built into WinGate. The following steps help you set up a port mapping connection. After that, we will cover using the SOCKS proxy.

To make a port mapping connection, follow these steps:

1. Open GateKeeper and log in.

2. Right-click on the Services selection in the right window pane, then select New, Service, TCP Mapping Service.

3. You will see a window appear.

4. If you want, you can change the Service Name and Description to something more descriptive. For the description you may want to put the name of the IRC server this mapping will connect to.

5. In the Accept connections on port field, enter 6667. If you already have an IRC server mapping on Port 6667, choose another unused port.

6. Check the Enable default mapping box.

7. In the Server and Port field, put the IP address and port number of the IRC server you want to use.

8. Click OK.

Port mappings can be used for many different applications that do not directly support a proxy. A port mapping takes a connection made to WinGate and extends that connection to a predefined server. In the above example, you told WinGate to forward any connection it receives on Port 6667 to the server IP and port number you specified.

To use this mapping, enter the IP address of the WinGate server into your IRC client as the server to connect to.

If you use the PiRCH client, you can use the SOCKS proxy built into WinGate. The advantage of this setup is that the PiRCH client can connect to any IRC server, not just those that you set up as port mappings in WinGate.

To configure PiRCH, follow these steps:

1. Load PiRCH.

2. Select IRC, and then Proxy Setup.

3. You will see a window appear.

4. Check the Enabled box.

5. In the SOCKS Host field, enter the IP address of the computer running WinGate.

6. In the port field, enter 1080.

7. Click OK.

SOCKS client

As I said earlier, WinGate has an integrated SOCKS version 5 proxy
server. This proxy allows any client that supports SOCKS to function
through WinGate flawlessly. All connections to the WinGate server are
handled behind the scenes away from the user. The application functions as though it was not working through a proxy and no extra configuration settings are needed.

When a SOCKS client application makes a request to a host outside
of the local network, the request is redirected to the SOCKS server. The
SOCKS server authenticates the user, if you have this enabled, and then
authorizes the request and establishes a proxy connection, and then
transparently passes data between the inside host and the outside host.

While SOCKS is a great thing, the problem is that most Internet
applications do not support it. But do not despair! Luckily there is a
free SOCKS client that replaces `Winsock.dll` in Windows 95 and
Windows NT. This allows most non-SOCKS applications to support
the SOCKS proxy. This all happens at the WINSOCK layer, without
affecting the application.

A few warnings before we start: First, be careful when replacing `Winsock.dll`. The instructions are simple, but if you mess up, par-
ticularly under Windows NT, you may crash your system. Second, not
all applications function with the SOCKS client. Almost all that I have
tested do, but it is not 100 percent. Do not let the warnings scare you.
The SOCKS client can be a great thing for WinGate users and is well
worth trying out.

First, you will need to get the SOCKS client, and then configure it.
The SOCKS client is available at `http://www.hummingbird.com/`
`products/socks/index.html`. This client is free.

To install the SOCKS client, simply run the `Install.bat` file that is
included. Once you have installed the client, you need to configure it.
SOCKS is configured by using a `Socks.cnf` file. This is a normal text
file that can be edited with any text editor. Below is a sample file.

Listing A-1: *Sample SOCKS Configuration File*

```
# Sample Configuration File
#
# Each line is one of:
#
```

```
# DENY [*=userlist] dst_addr dst_mask [op dst_port]
# DIRECT [*=userlist] dst_addr dst_mask [op dst_port]
# SOCKD [@=serverlist] [*=userlist] dst_addr dst_mask
[op dst_port]
# SOCKD4 [@=serverlist] [*=userlist] dst_addr dst_mask
[op dst_port]
# SOCKD5 [@=serverlist] [*=userlist] dst_addr dst_mask
[op dst_port]
# GSS encryption_type
#
# Where:
# userlist    is a comma separated list of users
(optional)
# dst_addr    is a dotted quad IP address
# dst_mask    is a dotted quad IP address
# op          is one of EQ NEQ LT GT LE GE
# dst_port    is the number or name of a destination
port
# serverlist  is a comma separated list containing the
name or IP addresses
#             of SOCKS servers (use IP addresses for
speed).     Each address
#             or name may be optionally followed by an
explicit port number
#             as follows:
#                 IPaddress:portNumber or name:portNumber
#             Note that the default port number is 1080.
# encryption_type is:
#                 0 - Authentication Only
#                 1 - Integrity
#                 2 - Confidentiality (Full Encryption)
# Note GSS is only available with the GSSAPI.DLL and
KRB5.DLL from MIT
#
```

```
# On connect each line is processed in order and the
first line that matches
# is used. If no line matches the address is assumed to
be Direct.
#
# Matching is done by taking the destination address and
ANDing it with the
# dst_mask. The result is then compared to the dst_addr.
If they match, then
# if the userlist exists the current username is
compared against this list.
# Also if the [op dst_port] exists, the destination port
is compared to
# dst_port and if the "op" is true, the line is used.
#
# DENY       means to disallow the connect attemp.
# DIRECT     means to attempt the connection as normal.
# SOCKD      means to go the specified SOCKD 4 server.
# SOCKD4     means to go the specified SOCKD 4 server.
# SOCKD5     means to go the specified SOCKD 5 server.
#
# If @=serverlist is not present the SOCKD server
specified by the registry
# value:
#   LOCAL_MACHINE\SOFTWARE\HummingBird\SOCKS_SERVER
# is used. Note that the IP address or name of the
server may be optionally
# followed by an explicit port number as follows:
#       IPaddress:portNumber or name:portNumber
# Note that the default port number is 1080.
#
# Installation is best performed by the accompanying
INSTALL.BAT file.
#
```

```
# To manually install under Windows 95 WITHOUT the
Winsock2 API added:
#
# Restart Windows 95 in DOS mode. Rename the file
\Windows\System\WSOCK32.DLL
# to WSOCK320.DLL and copy the new WSOCK32.DLL into
\Windows\System. Place
# this file (socks.cnf) in the \Windows\System
directory. Restart Windows 95.
#
# To manually install under Windows NT 3.51:
#
# Rename the file \Winnt\System32\WSOCK32.DLL to
WSOCK320.DLL and copy the
# new WSOCK32.DLL into the \Winnt\System32 directory.
Place this file
# (socks.cnf) in the \Winnt\System32 directory. It is
now installed.
#
#SOCKD4 @=192.75.152.8 130.113.68.1 255.255.255.255
#
```

To get SOCKS to work with your WinGate server, you need to modify this file. By default, all lines in the file are commented out, and so they are not used. You just need to add one or two lines at the bottom to make it work. The first line to add should look like the following:

```
SOCKD5 @=IP_OF_WINGATE_COMPUTER:1080 0.0.0.0
255.255.255.255
```

This will cause all traffic to be routed through the SOCKS proxy.

If you need to send some data directly to a computer, and not through the proxy, you may need to use the DIRECT keyword. You can find more information on this in the SOCKS client documentation.

Telecommuting

Another popular service being added to almost every network is the ability for users to dial in and work from a remote location. Microsoft provides the ability to let users dial-in under Windows 95 (with the Plus! pack) and Windows NT.

Both Windows 95 and Windows NT Workstation only allow you to set up one modem for dial-in users. Windows NT Server allows you to handle up to 255 dial-in users.

The first step in configuring this is to set up the dial-up server. You will do this separately for Windows 95 and Windows NT.

Dial-up Server

The dial-up server is the connection between your network and the remote user. Usually the sever uses some sort of security mechanism to make sure only authorized users are allowed to use the service. If you want high security, the answer is clearly Windows NT. Windows 95's dial-in security is a simple password.

Setting up a dial-up server under Windows 95

This section assumes you have installed the Plus! pack.

The first step in setting up a dial-up server for Windows 95 is to install the dial-up adapter. The dial-up adapter is a piece of software that acts like a network card. The difference is, instead of being attached to a network, it enables you to dial into other networks.

To install the dial-up adapter, follow these steps:

1. Go to Control Panel.
2. Double-click the Network icon.
3. You will see the Network Components list.
4. Click the Add button.
5. Highlight Adapter and click Add.
6. In the Manufacturer list, choose Microsoft.
7. In the model list, choose Dial-Up Adapter.

8. Click OK.

9. Click OK again. (You will be required to reboot.)

Now for the easy part. Enabling and configuring the dial-up server is simple.

To enable the dial-up server, follow these steps:

1. Open My Computer, and then the Dial-Up Networking folder.

2. Click Connections, then Dial-Up Server. You will see a window appear.

3. To enable callers to dial in, change the first option to Allow caller access. It is a good idea to enable password security for your server. Pick a password that is easy to remember but hard to guess.

The downside to this security on Windows 95 is that there is only one password. If you change the password, you must tell everyone that is dialing in.

4. To set or change the password, click the Change Password button. Enter the old password (blank if this is the first time) and then enter the new password.

5. Finally, click OK.

6. Click the Server Type button to set the parameters for the server. In most cases you would leave the two boxes at the bottom checked. In the Type of Dial-Up Server drop-down box, you may want to change this to PPP. This will allow any PPP host to dial in.

7. Click OK, and then click OK again to finish setting the parameters. Windows 95 is now set up as a dial-up server.

Setting up a dial-up server under Windows NT

Windows NT uses a piece of software called Remote Access Service to dial in and out to make network connections. Unlike Windows 95, Windows NT doesn't require you to install a fake network adapter, only a network service.

To install Remote Access Service, follow these steps:

1. Go to Control Panel.

2. Double-click the Network icon. You will see the Network window.

3. Click the Services tab.

4. Click the Add button.

5. Choose Remote Access Service and click OK.

6. You will see a window appear. Choose the modem you plan to use and then click OK.

7. In the window that appears next, click the Network button.

8. Choose the protocols you want to enable over the dial-up and click OK.

9. Click the configure button to display the next window.

10. Choose whether you will only dial in, dial out, or do both from this Windows NT computer.

11. Click OK.

12. Click Continue.

13. Click Close. (You will need to reboot your computer.)

The dial-in security for Windows NT is handled by the normal Windows NT security. A user must have an account on the computer or domain that they are dialing in to. You will also need to go into User Manager and enable the dial-in right for the users.

The nice thing about both of these dial-up servers is that they allow any PPP client to access them. All you need to do on either Windows 95 or Windows NT is to set up a new connection under Dial-Up Networking in My Computer.

Practice Exam

1. **What is the maximum cable segment length for thinnet Ethernet?**

   - ☐ A. 100 meters
   - ☐ B. 185 meters
   - ☐ C. 200 meters
   - ☐ D. 250 meters

2. **Which of the following statements best defines share-level security?**

   - ☐ A. It provides better security than user-level security.
   - ☐ B. Passwords are assigned to resources.
   - ☐ C. Each user has a separate login and password.
   - ☐ D. It is also known as access control.

3. **Which of the following devices can be used to translate protocols between networks?**

   - ☐ A. Router
   - ☐ B. Bridge
   - ☐ C. Gateway
   - ☐ D. Repeater

4. Your building has been experiencing many power problems lately, including brownouts and blackouts. What can you do to keep these from damaging your network equipment?

    ☐ A. Implement RAID 5.
    ☐ B. Implement disk duplexing.
    ☐ C. Put each device on a UPS.
    ☐ D. Enable write back cache on each server.

5. What happens to the MAC address on a frame when it passes through a router?

    ☐ A. No change is made.
    ☐ B. The source address is stripped off and replaced by the router's MAC address.
    ☐ C. The destination address is stripped off and replaced by the address of the next device.
    ☐ D. The source and destination addresses are switched.

6. You have just been hired as a network administrator at a growing company. Currently, there are only eight people in the company and they all use computers. Due to the growth of the company, they plan to hire ten more people in the next several months. Several computers store confidential data about customers, so security is critical. You are asked to design and implement a new network for your company. What type of network would you implement?

    ☐ A. Server-based network
    ☐ B. Peer-to-peer network
    ☐ C. Client/server network
    ☐ D. Workgroup

7. **Which of the following is used to connect a workstation to a piece of cable in a thinnet bus network?**

    ☐ A. BNC Terminator
    ☐ B. BNC T-connector
    ☐ C. BNC barrel connector
    ☐ D. Hub

8. **You have just installed several new workstations on a 10Base-2 network. Prior to this, the network was functioning flawlessly. Now that the new workstations have been added, the entire network is down. What could be the cause?**

    ☐ A. One of the client computers has malfunctioned.
    ☐ B. The new cable added for the workstations is not the correct type.
    ☐ C. The new workstations have an incorrect type of NIC.
    ☐ D. The network is now incorrectly terminated.

9. **Which of the following tools can you use to gather information about the different network systems' components and systems?**

    ☐ A. Performance Monitor
    ☐ B. Task Manager
    ☐ C. SNMP
    ☐ D. Microsoft Systems Management Server

10. **Passwords are very important and are usually the main defense for network security. Which of the following policies can be used to protect sensitive systems with passwords?**

    ☐ A. Minimum password length
    ☐ B. Assigning passwords based on users' names
    ☐ C. Forcing periodical password changes
    ☐ D. Setting Windows NT to automatically lock out accounts after several bad password attemptsh

11. You are planning to implement fault tolerance on all of your company's Windows NT servers. You want to get the best possible read performance you can. Which scheme should you implement?

   ☐ A. RAID 0
   ☐ B. RAID 1
   ☐ C. RAID 4
   ☐ D. RAID 5

12. Why do broadcast storms degrade performance on the network?

   ☐ A. Each broadcast message must be answered by every device.
   ☐ B. Routers automatically forward broadcasts to other network segments.
   ☐ C. Each device on the network must process the broadcast.
   ☐ D. Broadcast messages are larger than normal frames.

13. The NDIS and ODI standards were created to solve some problems with earlier driver models. Which features do they both have?

   ☐ A. They use less memory.
   ☐ B. One driver supports many network adapters.
   ☐ C. Multiple protocols can bind to one driver simultaneously.
   ☐ D. They can be used on any network operating system.

14. **You are employed by a mid-sized marketing firm. The business offices are in a separate building from the rest of the company. Each building has its own 10Base-T network. The buildings are approximately 1,500 feet apart. The company needs to connect the two networks together.**

    Required Result:

    You must decide how to connect the two separate networks together.

    Optional Desired Results:

    The network connection must be easy to install.

    The network connection must be immune to EMI.

    Proposed Solution:

    Connect the buildings using 10Base-FL.

    Which results does the proposed solution produce?

    - ☐ A. The proposed solution produces the required result and produces both of the optional desired results.
    - ☐ B. The proposed solution produces the required result and produces only one of the optional desired results.
    - ☐ C. The proposed solution produces the required result but does not produce either of the optional desired results.
    - ☐ D. The proposed solution does not produce the required result.

---

15. **Your company has some inportant data, the loss of which would irreparably hurt the company. What is the best way to safeguard this data?**

    - ☐ A. RAID 5
    - ☐ B. RAID 0
    - ☐ C. Fault tolerance
    - ☐ D. Daily backups

16. **Your company sometimes employs temporary contract workers to help finish projects quickly. You have set up several computers that are used by these contractors. You have become aware of several contractors copying sensitive data to floppy disks and leaving with them.**

Required Result:

You must keep the contractors from copying data to disks.

Optional Desired Results:

You want to set up virus protection for the entire network.

You want to monitor the network to see which users are using the most resources.

Proposed Solution:

Remove all floppy disk drives from the contract computers. Secure the computers with access restrictions. Only allow the contractors to use the computers during business hours.

Which results does the proposed solution produce?

- ☐ A. The proposed solution produces the required result and produces both of the optional desired results.
- ☐ B. The proposed solution produces the required result and produces only one of the optional desired results.
- ☐ C. The proposed solution produces the required result but does not produce either of the optional desired results.
- ☐ D. The proposed solution does not produce the required result.

17. You want to connect a Token Ring network to an Ethernet network. Both networks use the TCP/IP protocol suite. Which device would you use to do this?

☐ A. Router
☐ B. Bridge
☐ C. Gateway
☐ D. Connector

18. You have added several UNIX workstations to your existing Windows NT network. You want to standardize on a single protocol suite. Which should you choose?

☐ A. NetBEUI
☐ B. IPX/SPX
☐ C. TCP/IP
☐ D. DLC

19. Which of the following RAID strategies creates a stripe set but does not use parity for data recovery?

☐ A. RAID 0
☐ B. RAID 1
☐ C. RAID 4
☐ D. RAID 5

20. You want to start documenting your company's network. First, you want to get a picture of the performance of the network and how often certain protocols are being used. Which tool would you use to accomplish this?

☐ A. SNMP
☐ B. Cable tester
☐ C. Time-domain reflectometer
☐ D. Protocol analyzer

21. **Which protocol enables UNIX workstations to retrieve files shared by Windows NT hosts?**

   ☐ A. NFS
   ☐ B. SMB
   ☐ C. SNMP
   ☐ D. DLC

22. **One of your workstations is having trouble connecting to the network. All other devices on the network are functioning normally. Which of the following is the most likely cause?**

   ☐ A. Bad terminator
   ☐ B. Faulty NIC on the network server
   ☐ C. Overloaded network
   ☐ D. Faulty NIC in the client computer

23. **You have been assigned the job of installing new cable for your network. This cable will share the wiring conduits with the phone systems. The maximum cable segment you expect to run is 90 meters. Which type of cable should you choose?**

   ☐ A. Thinnet
   ☐ B. Cat 3 UTP
   ☐ C. Thicknet
   ☐ D. Fiber-optic

24. **Which of the following statements are true of repeaters?**

   ☐ A. Repeaters can be used to solve attenuation problems.
   ☐ B. Segments joined by a repeater must use the same type of media.
   ☐ C. Segments joined by a repeater must use the same type of media access.
   ☐ D. Repeaters can be used to solve cross talk problems.

25. **Which of the following is associated with broadband transmissions?**

    □ A. Single frequency
    □ B. Unidirectional
    □ C. Bidirectional
    □ D. Low bandwidth

26. **Which device can function at the Application Layer of the OSI model?**

    □ A. Router
    □ B. Gateway
    □ C. Bridge
    □ D. Repeater

27. **Which type of cable is required for 100Mb/s Ethernet?**

    □ A. Cat 5 UTP
    □ B. Cat 3 UTP
    □ C. STP
    □ D. Thicknet

28. **Routers are used to connect networks. Which of the following protocols can be used with a router?**

    □ A. NetBEUI
    □ B. IPX/SPX
    □ C. TCP/IP
    □ D. DLC

29. **Which type of media access is used by Token Ring?**

    □ A. CSMA/CA
    □ B. CSMA/CD
    □ C. Polling
    □ D. Token passing

30. **You are installing a LAN in a new office building. The company currently has 35 employees that will use the network.**

    Required Result:

    You must choose a network topology that has some built-in redundancy and future growth.

    Optional Results:

    Installation should be easy.

    The network cable type should be inexpensive.

    Proposed Solution:

    You install an FDDI network.

    Which results does the proposed solution produce?

    - [ ] A. The proposed solution produces the required result and produces both of the optional desired results.
    - [ ] B. The proposed solution produces the required result and produces only one of the optional desired results.
    - [ ] C. The proposed solution produces the required result but does not produce either of the optional desired results.
    - [ ] D. The proposed solution does not produce the required result.

31. **Your computer uses COM1, COM2, LPT1, and LPT2. The 3COM Etherlink NIC you are using has the following settings: IRQ 7, I/O 0x300. Which device has a conflict with the NIC?**

    - [ ] A. COM1
    - [ ] B. COM2
    - [ ] C. LPT1
    - [ ] D. LPT2

32. Your network uses NetBEUI as its primary network protocol. Which device could you use to reduce network traffic?

☐ A. Router
☐ B. Bridge
☐ C. Repeater
☐ D. Gateway

33. Which of the following happens when there is a serious error on a Token Ring network?

☐ A. Beaconing
☐ B. Jabber
☐ C. Cross talking
☐ D. Jittering

34. Which of the following devices can be used to combine multiple signals into one transmission?

☐ A. Transceiver
☐ B. Signal generator
☐ C. Redirector
☐ D. Multiplexer

35. Your company has three offices. The home office is in Raleigh, and the two remote offices are in San Jose and New York. You need to connect the three offices' networks with a WAN.

Required Result:

Implement a network that connects all three sites.

Optional Desired Results:

The WAN should have at least 512Kb of usable bandwidth.

The WAN needs to continue functioning if one link fails.

Proposed Solution:

Connect each site using T1 connections. Connect Raleigh to San Jose, San Jose to New York, and New York to Raleigh.

Which results does the proposed solution produce?

- [ ] A. The proposed solution produces the required result and produces both of the optional desired results.
- [ ] B. The proposed solution produces the required result and produces only one of the optional desired results.
- [ ] C. The proposed solution produces the required result but does not produce either of the optional desired results.
- [ ] D. The proposed solution does not produce the required result.

36. **Which of the following terms describes the process of signals crossing between adjacent wires?**

- [ ] A. Cross talk
- [ ] B. Attenuation
- [ ] C. Corruption
- [ ] D. Collision

37. **Which of the following is associated with connection-oriented transmissions?**

- [ ] A. Unreliable
- [ ] B. High performance
- [ ] C. Guaranteed delivery
- [ ] D. Compression

38. **Which type of connector is used by UTP cable?**

- [ ] A. BNC
- [ ] B. AUI
- [ ] C. DIN
- [ ] D. RJ-45

39. Which of the following is the name of the Microsoft version of IPX/SPX?

   ☐ A. NetBEUI
   ☐ B. Network Packet Exchange
   ☐ C. NWLink
   ☐ D. NetWare Services

40. What term is used for when the number of broadcast messages being sent outpaces the network bandwidth?

   ☐ A. Broadcast storm
   ☐ B. Attenuating
   ☐ C. Beaconing
   ☐ D. Convergence

41. Which type of backup only backs up files that were created or changed since the last full backup and then marks the files as having been backed up?

   ☐ A. Full backup
   ☐ B. Differential backup
   ☐ C. Incremental backup
   ☐ D. Extended backup

42. What is the most likely cause when one workstation can't communicate on a NetWare network?

   ☐ A. Incorrect packet size
   ☐ B. Wrong frame type
   ☐ C. Bit order
   ☐ D. Invalid CRC

43. You have begun auditing network access using Windows NT auditing. Which application do you use to view the audit reports?

   ☐ A. Security Manager
   ☐ B. Server Manager
   ☐ C. User Manager
   ☐ D. Event viewer

44. Which protocol is used to print to Hewlett-Packard network printers?

    ☐ A. DLC
    ☐ B. NetBEUI
    ☐ C. SMB
    ☐ D. NFS

45. Which of the following protocols can be used over a dial-up connection when using SLIP?

    ☐ A. IPX/SPX
    ☐ B. TCP/IP
    ☐ C. NetBEUI
    ☐ D. DLC

46. Which type of connector is used for 10Base-2 cable?

    ☐ A. RJ-11
    ☐ B. RJ-45
    ☐ C. BNC
    ☐ D. DIX

47. You are an administrator of a LAN with two segments. Both segments use the NetBEUI protocol and are connected via a bridge. You have just added several new client computers and a server, and now the network performance is unacceptable.

    Required Result:

    Replace the bridge with an internetwork device that will alleviate the performance problems.

    Optional Desired Results:

    Continue to support NetBEUI.

    The solution should be simple to implement.

    Proposed Solution:

    Replace the bridge with a switching hub.

Which results does the proposed solution produce?

- ☐ A. The proposed solution produces the required result and produces both of the optional desired results.
- ☐ B. The proposed solution produces the required result and produces only one of the optional desired results.
- ☐ C. The proposed solution produces the required result but does not produce either of the optional desired results.
- ☐ D. The proposed solution does not produce the required result.

---

48. **Which of the following devices does not distinguish between the protocols it passes and filters?**

- ☐ A. Router
- ☐ B. Bridge
- ☐ C. Gateway
- ☐ D. Switch

---

49. **Which category of cable is required for 10Base-T?**

- ☐ A. CAT 3
- ☐ B. CAT 5
- ☐ C. UTP 1
- ☐ D. UTP 3

---

50. **As your network grows, you are beginning to have problems with attenuation.**

Required Result:

You must install new hardware to fix the attenuation problems that are increasing.

Optional Desired Results:

Eliminate broadcast storms.

Filter traffic based on network addresses.

Proposed Solution:

Install a bridge to segment the network.

Which results does the proposed solution produce?

- [ ] A. The proposed solution produces the required result and produces both of the optional desired results.
- [ ] B. The proposed solution produces the required result and produces only one of the optional desired results.
- [ ] C. The proposed solution produces the required result but does not produce either of the optional desired results.
- [ ] D. The proposed solution does not produce the required result.

51. **As your network grows, you are beginning to have problems with attenuation.**

Required Result:

You must install new hardware to fix the attenuation problems that are increasing.

Optional Desired Results:

Eliminate broadcast storms.

Filter traffic based on network addresses.

Proposed Solution:

Install a router.

Which results does the proposed solution produce?

- [ ] A. The proposed solution produces the required result and produces both of the optional desired results.
- [ ] B. The proposed solution produces the required result and produces only one of the optional desired results.
- [ ] C. The proposed solution produces the required result but does not produce either of the optional desired results.
- [ ] D. The proposed solution does not produce the required result.

52. **What type of cable is used in ARCNET networks?**

- [ ] A. UTP
- [ ] B. STP
- [ ] C. RG-62
- [ ] D. RG-58

53. **You have a 10Base-2 network with four segments that are separated by repeaters. How many terminators are needed?**

- [ ] A. 2
- [ ] B. 4
- [ ] C. 8
- [ ] D. 16

54. **You have a 10Base-2 network with four segments that are separated by repeaters. How many grounded terminators are needed?**

- [ ] A. 2
- [ ] B. 4
- [ ] C. 8
- [ ] D. 16

55. You are an administrator on a network where available bandwidth is becoming an issue. You are about to add more clients to the network, which will add more traffic and also extend your network to a distance outside the Ethernet specifications. Management also wants to add a new e-mail system.

Required Result:

Choose a connectivity device that will reduce the traffic on your network segment and also regenerate the signal so your network distance is not a problem.

Optional Desired Results:

Filter traffic between segments.

Try to stop broadcast storms that may arise due to the increased network size.

Proposed Solution:

Install a repeater.

Which results does the proposed solution produce?

- ☐ A. The proposed solution produces the required result and produces both of the optional desired results.
- ☐ B. The proposed solution produces the required result and produces only one of the optional desired results.
- ☐ C. The proposed solution produces the required result and but does not produce any of the optional desired results.
- ☐ D. The proposed solution does not produce the required result.

Exam Key

1.	B	20.	D	39.	C
2.	B	21.	A	40.	A
3.	C	22.	D	41.	C
4.	C	23.	B	42.	B
5.	B & C	24.	A & C	43.	D
6.	A	25.	B	44.	A
7.	B	26.	B	45.	B
8.	B	27.	A	46.	C
9.	C	28.	B & C	47.	A
10.	A, C, & D	29.	D	48.	B
11.	D	30.	C	49.	A
12.	C	31.	C	50.	C
13.	C	32.	B	51.	A
14.	B	33.	A	52.	C
15.	D	34.	D	53.	C
16.	C	35.	A	54.	B
17.	A	36.	A	55.	C
18.	C	37.	C		
19.	A	38.	D		

Exam Analysis

1. Thinnet media is used in 10Base-2 networks. The "2" stands for approximately 200 meters. Don't be confused and answer 200 meters, though! The correct answer is 185. See Chapter 3, "Coaxial Cabling" section.

2. Each resource in a share-level security network is designated a password that controls all access to that resource. See Chapter 7, "Security Types" section.

3. Gateways operate at all seven layers of the OSI model and can translate between protocols and systems. See Chapter 6, "Internetworking Devices" section.

4. A UPS will provide continuous power in the event that you lose electricity. It also protects against surges and other power problems. See Chapter 8, "Power Problems" section.

5. The Physical layer uses MAC addresses. They are valid only for one hop through a network. When data is sent from a computer to another through a router, the first hop is from the computer to the router. The source MAC address is that of the computer, and the destination MAC address is that of the router. When the data arrives at the router, the source MAC address is removed and the router's address is added. The destination address is removed, and the MAC address of the next device on the path is added. The data is then sent out the network. See Chapter 2, "Data Link Layer" section.

6. A server-based network would provide the growth potential and security needed for your company. See Chapter 1, "Different Network Types" section.

7. T connectors are used to connect workstations to a thinnet bus network. See Chapter 3, "Network Adapter Ports" section.

8. If you added any new pieces of cable, they could be the wrong type of coaxial cable. This is a very common mistake. See Chapter 3, "Unbounded Media" section.

9. SNMP is used to gather information from devices on a network. See Chapter 5, "TCP/IP Protocol Suite" section.

10. Minimum password lengths ensure that users do not choose passwords that are too short and therefore easy to guess or decode. Periodic password changes, while sometimes aggravating to users, help to keep old passwords from being found out and passed around. Even if someone does get a password, once a change is forced, the old password is no longer valid. Locking out accounts after several bad attempts keeps someone from using password cracking tools to constantly try different passwords. See Chapter 7, "Passwords" section.

11. RAID 5 uses a stripe set with parity to provide fault tolerance. Although write performance is slower due to the parity information being generated, read performance is very fast because the parity is not read during a normal read. See Chapter 7, "Redundant Systems" section.

12. Every device on the network examines the packet to see the information it contains. Each device does not answer the broadcast message. Routers do not pass broadcast messages by default. See Chapter 8, "Common Network Problems and Solutions" section.

13. NDIS and ODI were created to enable users to use multiple network protocols at once. One driver supports only one adapter or set of adapters. The driver is written for a specific network operating system. See Chapter 3, "Adapter Drivers" section.

14. 10Base-FL will connect the networks with no problems. It is also immune to EMI. Fiber-optic cable is not easy to install, so it does not meet both optional requirements. See Chapter 5, "Ethernet" section.

15. Although RAID 5 will protect data, it should not be the main strategy. Daily backups are imperative and should be maintained. See Chapter 7, "Safeguarding Data" section.

16. The solution that is proposed stops the contractors from copying data from their computers. It does not, however, protect the network against viruses or help you monitor the network. See Chapter 7.

17. A bridge can only connect networks that use the same type of media access. In this case, you must use a router. See Chapter 6, "Internetworking Devices" section.

18. TCP/IP is the native protocol used by UNIX operating systems. Windows NT can also use this protocol, so this is the best choice. See Chapter 5, "TCP/IP Protocol Suite" section.

19. RAID 0 creates a stripe set across multiple disks, but does not use any parity for fault tolerance. See Chapter 7, "Redundant Systems" section.

20. A protocol analyzer can look at the network from a higher level than a cable tester or time-domain reflectometer. By looking at a higher level it can track utilization and how often different protocols are being used. SNMP is used to query devices on their statistics. See Chapter 8, "Network Troubleshooting" section.

21. Installing an NFS server on to the Windows NT computers enables the UNIX users to map drives and retrieve information. See Chapter 5, "TCP/IP Protocol Suite" section.

22. The first three choices given would affect more than just the one client workstation. Only a malfunctioning NIC in the client would account for this specific outage. See Chapter 8, "Client Troubleshooting" section.

23. CAT 3 would be the best choice, considering where the cable needs to be run. See Chapter 3, "Bounded Media" section.

24. Repeaters can connect networks that use the same type of media access. They are not intelligent enough to connect different types of networks, such as Ethernet to Token Ring. See Chapter 6, "LAN Connectivity Devices" section.

25. Broadband can only send signals in one direction. An easy way to remember this is that conventional cable television uses broadband and the signals all flow to the customer, but none go back to the company. See Chapter 3, "Data Transmission" section.

26. Gateways can function at all seven layers of the OSI model, depending on their purpose. See Chapter 6, "Internetworking Devices" section.

27. 100Mb/sec Ethernet requires Category 5 cable. CAT 3 cable is only capable of 10 Mb/sec. See Chapter 3, "Bounded Media" section.

28. IPX/SPX and TCP/IP are both routable protocols. NetBEUI and DLC are not — they can only be bridged. See Chapter 5.

29. CSMA/CD is used by Ethernet. AppleTalk uses CSMA/CA. See Chapter 2, "Data Link Layer" section.

30. FDDI has excellent growth ability and built-in fault tolerance. However, the installation is very difficult and expensive due to the fiber-optic cable. See Chapter 3, "Fiber-Optic Cable" section.

31. LPT1 uses IRQ 7 by default. See Chapter 3, "Installing and Configuring Network Adapters" section.

32. Since NetBEUI cannot be routed, the only other solution is a bridge. Repeaters and gateways do not filter traffic. See Chapter 5, "Microsoft Protocols" section.

33. When a device detects an error on a token ring network, it sends out a broadcast message to alert the other devices. This is known as a beacon. See Chapter 4, "Token Ring" section.

34. Multiplexers are used to combine multiple signals into one larger signal. See Chapter 3, "Multiplexing" section.

35. The proposed solution fulfills all requirements. T1 connections provide 1.544Mb/sec bandwidth, which is three times the requirement. Because the links would use routers (which make intelligent routing decisions), if one link fails, traffic could be rerouted another way. See Chapter 5.

36. Cross talk happens when one signal leaks to another cable. Twisting the cables as in UTP cable prevents this. See Chapter 3, "Electrical Properties" section.

37. While connection-oriented communications do have guaranteed delivery, they are slower than connectionless transmissions, which are unreliable. See Chapter 2, "What Is a Protocol" section.

38. An RJ-45 connector is similar to a telephone connector, but larger. See Chapter 3, "Network Adapter Ports" section.

39. In Microsoft applications and operating systems, IPX/SPX is referred to as NWLink. See Chapter 5, "IPX/SPX Protocol Suite" section.

40. Broadcast storms can cause severe degradation of network performance. See Chapter 8, "Common Network Problems and Solutions" section.

41. Full backups back up all files and set the Archive bit to "on." Differential backups only back up files that have changed since the last full or incremental backup, and do not set the Archive bit. See Chapter 7, "Safeguarding Data" section.

42. The most common solution to the problem of one client not talking to a NetWare server is the frame type. The frame types must match for communication to occur. See Chapter 3, "Ethernet" section.

43. Event Viewer is used to view the audit logs. These are stored in the Security log. See Chapter 7, "Auditing" section.

44. On the exam, DLC is used to print to HP network printers. See Chapter 5, "DLC" section.

45. SLIP only supports TCP/IP. PPP, on the other hand, supports almost any transport protocol. See Chapter 5, "SLIP & PPP" section.

46. 10Base-2 uses thinnet coaxial cable with BNC connectors. See Chapter 3, "Bounded Media" section.

47. A switch is an excellent solution to the problem. Switches provide dedicated data paths between sending and receiving devices. They act as a multiport bridge. They are easy to implement and support NetBEUI. See Chapter 6, "LAN Connectivity Devices" section.

48. Bridges operate at the Data Link layer of the OSI model. At this layer, they do not understand which protocols they are passing. See Chapter 2, "Data Link Layer" section. Also see Chapter 6, "LAN Connectivity Devices" section.

49. CAT 3 cable is the minimum requirement for 10Base-T. See Chapter 3, "Bounded Media" section.

50. The bridge will extend the network into two segments, thus alleviating the attenuation problems. However, bridges use hardware addresses to filter data, not network addresses. A bridge also passes all broadcasts, so it will not stop broadcast storms. See Chapter 6, "LAN Connectivity Devices" section.

51. A router would extend the network into two segments, which would alleviate the attenuation problems. Routers can also be set to filter on network addresses, and they do not pass broadcasts by default, thus eliminating broadcast storms. See Chapter 6, "Internetworking Devices" section.

52. ARCNET uses RG-62 coaxial cable. See Chapter 4, "ARCNET" section.

53. Each segment requires two terminators. See Chapter 4, "Bus" section.

54. Only one terminator from each segment should be grounded. See Chapter 4, "Bus" section.

55. The proposed solution only helps the attenuation problem. Repeaters do not filter or stop broadcasts. See Chapter 6, "LAN Connectivity Devices" section.

Exam Revealed

1. **What happens** to the MAC address on a frame when it passes through a router?

    A.   No change is made.

    B.   The source address is stripped off and replaced by the routers MAC address.

    C.   The destination address is stripped off and replaced by the address of the next device.

    D.   The source and destination addresses are switched.

This is a simple-looking question that turns out to be more difficult. The process of frames going through routers like this is never directly discussed in the text. The idea is that the reader should be able to take the information they learned and apply it to more real-world situations on the exam. There is no possible way to cover every possible real-world type question you will see. You must draw from all of the information you have learned.

2. You have just been hired as a network administrator at a growing company. Currently, there are only eight people in the company, and they all use computers. Due to the growth of the company, they plan to hire ten more people in the next several months. Several computers store confidential data about customers, so security is critical. You are asked to design and implement a new network for your company. What type of network would you implement?

    A.   Server-based network
    B.   Peer-to-peer network
    C.   Client/server network
    D.   Workgroup

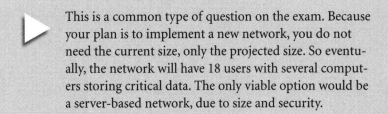

This is a common type of question on the exam. Because your plan is to implement a new network, you do not need the current size, only the projected size. So eventually, the network will have 18 users with several computers storing critical data. The only viable option would be a server-based network, due to size and security.

3. You have just installed several new workstations on a 10Base-2 network. Prior to this, the network was functioning flawlessly. Now that the new workstations have been added, the entire network is down. What could be the cause?

    A.   One of the client computers has malfunctioned.
    B.   The new cable added for the workstations is not the correct type.
    C.   The new workstations have an incorrect type of NIC.
    D.   The network is now incorrectly terminated.

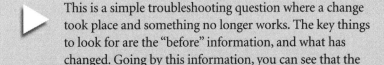

This is a simple troubleshooting question where a change took place and something no longer works. The key things to look for are the "before" information, and what has changed. Going by this information, you can see that the

network was working fine before, but then some workstations were added. Now the entire network is not functioning. You must then go through and see what may have
happened. Answer A should not bring the entire network
down, only that workstation. Answer C is also incorrect
because you can only use one type of NIC on 10Base-2.
If this had been a Token Ring network, this may be correct
due to speed issues. Answer D would not be correct,
because termination should not have changed. Answer B
is the solution, because more cable had to be used to add
workstations. This is the only answer that would affect
the entire LAN by adding these workstations.

4. **You are employed by a mid-sized marketing firm. The business
offices are in a separate building from the rest of the company.
Each building has its own 10Base-T network. The buildings are
approximately 1500 feet apart. The company needs to connect
the two networks together.**

Required Result:

You must decide how to connect the two separate networks
together.

Optional Desired Results:

The network connection must be easy to install.

The network connection must be immune to EMI.

Proposed Solution:

Connect the buildings using 10Base-FL.

Which results does the proposed solution produce?

    A.   The proposed solution produces the required
result and produces both of the optional desired
results.

B.   The proposed solution produces the required result and produces only one of the optional desired results.

C.   The proposed solution produces the required result but does not produce either of the optional desired results.

D.   The proposed solution does not produce the required result.

Be prepared for these questions on the exam! They are the toughest and most time-consuming. These questions give you a scenario and then a list of required and optional results. They then list a proposed solution, and you must answer how many of the required and optional results are satisfied.

First, you need to read the question for vital information. Make note of this information so you can apply it to the results and solutions. Next, look at the required and optional results. Note that the optional results may sometimes contradict each other, as in this question. Make sure the proposed solution satisfies at least the required result, and then match it to the optional result.

5. **Your company sometimes employs temporary contract workers to help finish projects quickly. You have set up several computers that are used by these contractors. You have become aware of several contractors copying sensitive data to floppy disks and leaving with them.**

Required Result:

You must keep the contractors from copying data to disks.

Optional Desired Results:

You want to set up virus protection for the entire network.

You want to monitor the network to see which users are using the most resources.

Proposed Solution:

Remove all floppy disk drives from the contract computers. Secure the computers with access restrictions. Only allow the contractors to use the computers during business hours.

Which results does the proposed solution produce?

A.   The proposed solution produces the required result and produces both of the optional desired results.

B.   The proposed solution produces the required result and produces only one of the optional desired results.

C.   The proposed solution produces the required result but does not produce either of the optional desired results.

D.   The proposed solution does not produce the required result.

This is another question similar to the one we just analyzed. We will cover a few of these, because they are the hardest on the exam and take the most amount of time.

Again, read the situation and get the vital information you need. You can see the vital information in the callouts. Next, read the required result and see how it relates to the situation. Finally, read the optional results and the proposed solution. This solution has multiple parts, so read each one separately. Remember that it is fine if the proposed solution does more than the required and optional results, just as long as those are satisfied. In this case, removing the floppy disks satisfies the required result. The other two solutions do not satisfy either of the optional results, even though they do go further and restrict the contractors' access.

6. One of your workstations is having trouble connecting to the network. All other devices on the network are functioning normally. **Which of the following is the most likely cause?**

    A. Bad terminator
    B. Faulty NIC on the network server
    C. Overloaded network
    D. Faulty NIC in the client computer

This is another fairly simple troubleshooting question. Again, look for the things that changed and the results of it. In this case, something happened so that the workstation can no longer talk on the network. You must sort through each of the solutions to see which one answers the problem.

---

7. Your computer uses COM1, COM2, LPT1, and LPT2. The 3COM Etherlink NIC you are using has the following settings: **IRQ 7, I/O 0x300.** Which device has a conflict with the NIC?

    A. COM1
    B. COM2
    C. LPT1
    D. LPT2

You are certain to see a similar question on the exam. The key to these questions is to know what devices use which IRQs, and then find one that isn't being used. It sometimes helps to list out the used IRQs on the paper you get for the exam.

---

8. As your network grows, you are beginning to have problems with attenuation.

Required Result:

You must install new hardware to fix the attenuation problems that are increasing.

Optional Desired Results:

Eliminate broadcast storms.   Filter traffic based on network addresses.

Proposed Solution:

Install a bridge to segment the network.

Which results does the proposed solution produce?

    A.   The proposed solution produces the required result and produces both of the optional desired results.

    B.   The proposed solution produces the required result and produces only one of the optional desired results.

    C.   The proposed solution produces the required result but does not produce either of the optional desired results.

    D.   The proposed solution does not produce the required result.

9. **As your network grows, you are beginning to have problems with attenuation.**

Required Result:

You must install new hardware to fix the attenuation problems that are increasing.

Optional Desired Results:

Eliminate broadcast storms.

Filter traffic based on network addresses.

Proposed Solution:

Install a router.

Which results does the proposed solution produce?

A. The proposed solution produces the required result and produces both of the optional desired results.

B. The proposed solution produces the required result and produces only one of the optional desired results.

C. The proposed solution produces the required result but does not produce either of the optional desired results.

D. The proposed solution does not produce the required result.

Usually, on an exam with the result/solution problems, you will get a series of them. Most of the time, the situation and results stay the same, but the proposed solution changes. This is the case with these two questions. Usually, on the exam, the solutions satisfy more of the results as you go further in the series, BUT THIS IS NOT ALWAYS THE CASE!

The best way to handle these questions is to do them just like any other result/solution questions, and do them individually.

10. You are an administrator on a network where available bandwidth is becoming an issue. You are about to add more clients to the network, which will add more traffic and also extend your network to a distance outside the Ethernet specifications. Management also wants to add a new e-mail system.

Required Result:

Choose a connectivity device that will be able to reduce the traffic on your network segment and also regenerate the signal so that your network distance is not a problem.

Optional Desired Results:

Filter traffic between segments.

Try to stop broadcast storms that may arise due to the increased network size.

Proposed Solution:

Install a repeater.

Which results does the proposed solution produce?

A. The proposed solution produces the required result and produces both of the optional desired results.

B. The proposed solution produces the required result and produces only one of the optional desired results.

C. The proposed solution produces the required result and but does not produce any of the optional desired results.

D. The proposed solution does not produce the required result.

Let's look closely at the question. The first thing you should do is read the scenario. Make a note of any important facts, and try to filter out any unnecessary info. You may find they tell you facts that aren't needed to answer the question, so don't assume that everything in the scenario must be involved in the answer. For example, the last sentence is extra information that is not required in the answer, since it is not listed as a required or optional result.

Glossary

100 VG-ANYLAN A network that uses voice-grade, fiber-optic cable, as well as Categories 3, 4, or 5 twisted-pair cable to provide a possible transmission rate of 100Mbps.

10Base-2 A network that uses RG-58 cable along with T connectors wired in a linear bus configuration to provide a transmission rate of 10Mbps.

10Base-5 A network that uses RG-8 cable with external transceivers and a vampire clamp. The clamp fastens directly into the cable, which is wired in a linear bus to provide a possible transmission rate of 10Mbps.

10Base-FL A network that operates over fiber-optic cable at 10Mbps using baseband signaling.

10Base-T A network standard that utilizes 22-AWG UTP cable with RJ-45 jacks arranged in a star configuration to provide possible transmission rates of 10Mbps.

Address Resolution Protocol (ARP) ARP is used to dynamically discover the low-level physical network hardware address that corresponds to the high-level IP address for a given host.

ADSP *See* AppleTalk Data Stream Protocol.

American National Standards Institute (ANSI) ANSI is the primary organization for fostering the development of technology standards in the United States.

amplitude shift keying (ASK) A method of encoding that uses changes in amplitude to represent data.

analog signal A signal that takes the form of a wave, which curves smoothly from one value to the next.

ANSI *See* American National Standards Institute.

AppleShare A group of client/server applications that provide access to network resources.

AppleTalk A set of communications protocols used to define networking on an AppleShare network.

AppleTalk Data Stream Protocol (ADSP) ADSP is a newer protocol that uses byte-streaming connections instead of transactions. It is part of the AppleTalk protocol suite.

AppleTalk Session Protocol (ASP). Grouped with AppleTalk Transport Protocol, ASP allows for reliable data transfer.

AppleTalk Transaction Protocol (ATP) ATP provides a connectionless transport layer protocol, but instead of being used strictly for data like others of this type, it is used for transactions.

Application layer The top layer of the network protocol stack. The application layer is concerned with the semantics of work.

archiving Creating a redundant copy of computer file data. Used to protect the data if the original copy is damaged or otherwise irretrievable.

ARCNET A proprietary token-bus networking architecture that supports coaxial, twisted-pair, and fiber-optic cable-based implementations and is capable of 2.5Mbps transmissions.

ARP *See* Address Resolution Protocol.

ASK *See* amplitude shift keying.

ASN.1 The language used by the OSI protocols for describing abstract syntax. This language is also used to encode SNMP packets.

ASP *See* AppleTalk Session Protocol.

asynchronous A data transmission method in which each character is sent one bit at a time. Each character has a start and stop bit to synchronize signals between the sending device and the receiving device.

Asynchronous Transfer Mode (**ATM**) A new type of network that uses fixed-size packets called cells and supports dynamic bandwidth allocation.

ATM *See* Asynchronous Transfer Mode.

ATP *See* AppleTalk Transaction Protocol.

attachment unit interface (**AUI**) A 15-pin connector that allows for the use of an external transceiver.
AUI *See* attachment unit interface.

attenuation The fading of the electrical signal over a distance.

auditing Allows an administrator to track users' successful and failed attempts to log on to the network, access resources, shut the system down, and so on.

B

back up Copying data to another location. Important data is often backed up to a tape device, which allows for restoration if the original data is lost.

baseband The transmission of a signal at its original frequencies — that is, unmodulated.

beaconing The process used in Token Ring networks to report an error. If a workstation detects a problem with its neighbor, the workstation sends its address, the address of its nearest active upstream neighbor, and the type of error known.

bit synchronization Coordinating timing between the sending device and the receiving device.

BNC connector A bayonet-type coaxial cable connector of the kind commonly found on RF equipment.

bridge An internetwork device used to split a network segment to control traffic. Data is passed through or rejected depending on the destination device's MAC address.

broadband A communications channel with a bandwidth characterized by high data transmission speeds (10,000–500,000 bits per second). Often used when describing communications systems based on cable television technology.

broadcast storm An incorrect packet broadcast onto a network that causes multiple hosts to respond all at once, typically with equally incorrect packets which causes the storm to grow exponentially in severity.

bus The connection the adapter cards have to the rest of the computer. *Bus* also refers to the physical network topology where each device connects to the same cable.

bus mastering This capability allows a card in a computer to communicate with other devices without the main CPU being involved.

Carrier Sense Multiple Access/Collision Avoidance (CSMA/CA) A network access method that sends request before sending to control media access.

Carrier Sense Multiple Access with Collision Detection (CSMA/CD) A network access method for managing collisions of data packets. This method checks the media for other devices before transmitting.

CAU *See* Controlled Access Unit.

centralized A computer network with a central processing node through which all data and communications flow.

Channel Service Unit/Data Service Unit(CSU/DSU) The special equipment that is used to connect a LAN to a Digital Data Service (DDS) line.

checksum A fixed-length block produced as a function of every bit in an encrypted message; a summation of a set of data items for error detection; a sum of digits or bits used to verify the integrity of data.

circuit switching A switching method in which a dedicated connection is made between the two communicating devices.

client One for whom services are provided.

CLNS *See* Connectionless Network Services.

coaxial A type of cable that uses two conductors — a central, solid wire core, surrounded by insulation, which is then surrounded by a braided wire conductor sheath.

collaborative A setup that allows computers to share processing power across a network.

collisions An event which occurs when two devices try to transmit at the same time and disrupt each other's signaling.

Connectionless Network Services (CLNS) A Network layer protocol in the DNA protocol suite.

Connection-Oriented Network Service (CONS) Network layer protocol that provides reliable data delivery.

CONS *See* Connection-Oriented Network Service.

contention A media access method that allows every device to transmit whenever it needs to. This freedom to transmit sometimes results in collisions on the network.

Controlled Access Unit (CAU) An intelligent MAU used in Token Ring networks.

CRC *See* cyclic redundancy check.

cross talk The leaking of signals between two adjacent network wires.

CSMA/CA *See* Carrier Sense Multiple Access/Collision Avoidance.

CSMA/CD *See* Carrier Sense Multiple Access with Collision Detection.

CSU/DSU *See* Channel Service Unit/Data Service Unit.

cyclic redundancy check (CRC) An algorithm designed to generate a check field used to guard against errors which may occur in data transmission. The check field is often generated by taking the remainder after dividing all the serialized bits in a block of data by a predetermined binary number.

D

DAP *See* Digital Access Protocol.

Data Link Control (DLC) A nonroutable protocol used primarily for network printers.

Data Link layer The conceptual layer of control or processing logic existing in the hierarchical structure of a station that is responsible for maintaining control of the data link.

datagram A finite-length packet with sufficient information to be independently routed from source to destination without reliance on previous transmissions; typically does not involve end-to-end session establishment and may or may not entail delivery confirmation acknowledgment.

Datagram Delivery Protocol (DDP) An organization of information processing such that both processing and data may be distributed over a number of different machines in one or more locations; a technique to enable multiple computers to cooperate in the completion of tasks, typically in a networked environment. Each computer that contributes to the completion of the total task actually does so by completing one or more individual subtasks independently of its peers, reporting the results from its subtasks as they are completed.

DDCMP *See* Digital Data Communications Message Protocol.

DDP *See* Datagram Delivery Protocol.

DDS *See* Digital Data Service.

de facto Latin for "existing in fact," means the protocol is controlled by the entire industry. These are also known as *industry standards.*

de jure Latin for "according to law," means the protocol was designed by one company or organization. Normally, this organization maintains control of the protocol and is responsible for any additions or changes.

DECnet A set of networking protocols developed by Digital Equipment Corporation used in its VAX family of computers to exchange messages and other data.

deterministic A network that has a system that determines transmitting order. Token Ring is deterministic.

differential backup A method of file backup in which you back up selected files that have changed since the last backup. This method does not mark files as archived.

Differential Manchester An encoding scheme that uses mid-bit transitions for clocking. Data is represented by the presence of a transition at the beginning of the bit. Token Ring LANs utilize Differential Manchester.

Digital Access Protocol (DAP) A proprietary data transfer protocol that is used with FTAM. It allows for file management such as deletion, retrieval, and storage.

Digital Data Communications Message Protocol (DDCMP) A protocol from the original DNA specifications. It is proprietary to DEC and is included in Phase V as an option to retain compatibility with older versions of DNA. A frame in DDCMP is known as a *message.*

Digital Data Service (DDS) Similar to telephone lines, these digital lines are used to connect computers and LANs using special equipment.

Digital Network Architecture (DNA) The Digital Network Architecture was developed by Digital Equipment, Inc. in 1974. It has been revised many times over the years and is currently in its fifth revision, called Phase V. Equipment by DEC (Digital Equipment) that operates within the specifications of DNA (Digital Network Architecture) is referred to as a *DECNet product.*

digital signaling Signals that can exist in only one of two values, so they go directly to the next value, typically changing between 0 and 1.

digital volt meter A tool that allows checking for continuity on a network cable to see if there are any breaks in the physical media. By connecting the DVM to the ground mesh and to the central core, you can check for a short in the cable that will cause disturbances in the communications.

direct memory access (DMA) DMA allows your adapter cards to work directly with the computer's memory.

distance vector routing A routing method that simply calculates the shortest number of hops between two points. Distance vector can take a considerable amount of time to configure and change on a large network.

distributed A computing method in which data storage and processing can be done on the local workstation.

DIX A 15-pin connector with two rows of pins created by Digital, Intel, and Xerox. This is the same as an AUI connector.

DLC *See* Data Link Control.

DMA *See* direct memory access.

DNA *See* Digital Network Architecture.

DNS *See* Domain Name System.

DoD The abbreviation of Department of Defense.

domain Domains are server-based networks that provide a higher level of security and central administration.

Domain Name System (DNS) The Internet naming scheme which consists of a hierarchical sequence of names, from the most specific to the most general (left to right), separated by dots — for example, nic.ddn.mil.

driver Drivers are software that allows the computer to access the hardware.

E

EISA *See* Extended Industry Standard Architecture.

ELAP The EtherTalk protocol that lets you build AppleTalk networks on the popular Ethernet network protocols.

electromagnetic interference (**EMI**) Commonly caused by fluorescent lights, transformers, power company on a bad day, and pretty much anything else that creates an electrical field.

EMI *See* electromagnetic interference.

end systems The source and destination devices of data on the network.

error control The process of finding errors in transmitted data that is implemented by using checksums and CRCs (cyclic redundancy checks).

Ethernet A network cable and access protocol scheme originally developed by DEC, Intel, and Xerox but now marketed primarily by DEC and 3Com; a local area network and its associated protocol developed by (but not limited to) Xerox. Ethernet is a baseband system.

Ethernet_802.2 The IEEE frame type that contains three additional one-byte values. These values add flow control, error checking, and reliability to the previous 802.3 frame type. These packets also range from 64 to 1,518 bytes. This is the default frame type for NetWare 3.12 and 4.1.

Ethernet_802.3 The IEEE frame type that was developed and used by NetWare for its IPX/SPX protocol before the IEEE finished developing the standard. The frame size used in 802.3 is between 64 and 1,518 bytes and includes CRC (cyclic redundancy check) for error checking. This frame type, which doesn't fully comply to the standards developed by IEEE, is used primarily by NetWare 2.2 and 3.11.

Ethernet_II The frame type that can be used by both IPX/SPX and TCP/IP. This frame type doesn't identify the length of the packet but the type. This is used to specify whether the packet is IPX/SPX or TCP/IP.

Extended Binary-Coded Decimal Interchange Code (EBCDIC)
Eight-bit code defined by IBM; includes values for control functions
and graphics.

Extended Industry Standard Architecture (EISA) This bus was developed by a group of industry leaders and released as an open standard.
The EISA bus ran at 8MHz and could transmit 32 bits at a time.

Fast Ethernet A network that uses star topology with UTP cable. Fast
Ethernet requires special adapter cards and hubs capable of 100Mbps
transfers.

FDDI *See* Fiber Distributed Data Interface.

FDM *See* frequency-division multiplexing.

Fiber Distributed Data Interface (FDDI) A network that uses fiber-
optic cable in a ring topology with token-passing. FDDI operates at
100Mbps and can support two counter-rotating rings.

fiber optic A cable that uses glass and light to transmit data instead of
copper and electrical signals.

File Transfer Access Method (FTAM) ISO 8571 is an OSI-compliant
file-access protocol. FTAM is not a complete protocol itself but
requires other protocol implementations to be complete. One such protocol is Digital Access Protocol. *See also* Digital Access Protocol.

File Transfer Protocol (FTP) FTP allows a user to transfer files electronically from remote computers back to the user's computer. FTP is
part of the TCP/IP software suite.

flow control The process of controlling the amount of data sent to a
device so that it does not exceed the capabilities of the receiving system.

frame The sequence of contiguous bits bracketed by and including
beginning and ending flag sequences. A typical frame might consist of a

specified number of bits between flags and contain an address field, a control field, and a frame check sequence. A frame may or may not include an information field.

frame relay A new WAN connection technology that took the features of X.25 and stripped the error control and accounting from it to increase performance. *See also* X.25.

frequency shift keying (FSK) This method of encoding allows the frequency to represent a data value. For example, FSK uses one frequency to represent 1 and another frequency to represent 0.

frequency-division multiplexing (FDM) A method used in broadband transmissions to transmit analog signals. The channels are on different frequencies with an area of unused frequency ranges separating them. These unused ranges are known as guardbands and they prevent interference from other channels. This is the form of multiplexing used in cable TV systems.

FSK *See* frequency shift keying.

FTAM *See* File Transfer Access Method.

FTP *See* File Transfer Protocol.

full backup A method of file backup used to back up all selected files. This process marks the files as archived.

full-duplex A conversation in which both sides can send data simultaneously.

gateway The hardware and software necessary to make two technologically different networks communicate with each other. A gateway provides protocol conversion from one network architecture to another and may, therefore, use all seven layers of the OSI reference model.

A gateway can also be a special-purpose, dedicated computer that attaches to two or more networks and routes packets from one to the other. The term is loosely applied to any machine that transfers information from one network to another, as in a mail gateway.

Finally, a gateway is another term for a hardware/software package that runs on the OSI Application layer and allows incompatible protocols to communicate. Includes X.25 gateways.

group accounts Special accounts that contain user accounts and are useful in combining users in the same department or with a similar function. When resources are shared, the group can be granted access instead of requiring that each user account be granted access.

half-duplex A conversation in which only one side can send data at a time.

High-level Data Link Control (**HDLC**) A communications protocol defined for high-level, synchronous connections to X.25 packet networks.

Hub A connection device that receives a signal and then transmits the signal to the connected devices.

I

I/O address A way for devices to communicate with the main board. Each device has a different I/O address that is used to identify the device.

ICMP *See* Internet Control Message Protocol.

impedance In a circuit, impedance is the opposition that circuit elements present to the flow of alternating current.

incremental backup A file backup method used to back up selected files that have been changed since the last backup. The files are then marked as archived.

Industry Standard Architecture (ISA) A bus designed by IBM and used in the IBM PC. This bus was originally designed to transfer 8 million bits per second (Mbps).

infrared Light frequencies that are just below the visible light spectrum and allow high data transmissions.

Integrated Services Digital Network (ISDN) Allows you to send voice, data, and video over normal copper telephone lines by sending digital signals instead of analog.

intermediate devices Devices on the network that data passes through.

International Organization for Standardization (ISO) Based in Paris, the ISO develops standards for international and national data communications.

International Telecommunications Union, Telecommunications Standards Sector (ITU-T) Formally known as Consultative Committee for International Telegraphy and Telephony, the ITU-T is an international organization in which governments and the private sector coordinate global telecom networks and services. ITU activities include the coordination, development, regulation, and standardization of telecommunications.

Internet Control Message Protocol (ICMP) Provides error reporting for TCP/IP.

Internet Protocol (IP) The Network layer protocol in the TCP/IP suite that provides connectionless data transmission.

Internetwork Packet Exchange (IPX) A protocol that allows the exchange of message packets on an internetwork. Designed by Novell.

internetworking devices Devices used to connect LANs to each other.

IPX *See* Internetwork Packet Exchange.

IRQ An interrupt request value is an assigned value that a device sends to the computer's processor to interrupt its processing when it needs to send some information.

ISA *See* Industry Standard Architecture.

ISDN *See* Integrated Services Digital Network.

ISO 8327 A generic OSI Session layer protocol. It handles half-duplex data transfer, connection establishment, and connection release.

ITU-T *See* International Telecommunications Union, Telecommunications Standards Sector.

J

jumpers Small pairs of metal pins that stick out of the adapter card. You change their configuration by putting small plastic covers with metal internal connectors over them. By doing this, you are actually completing the circuit between the two pins. A jumper with the plastic cover on it is considered "closed," and one without is considered "open."

L

LAM *See* Lobe Access Module.

LAN *See* local area network.

link state routing A routing protocol that takes more into account than just hop count. It usually considers link speed, latency, and congestion.

LLAP *See* LocalTalk Link Access Protocol.

LLC *See* Logical Link Control.

Lobe Access Module (LAM) A LAM (pronounced "lamb") allows intelligent expansion of CAUs. *See also* CAU.

local area network (LAN) A network in which communications are limited to a moderate-sized geographic area such as a single office building, warehouse, or campus, and that do not extend across public rights-of-way. A system that links computers together to form a network, usually with a wiring-based cabling scheme. LANs connect personal computers and electronic office equipment, enabling users to communicate, share resources such as data storage and printers, and access remote hosts or other networks.

LocalTalk Link Access Protocol (LLAP) A proprietary set of network protocols designed by Apple Computers. LocalTalk uses twisted-pair cable with a bandwidth of 230.4Kbps using the CSMA/CA contention system. With a maximum length of 300 meters and only thirty-two devices, it is well suited for a small workgroup network.

Logical Link Control (LLC) This sublayer of the Data Link Layer establishes and maintains data link connections between network devices. It is responsible for any flow control and error correction found in this layer.

MAC address The physical address assigned to the network adapter usually during production.

Manchester A means by which separate data and clock signals can be combined into a single, self-synchronizable data stream suitable for transmission on a serial channel.

Multistation Access Unit (MAU) A MAU (pronounced "mow," as in *cow*) is a Token Ring hub. This device is sometimes known as an IBM 8228 MAU and an MSAU. Devices connect to the hub in a physical star. The MAU internally links the workstations into a ring. MAUs have special ring in and ring out ports used to connect several MAUs to the ring. The ring out on one MAU is connected to a ring in on the next MAU. This continues until the ring out on the last MAU is connected to the ring in on the first MAU, forming a ring.

MAU *See* Multistation Access Unit.

media The means used to transmit data. Media can include cable, microwaves, radio waves, infrared rays, among other devices.

Media Access Control The portion of the IEEE 802 data station that controls and mediates the access to the medium.

mesh A network topology that uses separate cables to connect each device to every other device on the network providing a straight communications path.

message switching Data is sent from device to device in whole across the network.

metropolitan area network (MAN) A group of LANs located in a geographical city.

MicroChannel Architecture (MCA) A proprietary bus architecture developed by IBM. MCA operates at 32Mbps and uses software to configure the resource settings. MCA was not designed to be backward compatible with ISA, requiring people to buy new MCA adapters.

microwaves These waves travel at higher frequencies than radio waves and provide better throughput as a wireless network media.

MLID *See* Multiple Link Interface Driver.

modem MODulator/DEModulator. A device which modulates and demodulates signals transmitted over communication facilities.

multimode Fiber-optic cable with many light paths.

Multiple Link Interface Driver (MLID) Used in the IPX/SPX protocol suite, MLID is a network interface board driver specification. It is the software that makes the network card work inside a computer.

multiplexer A multiplexer is a hardware device that allows multiple signals to be sent across one transmission media.

N

Name Binding Protocol (NBP) Allows AppleTalk networks to use easily remembered names for devices, keep up with the dynamic changes in device addresses, and hide them from the user.

NBP *See* Name Binding Protocol.

NCP *See* NetWare Core Protocol.

NDIS *See* Network Device Interface Specification.

NetBEUI transport (NetBIOS Extended User Interface) A local area network transport protocol provided with various Microsoft operating environments.

NetWare Core Protocol (NCP) Handles most network services including file services, printing, file locking, resource access, and synchronization.

Network Basic Input/Output System (NetBIOS) A programmable entry into the network that allows systems to communicate over network hardware using a generic networking API that can run over multiple transports or media.

NetBIOS *See* Network Basic Input/Output System.

network congestion The amount of collisions and traffic on a network.

Network Device Interface Specification (NDIS) Created by Microsoft and 3COM. These requirements are used by most companies in the PC networking community and allows multiple protocols to work with one NIC driver.

network interface cards (NIC) Adapters responsible for moving data from the computer to the transmission media. The network adapter transforms data into signals that are carried across the transmission media to its destination.

Network layer This layer of the OSI model is responsible for routing information from one network device to another.

Network Link Services Protocol (NLSP) An advanced routing protocol using a link state routing mechanism to choose the best route.

Network Services Protocol (NSP) An original part of the DNA specification, and the only proprietary protocol in the middle layers. It is a full-duplex, connection-oriented protocol that is capable of prioritizing messages based on needs. It also implements flow control to handle the number of outstanding messages appropriately during times of congestion.

Network Virtual Terminal Service (NVTS) An NVTS provides terminal emulation over the network. It translates the data into a format that can be sent over the wire, and then handles the translating of the data back to its original form for the host or for display on a workstation.

NIC *See* network interface cards.

NLSP *See* Network Link Services Protocol.

noise Noise is interference on network cable caused by radio interference (RFI) or electromagnetic interference (EMI). *See also* RFI *and* EMI.

Non-return-to-zero A data-encoding scheme similar to Differential Manchester in that it uses a transition at the beginning of the bit to determine the value. A transition signifies one value while the lack of a transition signifies another value. This method does not use a mid-bit transition for clocking.

NSP *See* Network Services Protocol.

NVTS *See* Network Virtual Terminal Service.

object An entity (for example, record, page, program, printer) that contains or receives information.

ODI *See* Open Datalink Interface.

Open Datalink Interface (ODI) Novell's answer to the driver specification question. It allows for multiple protocols to use one NIC driver.

Open Shortest Path First (OSPF) A routing protocol that uses much more information than just the number of hops to make a decision. Usually OSPF is configured to figure in the hop count, the speed of the connection between the hops, as well as load-balancing to calculate the best way to route packets. OSPF is part of TCP/IP.

oscilloscopes An instrument used to show voltage over time. While used frequently in diagnosing problems with electrical equipment, they can also be used to test for faulty network cable.

OSI model A model for network communications consisting of seven layers that describe what happens when computers communicate with one another.

OSPF *See* Open Shortest Path First.

packet switching A discipline for controlling and moving messages in a large data communications network. Each message is handled as a complete unit containing the addresses of the recipient and the originator.

PAP *See* Printer Access Protocol.

parity A way to check for small errors in data that utilizes one bit to specify whether the byte has an even or odd value.

passive hub A hub that uses no power and sends the signal to all workstations with no regeneration or amplification.

patch cable A cable used to connect the workstation to a network jack in the office.

patch panel A set of jacks that allow the administrator to connect the individual wall jack cables to a network device such as a hub or router.

PCI *See* Peripheral Component Interface.

PCMCIA *See* Personal Computer Memory Card International Association.

peer Computer/communication systems capable of performing equal or comparable tasks within defined limits or parameters.

peer-to-peer The communication between two network entities considered to be of equal stature; the designation for a local area network in which the resources of some or all the connected machines may be shared.

Peripheral Component Interface (PCI) A bus type that runs at up to 33MHz and can transfer 32 bits at a time.

Personal Computer Memory Card International Association (PCMCIA) An interface used primarily in notebook computers. It uses a 68-pin connector.

phase shift keying (PSK) A signaling method in which a change (or absence of change) can present a data value. For example, a phase change can represent 1, while the absence of a phase change can represent 0.

Physical layer The first layer of the OSI model is the Physical layer. The function of this layer is the transmission of bits over the network media. It provides a physical connection for the transmission of data among the network devices. The Physical layer is responsible for making sure that data is read the same way on the destination device as it was sent on the source device.

Point-to-Point-Protocol (PPP) The PPP provides error checking to ensure the accurate delivery of the frames that it sends and receives. PPP also keeps a logical link control communication between the two connect devices by using the Link Control Protocol. PPP allows for dynamic host configuration and supports multiple protocols.

polar A data-encoding scheme that uses each level to represent a specific value. This scheme allows for a positive and a negative level to each represent a value.

policies Policies provide controls on user accounts. They can be used to manage passwords. Password length, duration, and uniqueness can be set. They can also control which computers a user can log in to and at what times.

polling systems A media access method in which a master device will go and check the other secondary devices on the network to see if they need to transmit. The order of the devices polled and their priority can be set by the administrator.

PPP *See* Point-to-Point Protocol.

Presentation layer The sixth layer of the OSI model, it negotiates and establishes the format that data is exchanged in.

Printer Access Protocol (PAP) A Session layer protocol that provides printing services to clients, but it can also do other services, as well. Printer Access Protocol is part of the AppleTalk suite.

profiles Profiles are used to set user variables such as defining a user's desktop settings.

protocol A specification for the format and relative timing of information exchanged between communicating parties.

protocol analyzer Device that you use to look at a network packet by packet and tell you exactly what is being transmitted. You may even use them to debug network applications by using it to look at the "conversation" that is in progress.

protocol stack A collection of networking protocols that provides the communications and services needed to enable computers to exchange messages and other information, typically by managing physical connections, communications services, and application support.

PSK *See* phase shift keying.

PSTN *See* Public Switched Telephone Network.

Public Switched Telephone Network (PSTN) PTSN is the telephone system in place and used for many years all across the country.

radio interference (RFI) Causes noise on network cable.

radio waves Radio waves that have frequencies between 10KHz and 1GHz.

RAID 0 Disk striping that separates the data into blocks and spreads the blocks across each drive or partition. All the devices combine to create one logical device.

RAID 1 Disk mirroring, duplicates all data and partitions to a separate physical disk. This provides two full copies of the system and all data.

RAID 5 Disk striping with parity. Data blocks are striped to several disks with a parity stripe written in varying locations. The data and parity are always written on different disks. The parity stripe contains information that can be used to reconstruct data.

repeater A device used to extend the length, topology, or interconnectivity of the physical medium beyond that imposed by a single segment, up to the maximum allowable end-to-end trunk transmission line length by copying electrical signals from one network segment to another.

resistance Resistance occurs when electricity moves through a media. Resistance causes loss of electricity.

resources Any item on the network that can be shared or accessed.

Return-to-Zero This current-state encoding method translates a high voltage to one value while a low voltage represents another. Return-to-Zero includes a mid-bit transition to zero for clocking purposes.

RFI *See* radio interference.

ring A network topology that looks like a circle in which the data travels from computer to computer in one direction.

RIP *See* Routing Information Protocol.

RJ-45 Cable that looks very much like a normal telephone connector but larger. It uses twisted-pair cabling with four pairs of wires.

router A software and hardware connection between two or more networks, usually of similar design, that permits traffic to be routed from one network to another on the basis of the intended destinations of that traffic.

routing The assignment of the path by which a message will reach its destination.

Routing Information Protocol (RIP) A routing protocol that uses the number of routers between you and the destination (hops) to decide the best way to route a packet.

Routing Table Maintenance Protocol (RTMP) A routing protocol that uses a distance vector algorithm to decide the best path.

RTMP *See* Routing Table Maintenance Protocol.

SAP *See* Service Access Protocol.

Sequenced Packet Exchange (SPX) A protocol by which two workstations or applications communicate across the network. SPX uses NetWare IPX to deliver the messages, but SPX guarantees delivery of the messages and maintains the order of messages on the packet stream.

Serial Line Internet Protocol (SLIP) A Physical layer protocol that provides no error checking and relies on the hardware (such as modem error checking) to handle this. It also only supports the transmission of one protocol, TCP/IP.

server A server is a computer in a network that is shared by multiple users such as a file server, print server, or communications server; a computer in a network designated to provide a specific service as distinct from a general-purpose, centralized, multi-user computer system.

Server Message Block (SMB) A communications protocol used by Microsoft clients to share files.

Service Access Protocol (SAP) An IPX/SPX protocol which requires computers sharing a resource on the network to send out a SAP packet telling about the resource and where it is located.

Session Control The Session Control protocol acts as an intermediary between the Application and Transport layers of the OSI model. It is used in protocol stacks that are not OSI compliant.

Session layer The fifth layer of the OSI model, this layer lets users establish a connection between devices. This connection is called a *session*. Once the connection has been established, the Session layer can manage the dialogue.

shared memory address Allows the network card and software driver to use a shared RAM memory address in the high memory range to communicate.

share-level security A security method that relies on assigning a password to resources that are shared on the network.

Shielded twisted-pair (STP) This cable has a mesh shielding that protects it from EMI which allows for higher transmission rates and longer distances without errors.

Simple Mail Transfer Protocol (SMTP) Responsible for making sure that this e-mail is delivered. SMTP only handles the delivery of mail to servers, and between them. It does not handle the delivery to the final e-mail client application. SMTP is part of the TCP/IP suite.

Simple Network Management Protocol (SNMP) Used to get statistics from network devices on usage and errors.

simplex One-way communications.

single mode Fiber-optic cable that allows for one light path through the cable.

sliding window A method of flow control that allows two communicating devices to negotiate the number of allowable outstanding frames.

SLIP *See* Serial Line Internet Protocol.

SMDS *See* Switched Multimegabit Data Service.

SMTP *See* Simple Mail Transfer Protocol.

SNA *See* Systems Network Architecture.

SNMP *See* Simple Network Management Protocol.

SONET *See* Synchronous Optical Network.

source-route bridge A source-route bridge is a Token Ring bridge that, instead of depending on MAC addresses, uses information in the Token Ring frame to determine whether to pass the data.

SPX *See* Sequenced Packet Exchange.

Star Star topology uses a separate cable for each workstation. The cable connects the workstation to a central device, typically a hub.

stop-and-wait flow control A green-light way of handling flow control. When the receiving device has no more memory left to store incoming data, it suspends transmission. When memory is free again, it sends a signal to the transmitting device to resume.

STP *See* Shielded twisted-pair.

switched connections Switched connections allow multiple people to use a connection at once. They require special hardware to manage the connections but give you the benefit of lower cost for the connection to the service provider.

Switched Multimegabit Data Service (SMDS) A combination of X.25 and ATM. It was designed by Bell Communications Research and released in 1991. It uses cells like ATM, and creates virtual circuits like X.25. *See also* X.25 *and* ATM.

switches Multiport bridges that filter traffic between the ports on the switch by using the MAC address of computers transmitting through them.

synchronous A data transmission mode in which synchronization is established for an entire block of data (message).

Synchronous Optical Network (SONET) Specifies how to deliver voice, data, and video over WAN connections at speeds in excess of 2Gbps. It is a Physical layer standard that defines the transfer of data over fiber-optic media.

Systems Network Architecture (SNA) SNA is the IBM network architecture, defined in terms of its functions, formats, and protocols.

T

T-carrier system A wide area network connection technology provided by the phone company. Speeds can reach 45Mbps.

TCP *See* Transmission Control Protocol.

TDM *See* time-division multiplexing.

TDR *See* time-domain reflectometer.

Telnet A portion of the TCP/IP suite of software protocols that handles terminals. Among other functions, it allows a user to log in to a remote computer from the user's local computer

time-division multiplexing (TDM) Type of multiplexing that uses time slots to separate channels. Each device is given a time slot to transmit using the entire available bandwidth.

time-domain reflectometer (TDR) A TDR is used to determine exactly where a media break occurred. The TDR uses a sonar-like pulse that is sent down the cable. The signal bounces back from a break in the cable. The TDR calculates the time that the signal took to go down the cable and back and computes the distance.

TLAP *See* TokenTalk.

Token passing A collision avoidance technique in which each station is polled and must pass the poll along.

Token Ring A very reliable topology based on some of the best standards available. It uses token passing in a physical star configuration connected in a ring using hubs.

TokenTalk Lets you build AppleTalk networks on the popular Token Ring network protocols.

translational bridge A bridge that allows connection of dissimilar networks.

Transmission Control Protocol (TCP) A connection-oriented protocol from the Transport layer of the OSI model. TCP opens and maintains a connection between two communicating hosts on a network.

transparent bridge An internetworking device that uses hardware network card addresses to determine when to pass or filter data.

Transport layer The fourth layer of the OSI model. It provides a transport service between the Session layer and the Network layer. This service takes information from the Session layer and splits it up if necessary. It then passes this information to the Network layer and checks to make sure that it arrived at the destination device successfully.

twisted-pair Two wires of a signaling circuit that are twisted around each other to minimize the effects of inductance.

UDP *See* User Datagram Protocol.

uninterruptible power supply (UPS) A backup power unit that provides continuous power even when the normal power supply is interrupted.

unipolar A scheme of encoding data uses a zero level to represent one value, while either a positive or a negative level represents the other value.

Unshielded twisted-pair (UTP) Twisted-pair cable that can be either voice grade or data grade depending on the application. UTP cable normally has an impedance of 100 ohms. *See also* twisted-pair.

UPS *See* uninterruptible power supply.

user A human being or computer process that possesses the right to log in to a particular computer system.

User Datagram Protocol (UDP) A connectionless transport protocol that is used when the overhead of TCP is not needed. UDP is just responsible for transporting datagrams.

user-level security Requires the proper user name and password to access a resource.

virtual circuit A communication arrangement in which data from a source user may be passed to a destination user over various real circuit configurations during a single period of communication (during a single session).

WAN *See* wide area network.

wide area network (WAN) A WAN consists of two or more LANs (local area networks) in separate geographic locations connected by a remote link.

workgroup Group of users on a network who have information or resources that they wish to share among themselves.

X.25 Developed in 1974 by the CCITT as a Network layer packet-switching protocol. It specifies how internetwork devices connect over a packet switched network.

X.400 A messaging standard that allows different e-mail systems to communicate seamlessly.

X.500 An international address-to-name resolution and directory services standard.

Index

A

Notes

Notes

Notes

Notes

Notes

Notes

Notes

my2cents.idgbooks.com